LUCKY BY DESIGN

**THE HIDDEN ECONOMICS YOU NEED
TO GET MORE OF WHAT YOU WANT**

JUDD KESSLER

Little, Brown Spark
New York   Boston   London

Copyright © 2025 by Judd B. Kessler

Hachette Book Group supports the right to free expression and the value of copyright. The purpose of copyright is to encourage writers and artists to produce the creative works that enrich our culture.

The scanning, uploading, and distribution of this book without permission is a theft of the author's intellectual property. If you would like permission to use material from the book (other than for review purposes), please contact permissions@hbgusa.com. Thank you for your support of the author's rights.

Little, Brown Spark
Hachette Book Group
1290 Avenue of the Americas, New York, NY 10104
littlebrownspark.com

First Edition: October 2025

Little, Brown Spark is an imprint of Little, Brown and Company, a division of Hachette Book Group, Inc. The Little, Brown Spark name and logo are trademarks of Hachette Book Group, Inc.

The publisher is not responsible for websites (or their content) that are not owned by the publisher.

The Hachette Speakers Bureau provides a wide range of authors for speaking events. To find out more, go to hachettespeakersbureau.com or email hachettespeakers@hbgusa.com.

Little, Brown and Company books may be purchased in bulk for business, educational, or promotional use. For information, please contact your local bookseller or the Hachette Book Group Special Markets Department at special.markets@hbgusa.com.

ISBN 9780316566827
LCCN 2025932672

Printing 1, 2025

LSC-C

Printed in the United States of America

To Ilana, Cass, Isla, and Natalie

Contents

Introduction: The Hidden Markets All Around Us	3
CHAPTER 1: The Three *Es* in Ice Cream	21
CHAPTER 2: The Need for Speed	43
CHAPTER 3: The Waiting Game	70
CHAPTER 4: That's So Random!	100
CHAPTER 5: Ranks a Bunch	129
CHAPTER 6: Choose-Me Markets	170
CHAPTER 7: Speculation and the Aftermarket	202
CHAPTER 8: You Are a Market Designer	230
Coda	257
Acknowledgments	258
Notes	261
Index	267

**LUCKY
BY
DESIGN**

INTRODUCTION

The Hidden Markets All Around Us

"Rock smashes scissors. Scissors cut paper. Paper covers rock."

I used both hands—playing both the winning and losing side—as I showed my four-year-old daughter, Natalie, the possible outcomes of the game rock-paper-scissors. Natalie stared intently. Her eyes, peering out from under her light brown bangs, were glued to my hands.

We had already gone over the hand motions: a fist for rock (ready to slam on a pair of scissors), two fingers in the shape of a V pointed at your opponent for scissors (open, to easily slice through a piece of paper), and a downward-facing palm for paper (poised to pounce on an unsuspecting rock).

Learning the game of rock-paper-scissors was a rite of passage for Natalie. Her nine-year-old brother and six-year-old sister were already experts. They had each learned to play at around four years old as well.

First, they learned to play just for fun. The remarkably simple game can fill a surprising amount of time while kids are waiting for a city bus (when Dad cannot think of anything better to do). Once they both knew how to play, however, they started to use it for its ultimate purpose: to settle disagreements (blessedly without having to involve a parent). Who chooses which cartoon they watch next? Do we have tacos or pizza for dinner? Who gets the last can of seltzer in the fridge? To the victor—of two out of three rounds—go the spoils.

Without knowing the rules of the game, my youngest was left out, fated to just watch her older siblings make incomprehensible hand gestures at each other until one laughed giddily in victory and the other groaned in defeat.

Natalie practiced the hand gestures and once she seemed to understand the rules, her older sister, Isla (pronounced "Eye-la," not "Is-la," as she would confidently correct you), volunteered to challenge Natalie to her very first real game.

Knowing that Natalie was eager to get into the tub in the bathroom they shared, Isla decided to make things more interesting: "Whoever wins gets to take a bath first." Natalie lit up with excitement.

I watched as my new protégée took on my old protégée for the very first time.

The game was over almost as soon as it began. Natalie proceeded to throw scissors on every turn. Her older sister figured this out rather quickly and then won decisively with a few throws of rock.

As I saw the disappointment creep onto Natalie's face, it was clear that her failure was mine. I had taught her the rules of the game, and I had demonstrated how it was played, but I had neglected to teach her any strategy. Playing scissors on every turn was too predictable, even against a six-year-old opponent.

The stakes of her game were low, even if it didn't feel like it to Natalie at the time. But we all go through versions of this experience with outcomes far more consequential than who gets their preferred bath time.

We are routinely in situations where scarce resources are allocated in ways that we do not fully understand. Who gets lifesaving organ transplants when they're needed? Who gets spots in the most desirable elementary schools, high schools, and colleges? Who gets hired for the most coveted jobs after graduation? Who gets tickets to popular concerts or reservations at hot restaurants? Who finds that special someone and who ends up alone?

Without understanding the rules of the game, you might assume that your outcomes are determined mostly by luck. But there are rules — often hidden and complex rules — that determine who gets what. When you aren't aware of them, you often wind up just like Natalie: using a suboptimal strategy and losing to people who seem to know tricks that you do not.

People who end up unhappy about what they get conclude that they were unlucky or that the system was rigged against them. After enough of these experiences, they believe that's just how the world works.

But it doesn't have to be.

A BRIEF INTRODUCTION TO (HIDDEN) MARKETS

And to me and my mentor, Al

More than two decades before I became a rock-paper-scissors instructor to my third child, I was a student in economics at Harvard University.

While still an undergraduate, I had been encouraged to take a PhD class taught by Alvin Roth, a brilliant and exceptionally kindhearted economist with distinctive rectangular glasses and a light gray beard.

Al's class met weekly on Fridays from 9:00 a.m. to noon on the business school campus, a twenty-minute walk from the main campus that could chill your bones during a Boston winter. That meant that if you were not willing to wake up at 8:00 a.m. and get whipped by the wind walking over the Charles River, you wouldn't be in his class.

This was the first—albeit unstated—lesson about who gets what (and why) that I learned from Al. Harvard had criteria determining who could enroll in his class, but because the number of eligible students who wanted to take it invariably exceeded the maximum enrollment allowed, only a small portion of students actually got in. By picking an early class time and an inconvenient location, Al ensured that he was surrounded by only the most interested and dedicated students. I was one of them; in fact, I enjoyed it so much, I returned to Harvard Business School to work under Al's supervision for another six years while I got my PhD.

Al was at the forefront of a new subfield of economics called market design. The subfield excited me in a way that other branches of economics did not. At its core was a big idea that changed the way I thought about the world.

Economists—myself included—think of the world as a set of markets in which individuals try to get the best outcomes they can. Before studying with Al, I associated these markets with prices. Markets were where buyers paid sellers a price and got something in return. At the farmers' market, I could pay a price for produce. On the stock market, I could pay a price for equity in publicly traded companies. If I was willing to pay the price, I got the pears or the shares. If I was not, I left empty-handed.

But the field of market design had a keen interest in different kinds of markets—markets that allocate valuable, scarce resources *without* relying on prices (or at least, without relying exclusively on them).

Without prices, these markets need some other criteria to determine who gets what, and because the criteria are not always obvious or visible the way that prices are, I call them *hidden markets*. Seats in Al's class, for instance, were not allocated based on willingness to pay for access but by an unstated criterion: a willingness to wake up to an early-morning alarm and brave Boston's chill.

Once I better understood what a hidden market was, I started to see them everywhere, hiding in plain sight all around us.

· Introduction ·

WHEN THERE ISN'T ENOUGH TO GO AROUND

Introducing the problem of scarcity and how prices can resolve it

At their core, markets allocate scarce resources.

Scarcity is an unavoidable fact of life. There is often not enough of what we want to go around. I would love to live in a palatial apartment in the most desirable location in New York City, go on fabulous vacations each school break, eat delicious meals at fancy restaurants once a week, and have a personal trainer work with me each day to keep me physically fit (even more important, given all the fancy meals I'm eating). But lots of other people also want these things, and there is a limited supply of each of them.

If the market offered these desirable resources free of charge to whoever wanted them, there would undoubtedly be more people asking for fancy apartments, vacations, dinners, and personal trainers than were available to give out.

Economists call this phenomenon *excess demand*, because there are more people demanding the good than there are goods available. As a result, people usually do not give scarce resources away for free. Instead, they are sold at a price, often a very high price.

An available apartment in a desirable neighborhood of New York City might get dozens of people showing up to an open house, each hoping to be the one to rent it. In the presence of such excess demand, a savvy landlord will raise the rental price. The higher price reduces the number of people who are interested in the unit, as fewer people will decide it is worth it—or even feasible—to pay the new, higher price for the apartment. The higher price also puts more money in the landlord's pocket.

That the quantity of people who demand something falls as the item's price rises is so predictable that economists call it the *law of demand*. This law of demand is how prices allocate scarce resources;

as the price of that good or service rises, only a select few are willing and able to pay for it.

When a price is high enough that demand no longer exceeds supply, economists call that the *market-clearing price*. Like a physical space that has cleared out, at the market-clearing price, the market is empty—everyone willing to buy that good at the price has it, and there are no customers or goods left in the market.

Economists' models generally assume that most sellers will act like the landlords, charging the highest prices they can until demand no longer exceeds supply. In other words, goods end up being sold at market-clearing prices.

But not all scarce resources are allocated by raising prices until supply and demand meet.

THE PROBLEM(S) WITH PRICES
What happens when prices fail to clear the market

On November 1, 2022, Taylor Swift announced a new tour—the Eras Tour—that would kick off the following March.

It was clear to everyone that tickets for the tour were going to be in exceptionally high demand. Beyond the fact that Swift was arguably the most popular pop singer on the planet, it was her first tour in five years (she had been forced to cancel her previous tour due to the pandemic), and her tenth studio album, *Midnights*, had broken Spotify's record for the most streamed album in a single day. (Its songs were streamed over 180 million times on the platform on the day it was released.)

Although the shows would be in massive stadiums, many more people wanted to see Swift perform live than there would be seats available. Like many megastars before her, Swift was faced with a dilemma. How should she allocate the available tickets to those who wanted them?

One option for Swift and her team was to set exorbitantly high prices for the tickets. Like the New York City landlords, they could even pick the market-clearing price for each performance. Set the price high enough and only one person would be willing to pay that price for each available seat.

Setting the price as high as possible while still selling out each stadium obviously makes an artist more money (often a lot more money) from each performance than pricing the tickets lower. But Taylor Swift did not follow this strategy.

Instead, Swift set prices much lower. Face-value prices (the prices charged by the venue) for tickets to the Eras Tour ranged from $49 for the nosebleed seats to $499 for the seats by the stage. With tickets at these prices, the number of people who wanted to attend each performance far exceeded the supply of seats.

Why did Swift leave money on the table when she could easily have raised ticket prices and still sold out the tour? You typically hear two explanations for this pricing strategy.

The traditional economist narrative assumes people are always looking out for their own interests. In the short term, this might mean maximizing profit by charging as much as they can. But in a world where the popularity of a restaurant, musical act, or show helps build buzz that increases future demand, excess demand today (a line around the block or stories about how hard it is to get tickets) might bolster even more demand tomorrow (and the day after that, and the day after that). This may be why restaurateurs, musicians, Broadway producers, and others regularly set prices lower than needed to fill the seats at their restaurants, concerts, and theaters; these sellers are still trying to maximize their profits, but they are taking a longer-term view of it.

While a megastar like Swift does not need to build this kind of buzz, she might still have long-term considerations in mind when she prices her tickets. Beyond maximizing profits from her tour, Swift likely wants to keep her fan base of Swifties loyal and devoted so they continue streaming her songs, buying her merchandise, and seeing her shows for years to come. The loyalty of her fans also ensures that she can get lucrative advertising gigs, such as her multi-year deal with Capital One. Unlike the New York City landlord who doesn't care if you like him and just wants your rent check on time, Swift is a celebrity whose future career success relies, at least partially, on people liking her. And it's easy to see how an artist with a net worth of $1.6 billion (as estimated by *Forbes* in 2025) could be seen as greedy and exploitative if she charges her fans an exorbitantly high price to see her perform.

The second reason an artist like Swift might leave money on the table does not rely on the self-interest-above-all logic of traditional economics models, although the two explanations are not mutually exclusive. This view assumes the seller has other considerations besides profit maximization in mind.

In Swift's case, she might not like what happens when she sets the market-clearing price for her tickets. She might view it as unfair that at the market-clearing price, only her wealthy fans—those who are all too well off—can afford to see her tour while her less moneyed fans get priced out.

According to this narrative, Swift's desire to price her tickets affordably is related to concerns about inequity. And these concerns are not unique to Swift. Concerns about inequity can lead society to decide that it is more fair to allocate a scarce resource without prices at all.

WHEN PRICES ARE INEQUITABLE

Explaining what I mean by inequitable

For an allocation mechanism to be *equitable*, it must treat people fairly. Instead of awarding benefits only to those who can afford it, an equitable mechanism spreads benefits as evenly as possible.

· Introduction ·

In a world where everyone had the same access to resources (if, say, we each had the same amount of money to spend) and where we all were charged the same prices for goods and services, using prices to allocate things would be exceedingly fair. No one could have everything, but we could each get what we wanted most, and no one would be at an advantage or disadvantage. If you prioritized a centrally located apartment and I prioritized fancy dinners, we would both use our money to buy what we valued most, even if we could not have it all.

But that is not the world we live in.

Instead, we live in a world with significant wealth and income inequality, a world where different groups have very different financial assets.

Whenever prices determine access to scarce resources, that financial inequality will be reflected in the allocation of resources. Regardless of what is being allocated, certain people—poorer people—will always be at a disadvantage.

Just as Taylor Swift might decide that she does not want to price her tickets so high that only the rich can buy them, society often decides that it wants to allocate certain goods *without* prices at all, so that people have *more equal* chances to access them.

For example, many public-school systems have more desirable and less desirable elementary schools (some schools might have more experienced teachers, better facilities, or more convenient locations), but desirable public schools do not cost more than undesirable ones, and they don't post prices and let parents buy seats in the public schools. Rich and poor parents all send their kids to public schools for free, and they all go through the same admissions process.

At the Wharton School, the business school at the University of Pennsylvania, where I teach, there are more and less popular courses. Some courses are so popular that there are not enough seats to meet student demand. But even though we are a business school, we do not sell the seats in desirable classes to those with the deepest pockets. Once you are a student at Wharton, we want you to have equal access to all our classes, regardless of your wealth or income.

Over one hundred thousand people in the United States are currently waiting for a lifesaving organ transplant, and similar shortages exist around the world. As a result, people routinely wait for years on the organ-donor list for a chance to get one, and over ten thousand people per year die or become too sick to get a transplant while they are waiting. But despite the massive excess demand, society does not determine who gets lifesaving transplants based on how much money people are willing to pay.

Similarly, at the height of the COVID-19 pandemic, when hospital beds and ventilators were in short supply, people arriving at the hospital did not pay more to secure the last of the lifesaving treatments. And once COVID vaccine production began but before there were enough shots to go around, medical facilities did not sell vaccines to the highest bidder. Letting the rich have exclusive access to lifesaving organs, ventilators, and vaccines would have been deeply inequitable. Instead, society had to come up with other mechanisms for allocation.

Of course, the rich still have advantages in these markets. They can afford housing in better public-school districts or they can send their kids to private school; during COVID, they could take trips to states where they were eligible to receive the vaccine, and they could even get ventilators for private use. Still, concerns about inequity help guide the rules society places on how these resources can be accessed as we attempt to mitigate the influence of unequal financial resources.

WHEN PRICES ARE INEFFICIENT

Explaining what I mean by inefficient

Another reason to forgo using prices is that using prices to allocate goods can be inefficient.

• Introduction •

For an allocation mechanism to be *efficient*, it should make the best possible use of the resources available. This includes not squandering any of the scarce resources available as well as allocating scarce resources to the people who value them most.

At first blush, it might seem that prices would allocate scarce resources efficiently. One might presume that a person willing to pay $499 for a Taylor Swift ticket cares more about seeing her perform live than someone willing to pay only $49.

But the same wealth and income inequality that makes allocations based on prices inequitable can also make them inefficient. If someone is not willing to pay more than $49 for a Taylor Swift ticket, that might be because it's all he can afford—not because he is less eager to see her perform than the person willing to spend $499.

It is hard to claim that a wealthy but casual baseball fan who did not attend a single game all season gets more value from a World Series ticket than does a die-hard fan who sat in the cheap seats for every home game but cannot afford the sky-high prices for the championship series. Similarly, a billionaire who buys up hundreds of acres of a tropical paradise probably does not value the last tenth of an acre as much as an indigenous person who wants to stay on her homeland but can't afford the rising housing costs. It might seem more efficient if the ticket went to the diehard and the tenth of an acre went to the local. Because of inequality in financial resources, how much people are willing to pay for things is not always a good proxy for how much they value them.

A second reason that using prices to allocate goods can be inefficient is that using prices can distort—and perhaps even undermine—the value of the resource being allocated.

In dating markets, you might be deemed more desirable if you make more money than others or take your partner on more expensive dates, but as the Beatles' 1964 song and the 1987 movie starring Patrick Dempsey tell us, money can't buy you love. Nor can you pay someone to be a true friend. Sure, the rich and famous have hangers-on, but when you buy people's companionship, you cannot know if they accepted your invitation because they genuinely want to spend time with you or for the perks of doing so. This is why the rich and famous might wonder who their *real* friends are or worry that a romantic partner might just be digging for the proverbial gold.

Introducing money into a relationship, be it romantic or platonic, can change its nature and make it less valuable. Even Niccolò Machiavelli, perhaps best known for strategic ruthlessness and using people instrumentally, is credited with the observation "The friendships which we buy with a price, and do not gain by greatness and nobility of character, ... fail us when we have occasion to use them."

Similarly, in addition to being inequitable, it would be inefficient to auction off the seats at the best colleges to students whose parents are willing and able to pay the most. It is far from guaranteed that the students who derive the most value from that education are the offspring of the parents with the deepest pockets. Moreover, a big benefit of going to one of these elite schools is being surrounded by excellent students and developing a network of people who are poised to succeed in the decades to come. Excellent students would not value admission as much if they were surrounded by less excellent students who had bought their way in. This is why, even when the sticker prices of many colleges appear prohibitive to less wealthy students, the best schools devote millions to need-based scholarships to make sure students of modest means can attend as well.

Efficiency concerns are also why the labor market does not rely exclusively on prices. Google does not decide which engineers to hire based on who asks for the lowest salaries; it is far more efficient for Google to hire the people with the most skill and talent, even if the company ends up paying a bit more for them. And the best hospitals do not pick their new doctors based on who will accept the lowest pay. There are far better ways of determining which candidates will deliver the most value.

• Introduction •

WHEN PRICES ARE TOO DIFFICULT

Explaining what I mean by too difficult

Beyond inequity and inefficiency, there is a third reason why markets might forgo prices: Sometimes it is just too difficult to use them.

While prices are relatively easy for market participants—typically all you need to do in a market with prices is decide whether something is worth the money—there are often additional costs associated with setting and collecting market-clearing prices that can make doing so not worth the trouble.

For example, parking spots in public lots and on certain city streets are often all free, despite some being in higher demand than others. While a municipality might like the idea of raising revenue by charging for parking in desirable areas, it might be too expensive or too much of a hassle to hire parking attendants or install and maintain parking meters for each spot. (Additionally, it might be too politically costly to start charging people for something, like street parking, that had previously been free.)

Similarly, while ticket prices at my local movie theater vary quite a bit—they are lower for my kids than for me, they are cheaper for morning than evening movies, they are higher for IMAX showings—all adult seats at a given showtime cost the same amount, even though watching from the first few rows can put a crick in your neck. In theory, the movie theater could charge more for the better seats (AMC theaters tried that in 2023 with a program called Sightline). But for shows that do not sell out, managers would have to hire ushers to stand in each theater and prevent people from buying the cheaper seats and then moving to empty premium seats once the lights went down. Stadiums that charge vastly different prices for different sections—think of the grandstand versus the field level—must hire staff to check tickets in front of the desirable sections to prevent such moves.

These headaches may also be why airlines, which are happy to charge you different prices for different sections of the airplane, often sell all seats in the same economy-class row (for instance, the window, middle, and aisle seats in row 32) for the same price, even though sitting in the middle seat can be much less comfortable. The crew might be willing and able to prevent coach passengers from sneaking into empty first-class seats and to upgrade customers to ensure the most desirable seats are filled, but what flight attendant wants to try to make a customer sit in the middle seat she paid for when the window seat next to her is empty?

It also might be too hard—or might introduce additional, perhaps hidden costs—to use prices for certain allocations in the household. Allowing my children to pay money for the most desirable bath time instead of settling the matter with rock-paper-scissors would not only be unfair to the youngest child with the smallest allowance but might also distort their views of how a well-functioning family operates. It would also put a massive strain on my marriage, one that would require a messy untangling of our finances, if my wife, Ilana, and I tried to allocate household chores by paying each other to do the dishes or put the kids to bed.

In the many situations where we deem prices too inequitable, too inefficient, or too difficult when determining who gets what, we need to resolve scarcity in some other way.

MARKET RULES

Introducing the concept of market rules, which determine allocations in hidden markets

Whenever we decide not to let prices determine allocations, either because we set prices low enough that there is excess demand or because we decide to forgo prices altogether, we need some other way to allocate scarce resources. In these cases, hidden markets arise.

· Introduction ·

Hidden markets decide who gets access to the best doctors, who gets seats in the best public elementary schools and in the best college classes, and who gets the most desirable restaurant reservations and the hottest concert and theater tickets. Hidden markets decide who gets the organs available for transplant, who gets the last hospital beds and ventilators, and who gets the earliest access to vaccines.

Hidden markets decide who is admitted to the most prestigious colleges and who gets to work at the best firms—and, therefore, who ends up with the most power. They allocate seats in movie theaters and on planes, trains, and automobiles. They even decide who gets to marry the most desirable partners and who must do what within the households they form.

The allocations we observe—who gets a donated kidney, a seat in the best elementary school, or a job at Google—can seem arbitrary and unfair. But there are rules that dictate how things are allocated in hidden markets, even if we aren't always aware of them.

Just like Natalie learning rock-paper-scissors, understanding why certain people get the best outcomes requires knowing these *market rules*. And once you know these rules, you can develop an optimal strategy so the best outcomes start going to you.

Doing academic research as a market designer opened my eyes to the world of hidden markets and the rules that guide them. In this book, I aim to show you how you, too, can develop the ability to spot the hidden markets all around you. Each chapter will provide guidance about how to play in certain types of markets and will arm you with a set of strategies to increase your chances of getting more of what you want from them.

Market rules are dictated by whoever controls access to the scarce resource. These rules might be chosen deliberately, or they might be based on historical accident or operational expediency. Market rules can be formalized, or they can be left unstated; they might be enforced by people or coded into software. And they can be designed poorly or designed well.

What does it mean for market rules to be designed poorly or well? If we forgo prices because they introduce inequity or inefficiency or are too difficult, we should strive to make sure that the market rules that we use instead do better on these same three dimensions. So when academic economists are involved in evaluating or designing market rules, we like rules that satisfy what I call the three *E*s. We want rules that allocate things in a way that is equitable, efficient, and easy.

First, we'll look at the three *E*s more closely, highlighting the trade-offs we face in trying to achieve them. This will help you see the hidden markets all around you and the market rules that dictate them (chapter 1), the first step in learning how to improve your outcomes in those markets.

Market rules can be some version of first come, first served, rewarding people who sign up the fastest (chapter 2) or queue up the earliest and wait the longest (chapter 3). The rules can involve randomization or a lottery, including some cases in which you might be able to improve your odds over others (chapter 4). They can allow participants to rank their preferences (chapter 5), or they can require participants on both sides of the market to agree on who gets what (chapter 6).

Certain market rules can introduce secondary markets — allowing prices to play a bigger role in allocating resources, despite attempts to avoid that — or permit speculation that is in some participants' interests but can be bad for the market as a whole (chapter 7).

By the time you get to the end of the book, you will realize that you are also a market designer. For the markets you control — including the market for your time and attention — you have a chance to create market rules that elevate your preferences and make it easier to achieve your goals (chapter 8).

In many hidden markets, the stakes are too high for you to go in blind. This book is written to help you better understand and master the rules governing the hidden markets that you interact with every day.

To others, it might seem like you just got lucky, but by better understanding these markets—and how to play in them—you will know you were lucky by design.

CHAPTER 1

The Three *Es* in Ice Cream

"HOLD THE CONE!"

My three kids all yell out the same pun.

They aren't being clever; none of them is old enough to have heard the expression "Hold the phone." Instead, they are clamoring for their favorite dessert, an original product from the grocery store chain Trader Joe's.

A Hold the Cone is a miniature ice cream cone about four inches long with its top dipped in chocolate. The chocolate hardens around the small scoop of ice cream and helps ensure the dessert keeps its shape, even if it melts a bit on the trip home from the grocery store and needs to be reconstituted in your freezer (I tip my hat to whatever genius food scientist thought of that).

These delectable treats come eight to a pack. Our kids will all happily have them for dessert two nights in a row, and I've been known to sneak one now and again. As a result, we sometimes end up with one Hold the Cone left and three kids angling for it after dinner.

As an economist and a market designer, I have a framework that I use for thinking about allocation problems like this one: the three *Es* I mentioned in the introduction. I consider whether the market rules for allocating resources are equitable, efficient, and easy.

Any parent facing this type of allocation problem—one dessert and three kids who want it—has a goal that is exceedingly simple to describe but incredibly hard to achieve. You want to allocate the single ice cream cone in whatever way will keep your kids as happy as possible, whether from an altruistic desire to maximize your kids' happiness or because happier kids complain less and you just want some peace and quiet after dinner (for me, it's a little from column A and a little from column B). Either way, when I think about how to keep my kids as happy as possible (short of heading out to Trader Joe's to procure more Hold the Cones), it boils down to the three *E*s.

Efficiency matters because they will be less happy if the cone goes to waste. Equity matters because if my kids think the rules are unfair, they will complain about the injustice (subjecting me to the kind of whining that I hope to avoid). And I want market rules to be easy on the market participants because the kids' happiness isn't determined only by what they get for dessert but also by the amount of hassle involved in getting it.

I could award the cone by birth order, but my market rules would not be equitable if they always awarded the ice cream cone to my firstborn and never my younger kids, just as they would not be equitable if they always awarded it to one of my daughters and never to my son.

Alternatively, I could conduct a mini-lottery. While this would be equitable in the sense that every child would have an equal chance of winning, the results might not be perceived as equitable if the winner turned out to be the same child who had won the Hold the Cone lottery last week.

Or I could decide that if I can't give a Hold the Cone to everyone who wants one, no one can have one. This would be equitable (all three kids would be treated equally) but inefficient. It would fail to make the best possible use of the resource available.

I could hold a contest and award the ice cream cone to whichever child could wash their dirty dishes the fastest or draw the most flattering portrait of me after dinner. But as easy as I am to portray in a favorable light, making my kids inflate my ego in colored pencil for a chance to have their top-choice dessert would require a lot of unnecessary effort from them for an uncertain outcome. For an allocation mechanism to be easy, it must not put too much of a burden on the market participants trying to use it to get what they want.

If I decided to use this dilemma as an opportunity to encourage healthy eating habits, I could ask my kids to pick their *second*-choice dessert and secretly decide to award the Hold the Cone to whoever named the healthiest option. But it would not be easy to participate in a market where falsely claiming you wanted a bowl of berries—which might actually be your fifth or sixth choice of dessert—was rewarded with a higher chance of getting ice cream. If the allocation mechanism is easy, participants should be able to be honest about what they want without fear that communicating their true preferences will be held against them. A rule that punished honesty would add complexity and make the market harder for them to navigate.

So, while each of these strategies has advantages, they all come with significant drawbacks. What is a well-meaning parent with three kids and one ice cream cone to do?

THE REALITY OF TRADE-OFFS

Explaining why no allocation mechanism can reliably satisfy all three Es

One potential way to satisfy the three *E*s is a classic parental go-to: If the three kids all want the same dessert, they should share it. And if the dessert is something that can easily be divided in three, like a piece of cake, finding an allocation rule that satisfies all three *E*s—that is efficient, equitable, and easy—is...a piece of cake.

Sharing is easy for participants: All the kids have to do is tell you what they want, and they can all honestly tell you that they want cake. It is efficient, since no cake is wasted (save for a few crumbs that might get lost in the cutting process). It can also achieve equity, since, as long as you have a steady hand and a good eye, each of the kids will get the same amount.

I would argue that sharing is a parenting go-to precisely because of its three-*E* properties. Perhaps unsurprisingly, when market designers consider allocation mechanisms, their first question is usually whether the resource being allocated can be divided up. If so, sharing is likely the best bet.

But many of the scarce resources that get allocated through hidden markets are not shareable. A donated kidney can go to only one recipient. People do not share single seats at Broadway shows, Taylor Swift concerts, or popular restaurants. Students do not share their spots in elementary-school classrooms or in the popular classes taught at Wharton. Attempts to share these resources would be impractical and would degrade them, resulting in both inefficiency and a terrible experience for everyone.

The Hold the Cone is not particularly shareable either. Cutting it into two pieces, let alone three, is a nonstarter. It's frozen solid, conical, and not very large. And if you were able to cut it, the ice cream inside would fall out (and likely end up melting into little pools on the counter, creating more post-dinner cleanup for Dad).

Much like telling a musical theater fan he must relinquish his seat after act 1 or telling a Wharton student she can attend class only every third week, giving each kid a minuscule piece of a deconstructed cone that's difficult to eat would make the cone much less valuable for everyone. So sharing, even if feasible, would be inefficient.

Once we realize the thing we want to allocate cannot be shared, we must swallow a bitter pill (pills being another thing that cannot be easily shared): No market rules can guarantee an allocation that is at once efficient, equitable, *and* easy. When indivisible objects need to be distributed without the use of money or other currency, we must accept that we cannot simultaneously achieve all three *E*s.

The Hold the Cone example makes the trade-off apparent. The most efficient way to allocate the dessert would be to give it to the child who derives the biggest benefit from it. But giving one child a favorite dessert while the other two receive disfavored options will fail to achieve equity.

Because no single rule can satisfy all three *E*s, any rule will have trade-offs. Some rules generate more efficient outcomes at the expense of ease or equity, some sacrifice efficiency in the name of equity, and so on.

When we are participating in a market for a scarce resource, we can evaluate how successfully the rules of that market generate outcomes that are efficient, equitable, and easy. Thinking about markets this way will let us better understand what game we are playing—the first step in crafting a strategy that will improve our chances of getting what we want.

UNDERSTANDING EFFICIENCY
Introducing efficient mechanisms

Earlier, I said that to be efficient, an allocation mechanism needed to make the best possible use of the resources available. But there are different ways of interpreting *best possible use*, which is why economists have two specific ways of thinking about efficiency.

Pareto Efficiency
NO OBVIOUS IMPROVEMENTS

The first way we think about efficiency is to consider whether there are obvious improvements—in other words, whether it is possible to reallocate things to make someone better off without making anyone else worse off. If the answer is no, the allocation satisfies *Pareto* *efficiency* (named for the economist Vilfredo Pareto).* Pareto argued that if it is possible to reallocate resources to make someone happier without making anyone else less happy, the original allocation was clearly wasteful and therefore inefficient.

I often achieve Pareto efficiency at breakfast when I dole out the last two bags of Quaker Instant Oatmeal to my son, Cass, and his sister Natalie. I know they each would take whatever kind of oatmeal is available over any other breakfast option, but I also know Cass prefers the original variety while Natalie prefers apples and cinnamon. If I am graced by good fortune and have one of each variety left in the multipack, I could dole them out at random, but that would mean a 50 percent chance that they both end up with their second choices — Natalie with original and Cass with apples and cinnamon. This outcome would fail to satisfy Pareto efficiency because I could make them both better off (while not making anyone worse off) if I gave them each their first choice instead.

Allocative Efficiency
Who wants it most?

While Pareto efficiency has a natural appeal, in my class at Wharton, I demonstrate its limitations with a thought experiment about the most efficient way to allocate twenty thousand dollars to the students in the class. (They like the example more in the few seconds before I emphasize it is a *hypothetical* twenty grand.)

Any allocation where I give out all the money is Pareto efficient, regardless of who wants or deserves that money the most. Whether I give it all to the best student, the worst student, the richest student,

---

* This heavily bearded Italian with the rhyming name, born in the mid-nineteenth century, is also known for the 80-20 rule, sometimes called the Pareto principle, which posits that 80 percent of output comes from 20 percent of inputs (for example, when 80 percent of a company's sales come from 20 percent of its products). Pareto developed this principle upon observing that 80 percent of Italian wealth was held by 20 percent of its population.

or the poorest student or spread it all around the room, after all the money is given out, I cannot make anyone better off without making someone else worse off (that is, I can't give anyone more money without taking money away from someone else).

The problem with thinking about efficiency Pareto's way is that while Pareto efficiency tells me that I should not let any of that (hypothetical) twenty thousand dollars go to waste, it does not tell me anything about whom to give the money to or in what proportion.

If I posed the thought experiment to you, you might argue that the most efficient way to allocate the twenty thousand dollars is to give it to the student who needs it the most. This precise determination about what to do with the scarce resource goes beyond Pareto efficiency and aims to maximize what economists call *allocative efficiency*.

In this case, allocative efficiency considers not only whether all available resources are being used but also whether we are putting them to their *best* use.

Imagine Isla wants the Hold the Cone much more than she wants her second-choice dessert, whereas Cass and Natalie will be nearly as happy receiving their second-choice dessert (say, a Tate's Bake Shop chocolate chip cookie, also a hit in our house). While giving the last Hold the Cone to anyone would achieve Pareto efficiency, giving it to Isla, who derives the greatest benefit from it, would achieve allocative efficiency.

Allocative efficiency is desirable, since it allows us to maximize happiness. But achieving it is hard because of the fundamental challenge of quantifying and comparing the value people derive from something.

The first issue is with measurement. How could I tell *how much* Isla preferred the Hold the Cone over the chocolate chip cookie? Could I tell from her impassioned plea? The look on her face? Her amount of whining about it? These might capture some true desire for the dessert, but each is an imperfect measure of how much happier she would be from receiving it.

Moreover, if my kids knew that I was using these measures, they might play up the intensity of their preferences. Their pleas for the Hold the Cone would become more impassioned, their faces more expressive, their whining more intense. (The first two strategies might have an upside, training them for future careers as litigators or dramatic actors; the last is a quick way to end up with a brood of spoiled brats.) And if I used the difference in value derived from first-choice versus second-choice options, Isla would have every incentive to misrepresent how much she likes Tate's cookies. Why not say she hates them if it increases her chance of getting the Hold the Cone she prefers?

The second issue is that trying to compare relative happiness and unhappiness across individuals is notoriously difficult. When I teach this in my course, I use the Wong-Baker FACES Pain Rating Scale as my example. The rating scale shows six simple, line-drawn faces exhibiting various states of distress, from "no hurt" to "hurts worst."

The first face looks perfectly happy, the fourth looks mildly uncomfortable, and the sixth has a giant frown with tears coming out of both eyes. These faces are likely familiar to anyone who has spent time in a pediatrician's office or anyplace where medical professionals need to treat patients across a language barrier, such as in an emergency department. The idea is that even someone who cannot verbally describe their pain to the doctor can still rank it by pointing to the face that most closely matches the way they feel.

While a useful tool for gauging an individual's subjective level of pain, the scale is less helpful for determining an individual's pain relative to others. To drive this point home, I describe to my class how two of my kids might use the scale. Imagine that Isla chooses the second face ("hurts little bit") and Natalie picks the fifth face ("hurts whole lot"). Can we say definitively that Natalie is in more pain than Isla? Your first instinct might be yes—Natalie's pain level is much higher on the scale than Isla's is. But what if I told you that when Isla broke her wrist (at around two years old), she barely cried, insisted that she felt fine, and showed so few signs of distress that it took us a few hours of observing her not using her right hand to realize we had to take her to urgent care, and that Natalie, by contrast, screams bloody murder whenever a comb touches the knots in her hair? You might think differently about how they are each using the scale.

Comparing happiness is as difficult as comparing pain; in both cases, different people will not necessarily express how they are feeling in the exact same way.

So, while we might want to identify the person who gets the most benefit from a scarce resource, we rarely try to figure out allocative efficiency by asking. Instead, we need to get more creative: We measure how much people want things by making them show us what they are willing to give up.

Sold to the Highest Bidder
DISCUSSING ONE WAY TO ACHIEVE ALLOCATIVE EFFICIENCY

These issues with measuring and comparing happiness are why economists are often tempted to use money to establish how much someone values a scarce resource. When we believe that willingness to pay is a good proxy for who values something most, we can achieve allocative efficiency by selling the good to whoever is willing to pay the most for it.

While I cannot confidently measure happiness, I can easily observe whether someone is willing to buy something at a given price. And while happiness levels are not comparable across people, money is (at least to the extent that it is always possible to determine which amount is more than another).

Prices also eliminate the incentive to inflate how much you value something, as it is costly to misrepresent your true preferences when money is at stake. With money, indicating you value something more requires paying more for it—you need to put your money where your mouth is.

The simplest way for sellers to take advantage of the logic that money can help measure the value people place on a scarce resource is to hold an auction and sell the resource in question to the person willing to pay the most for it.

Auctions are ubiquitous tools to allocate scarce resources. Sellers use them to allocate everything from livestock to fine art to rare items on eBay. The government often uses them to allocate timber rights, mining rights, and control over the wireless spectrum (the right to broadcast at certain wavelengths, which phone companies buy to enable them to provide cell service). In the world of finance, auctions are used to sell private companies and US Treasuries. Some initial public offerings use auctions to allocate shares to potential investors, as Google did in 2004.

While there are many auction formats, a classic one—as seen in the movies, at many charity galas, and on my all-time-favorite reality show, *Storage Wars*—starts with the auctioneer soliciting or offering an opening bid and then allowing participants to declare an amount they are willing to pay that is above the prior bid or to agree to pay a higher price suggested by the auctioneer (in more dignified art auctions, a bidder holds up a hand or a paddle to indicate their willingness to pay a higher price than the one offered by a previous bidder). The auction ends when no one is willing to outbid the current highest bidder. Since that bidder has offered to pay a price that no one else will top, the bidder gets to buy the item at that price.

In 2017, when Russian oligarch Dmitry Rybolovlev decided to sell his painting *Salvator Mundi*, attributed to Leonardo da Vinci, he engaged Christie's, a large auction house that specializes in fine art, to sell the work. If money is a good representation of how much someone values something, this auction efficiently put this rare painting into the hands of the person who valued it the most. The buyer, according to reports, was the Saudi prince Mohammed bin Salman, who paid over $450 million for the painting, the all-time record for a piece of art sold at auction.

But as we already noted in the introduction, the logic of using money as a proxy for how much people value something does not always hold. Imagine I am an art collector bidding against a member of the Saudi royal family. The Saudi royal family is estimated to be worth $1.4 trillion. To them, my entire net worth may be a rounding error. It is therefore possible that I value the painting just as much as the Saudi prince, but even if I went on a bank-robbing spree, I could not get my hands on the sum of money that he was able to bid for it.

A similar, if less pronounced, inequity would play out if I decided to use a monetary auction to allocate dessert to my kids. Cass has had many more birthdays, and thus many more cash birthday gifts from Grandma, than his sisters. Natalie has had far fewer birthdays than her siblings and doesn't even have access to Tooth Fairy money (she still has all her baby teeth). Unless he burns through all his savings, Cass will always be able to outbid his little sisters, even if they value something more.

In the face of inequity in wealth and income, the traditional auction does not necessarily achieve allocative efficiency, and it can also introduce inequity, thereby failing on another of the three *E*s. Maybe we can do better?

On the Auction Block

Discussing how we can use different types of auctions to achieve allocative efficiency

A clever market designer might suggest that if we want to avoid the inequity associated with money, we can measure how much market participants value something using some other form of currency. Let's say I identify something that I strongly suspect all my kids value equally, like the use of my iPad. (Much like adults value money, my kids value screen time and would happily accept an unlimited amount of it if Ilana and I were willing to grant it.)

If I gave them each the same number of iPad minutes before the start of the auction, I could auction off the last Hold the Cone in that currency. In this scenario, whichever child was willing to give up more of that sweet, sweet screen time in exchange for the last Hold the Cone could be assumed to value the dessert the most.

This kind of auction would achieve allocative efficiency by giving the Hold the Cone to the kid who valued it the most, and it would also be equitable, since everyone starts with the same amount of currency, and everyone walks away with something—either more screen time and their second-choice dessert or less screen time and their first-choice dessert.

But while I might be prepared to declare victory, this allocation method would be a burden to implement. It would require my being hypervigilant about screen-time budgets (everyone's screen time would need to be strictly enforced and monitored to the minute, accounting for any minutes deducted in exchange for Hold the Cones), and I am admittedly not up for that.

More broadly, it would feel inappropriate; a household where screen-time minutes are used as a currency and where dessert is sold by auction to the highest bidder seems more like the plot of an episode of *Black Mirror* or *The Twilight Zone* than a recipe for raising well-adjusted kids. I am no child psychologist, but my proposed auction strikes me as having the potential to lead my children to develop unhealthy attitudes toward both food and screen time, and market rules that risk causing psychological harm to market participants cannot reasonably be described as *easy*.

Finally, while I might be able to find a nonmonetary currency in my household, in practice, market participants rarely have a currency besides money to spend. So we must look elsewhere for ways to achieve allocative efficiency.

UNDERSTANDING EASE

Introducing easy and not-so-easy mechanisms

In markets without prices, economists often look to time and effort—things we all have and are not keen to give up—to assess who values things most. Those willing to sacrifice the most time or effort to obtain a scarce resource are assumed to value the good most.

This highlights another trade-off that makes it hard to achieve the three *E*s: Many market rules that might help us get closer to allocative efficiency do so by making market participation less easy.

First Come, First Served
INTRODUCING A MECHANISM THAT AIMS TO ACHIEVE
ALLOCATIVE EFFICIENCY BY MAKING THINGS DIFFICULT

At noon on the sixteenth of September, 1893, a pistol shot signaled the start of the United States' largest land run, the Cherokee Outlet Opening. Roughly one hundred thousand settlers raced across the border of Kansas into a six-million-acre strip of Oklahoma. This land, which the Cherokee Nation had been compelled to sell to the United States under pressure from the US government, was now being opened for settlement.

The land was partitioned into 160-acre homesteads, each about a quarter mile square. The homestead borders were on record at local land offices, of which there were a handful scattered around the region. Some of these plots were particularly coveted because of the quality of the land for farming or because of their proximity to the towns being built in the area, but the government was not charging more for the better plots. The federal Homestead Act of 1862, signed by Abraham Lincoln, gave the land away to settlers for free (beyond a filing fee, a residency requirement, and a trivial improvement requirement).

The government wanted to ensure that the homesteads went to

those who valued them most, so the process for claiming a parcel involved several steps. Before the land run began, you had to secure a certificate to participate, which required standing in a long line for days at a time in the hot summer sun. During the land run, you had to physically get to the parcel first and stake your claim by placing a literal stake in the ground. Finally, you had to race to the local land office to register that claim before anyone else did so.

To make sure people did not enter the territory before the designated time, eight cavalry troops and four infantry units were brought in to maintain law and order. But despite these efforts, the land run—like those that had occurred before it—quickly devolved into chaos.

Fights erupted among settlers jockeying to board trains into the territory. People jumped off moving trains, trying to stake claims on the best land before the train stopped at the next station to let people safely disembark. Settlers raced into the territory on horseback before the designated start time, despite the army's attempts to hold the line. In a famous incident, a man named John R. Hill protested that the army had let some settlers wait for the noon start time at a spot inside the territory, giving them an advantage. So he, along with a mob of other settlers, jumped the gun, galloping into the territory shortly before noon. He was promptly shot and killed.

Cheating was widespread. Settlers who thought that they had successfully secured a claim arrived at the land office to learn that their 160 acres had already been claimed by someone who had flouted the rules. These cheats, who sneaked past the army and staked their claims sooner than everyone else, were dubbed "sooners," a moniker that lives on as the name of the sports teams at the University of Oklahoma and in the nickname of the state.

The chaos of the Oklahoma land run illustrates a clear weakness of first come, first served as an allocation mechanism: Getting what you want can be an ordeal. While modern-day versions of the Oklahoma land run—such as queuing up outside the box office to get tickets to a show, standing in line for the chance to buy an iPhone, or racing to try to get a reservation at a hot restaurant—are not quite as onerous or chaotic, they often still require people to arrive early and devote significant time to the endeavor. And unlike money, which can be transferred from buyer to seller, the time and effort spent by market participants does not benefit anyone else. When I wait in line, I suffer, but no one else benefits.

Moreover, these allocation rules tend to bring out our competitive nature and can incentivize participants to seek unfair advantages over others. For a parent looking to allocate dessert (or, for that matter, a store trying to allocate iPhones or a theater trying to allocate tickets), this can be a risky proposition. Like the mobs fighting for spots on trains into the Cherokee land, a race to stake a claim to the last Hold the Cone could lead to a shoving match in front of the freezer. Or it could incentivize the kids to rush through dinner—perhaps the only time a busy family gets to spend together on a given day—to make sure they secure the treat sooner than their siblings.

These drawbacks are why market designers who want to use first-come, first-served market rules will often try to lower the cost to market participants.

Dibs!
Lower-Cost Versions of First Come, First Served

When I was growing up, the privilege of sitting in the front passenger seat on a car ride went to the first person who yelled "Shotgun" (as if it were a wagon train headed to Oklahoma for the land run). For your claim to be valid under our family rules, you had to be close enough to see the car when you said "Shotgun," and the driver had to hear you say it.

Any system involving dibs (a slang term for claiming something in advance) needs to have rules around when and how a claim can be made. Dibs is essentially a race, and if you're going to have a race, you need to agree on where and when the race begins and grant someone the authority to declare a winner.

Dibs has the potential to be equitable and efficient. Everyone has an equal opportunity to call dibs, and if people who value the resource the most make an extra effort to get it (like reaching the car first and being ready to yell when the driver is within earshot), dibs can achieve allocative efficiency as well.

But while racing to say dibs might be an improvement over standing in line—or a physical miles-long race to an Oklahoma land office—it still has costs for market participants. And when these races play out in practice, market participants will often make expensive investments to be just a little bit faster than the competition.

UNDERSTANDING EQUITY

Introducing equitable mechanisms

One way to guarantee equality in allocations is to provide the same thing—or nothing—to everyone.

In my ice cream example, achieving this type of equity would mean that if I can't give everyone a Hold the Cone for dessert, no one should be able to have one.

Achieving equity this way is a common tactic, particularly in classroom settings. Elementary-school teachers at many schools regularly prevent individual children from eating their own snacks or using their own school supplies (like colored pencils they bring from home) unless they can provide enough for all students to have the same experience. These rules arise from fears about the emotional consequences of some children feeling left out, concerns that appear to be growing over time.

When I was a kid, celebrating Valentine's Day at school was both exciting and stressful. Exciting because there was a chance of getting both candy and adoration; stressful because there was no guarantee of either. In my day, there was always the risk of not getting a valentine missive from anyone. Most people gave cards only to friends or—once we were old enough to have them—actual crushes. When you got a card, it often meant something special. But it also meant that you might receive only one or two cards while your more popular classmate (with his slicked-back black hair and charming smile) got one or two dozen.

Today, a generation later, all the schools that my kids have attended have enforced Valentine's Day equity. To avoid hurting classmates' feelings, students can either bring in Valentine's Day cards for the whole class or bring in none at all. As a result of these policies, each February 13, I check people off class lists as my kids scribble their classmates' names on little cardstock rectangles with assorted Valentine's-related puns like *Donut you just love Valentine's Day?* and *You have a pizza my heart*. (Thankfully, the kids are too young to notice the irony of giving a card that says *I only have fries for you* to seven different classmates.) Often these cards are sold in packs of twenty-eight, enough for the typical elementary-school class.

While equitable, this system isn't exactly easy for market participants (or their parents), who must remember to buy the cards, then take the time to personalize them for two dozen or more students. And the number of cards that get immediately discarded by their recipients—who want to receive cards from their least favorite classmates about as much as the senders want to bestow them—calls the efficiency of the exercise into question.

While we can buy more Valentine's Day cards and ensure we have enough participation trophies for a whole team, some resources are finite. Take, for example, the spots in a school's gifted-and-talented program. Schools can admit only a certain number of students to these programs; if entry was granted to everyone, the *gifted-and-talented* distinction would be meaningless. Administrators sometimes decide to offer that resource to no one—a number of school districts have done this—because of inequities in access to gifted programs or advanced placement courses. So in practice, efficiency and other considerations can lose out to concerns about equity and the desire to level an uneven playing field (or protect the feelings of second-graders).

The Two Xs
INTRODUCING EX-ANTE AND EX-POST EQUITY

It might be obvious that when we have a scarce resource that cannot be divided, any rule that allocates that resource to a subset of those who want it is going to introduce inequity by leaving others empty-handed.

But just as there are two ways of thinking about efficiency, economists have two ways of thinking about equity. We consider whether things are equitable *ex ante* (Latin for "before the event") as well as *ex post* (Latin for "after the event"). In other words, we look at whether market participants have an equal opportunity to obtain a resource (ex-ante equity) and at whether there is equality in the outcome (ex-post equity).

Ex-post equity cannot be achieved when an indivisible good is allocated to a subset of potential recipients. After you pick someone to receive the coveted dessert, you end up with one kid holding the Hold the Cone and two looking on with envy.

But even when we cannot achieve ex-post equity, we can still achieve ex-ante equity. That is, instead of giving each kid a third of the ice cream cone, you can give every child the same one-in-three chance of being the one who gets the whole thing.

Chosen at Random
INTRODUCING A MECHANISM THAT AIMS TO ACHIEVE EX-ANTE EQUITY

With roughly twenty-two million inhabitants, Beijing is the most populous world capital. Like many large urban areas with growing populations, Beijing has issues with air pollution. One of the biggest contributors is the city's nearly six million cars, which estimates suggest are responsible for 70 percent of the city's smog. In 2011, the city decided to take steps to reduce the number of cars on the road and improve breathability. It implemented a lottery.

If you want to drive a private car around the city during business hours, you need a Beijing license plate. But not everyone who wants a plate can get one—you must be randomly chosen. The lottery takes place every two months and currently doles out one hundred thousand new plates a year. With millions of people applying for a plate, participants have a less-than-one-in-two-thousand chance of winning one in a lottery (which works out to a less-than-one-in-three-hundred chance in any given year). Though not great odds, each person has an equal chance of winning.

Lotteries like this one have advantages. They can be ex-ante equitable by giving each person an equal chance of being selected to get the thing they all want. They can also be easy to participate in (so long as the paperwork to enter is not too onerous). And because all one hundred thousand plates that the city wants to give out get allocated to drivers, the lottery also achieves Pareto efficiency. But by randomly picking from all entrants, the lottery does not achieve allocative efficiency; someone who is desperate for a license plate—perhaps because she has a large family or a painful commute by public transportation—does not get priority over someone who wants the license plate less.

The market for Beijing license plates has another rule that prioritizes equity at the expense of efficiency: Plate holders are forbidden to drive gas-powered cars one day a week, and that day is assigned randomly, based on the last digit of their license plates. To see that this policy is inefficient, imagine that I really value driving on Friday but am willing to take public transit on Tuesday while you are willing to take the train on Friday if it means you can drive on Tuesday. Depending on the luck of the draw, we could both end up unable to drive on our desired days and be unable to swap, which would violate Pareto efficiency.

Taking Turns
Describing the deceptively simple solution to the Hold the Cone allocation

At one point in my quest to solve the Hold the Cone problem, I bought myself a three-sided die from Amazon, figuring that it would let me off the hook—instead of me picking a child to get the dessert, I could let the universe decide. But as it turns out, my young kids did not value randomization as an allocation mechanism as much as an economist like me might hope.

Unfortunately it is cold comfort to know that you had an equal shot at ending up with the dessert when you're watching your sibling eat it, particularly when you are a four-year-old who has watched her older sister win through the luck of the draw a few times in a row. This highlights a significant drawback of lotteries that achieve ex-ante but not ex-post equity: While the rules might be fair in theory, participants will not necessarily perceive them as fair if the outcomes are uneven.

How do we resolve the Hold the Cone problem in a way that is at least somewhat equitable and, importantly, also *perceived* as equitable by all participants? When my kids face a shortage, they *take turns* getting their first-choice dessert.

Taking turns leverages a key feature of many markets you will read about in this book: Organizations face the same allocation problem often, and they can remember the outcomes of previous allocations to help ensure that participants are treated somewhat fairly across a longer time horizon.

Taking turns is not completely equitable. If you zoom out far enough, it looks equitable: Each kid gets the cone a third of the time. But if you're going to take turns, you need to establish who gets to go first. To determine this in our household, we (perhaps uncreatively) followed centuries of tradition and used birth order, which meant that Cass (our oldest) is treated slightly better than Isla (the second oldest), who is treated slightly better than Natalie (the youngest), who must watch her two siblings get the last cone before her turn rolls around. It then becomes Cass's turn again, meaning he is slightly favored in each set of three turns.* But unlike rolling a die—which has no memory and might by chance make one child a winner multiple times in a row—taking turns gives everyone something. On any given evening, one of the kids gets the cone, and the other two get one step closer to their turns.

Taking turns is also not completely efficient. It achieves Pareto efficiency: The ice cream always gets eaten. But it doesn't always satisfy allocative efficiency: If Natalie is less in the mood for ice cream on the night that it happens to be her turn, she might not be the one who would get the most value out of the dessert (although she will almost always end up eating it anyway).

Taking turns is also not completely easy for the market participants, because it relies on memory of previous allocations to ensure participants are treated fairly. Having to remember whose turn it is is a cost (albeit a small one), and I cannot do this myself; I might not have been present the last time they settled this dessert allocation (they might have been with my wife, Ilana, or with a babysitter). This means that the cost of remembering who got the cone last is outsourced to the kids. Luckily, they seem to have an uncanny ability to always remember whose turn it is.

---

* This slight favoritism is why some turn-taking rules use a snake draft, in which the order of picking reverses each round. The snake draft is common for fantasy-football drafts (in that case, getting to pick first overall gives you a chance to snag the league's best player, but then you must wait for everyone else to pick twice before it's your turn again). If we applied a snake draft to the Hold the Cone problem, this would eliminate Cass's perpetual advantage. That said, this is harder to explain to young children than the traditional turn-taking rules and requires a better memory (in addition to remembering who got the cone last time, you need to remember who got it the time before that, which tells you which direction you're going this round).

But while taking turns is not guaranteed to perfectly satisfy any of the three *E*s, it gets as close to satisfying each one as it can without sacrificing too much on the other two.

Though it is often the best solution for solving simple household disputes, taking turns, or some variant of it, is not always practical for more complex allocation problems. Sometimes things are allocated only once. Other times, different people are competing for the goods at different times. As a result, taking turns is just one of the many sets of rules that dictate the hidden markets around us.

Indeed, mechanisms can get quite complicated as the allocation problems they aim to solve become more complex than assigning a single dessert to one of three kids. Often, they have dramatically more market participants with varied preferences for a wide array of available options. And unlike the Hold the Cone, which does not care who eats it, in some markets participants are trying to match with others who have preferences of their own. Other times, market participants will be angling for a resource for the purpose of reselling or trading it in an aftermarket.

Thankfully, as we become able to see the hidden markets around us with more clarity, we can determine our optimal strategy no matter how complex the rules may get.

CHAPTER 2

The Need for Speed

First-Come, First-Served Races

WHEN ILANA TURNED FORTY, HER BIG PRESENT TO HERSELF WAS A trip with two girlfriends to the Napa Valley in Northern California. My main gift to her was taking care of our three kids for the long weekend. But as a perennial overachiever, I wanted to go above and beyond. I knew that one of Ilana's dreams was to have a meal at the French Laundry, and my plan was to surprise her with a reservation for her and her girlfriends.

For the uninitiated, the super-fancy French Laundry, operated by restaurateur Thomas Keller, is one of only fourteen restaurants in the United States with three Michelin stars. It is located in Yountville, a cute town nestled among Napa Valley vineyards. Because of the restaurant's reputation and because it has only seventeen tables in its dining room (with a total seating capacity of sixty), it is notoriously difficult to get a table there, so much so that it regularly makes lists of the hardest reservations to obtain in the world.[*]

---

[*] It is also where California governor Gavin Newsom attended an unmasked dinner party in November 2020, during the COVID-19 pandemic, after his administration had issued guidelines that restricted dining to smaller groups. It led to significant outrage and was a point of contention during the 2021 gubernatorial recall election that

The restaurant is also obscenely expensive, but since the birthday Ilana was celebrating had a zero in it, it satisfied our family's unwritten rule about when it's okay to spend so much on a meal.

I assumed that with a little bit of research, I could figure out how to secure my wife and her two friends a reservation for one of the days they were in Napa. I learned that the restaurant's policy was to release all the open reservations for a calendar month on the first day of the preceding month at 10:00 a.m. Pacific time. I put it in my calendar and set a reminder, and on June 1, a few minutes before 1:00 p.m. eastern time, I headed to the website and refreshed the page repeatedly until all the July reservations were released for booking.

When the reservation page went live, each possible mealtime slot lit up as a blue rectangle, inundating me with a wide variety of options. Channeling my wife and her friends, I figured that their first choice would be dinner on Saturday, their second choice would be dinner on Friday (when they arrived in Napa), and dinner on Sunday would be acceptable, if not ideal. I quickly clicked on a 7:30 reservation for three people on Saturday night—but not fast enough. The blue rectangle had turned gray, indicating that the time slot was unavailable. The page reloaded, and all the desirable Saturday dinner times were gone.

All that was left on Saturday were two undesirable dinner times: 4:00 and 4:30. Figuring that an early-bird seating was better than nothing, I clicked on the 4:30 p.m. reservation. But this too was now gone, as was the 4:00 p.m. option. In just a few moments, the sea of blue had been replaced by a wall of gray. The Friday and Sunday reservations were also all taken. By 10:01 a.m. Pacific time, my search was over, and I had received an email from the French Laundry confirming that I had been added to the waiting list for all possible seatings over my three selected dates in July. I never heard from them, and a meal at the French Laundry remains on my wife's bucket list.

---

happened a few months after my wife's visit. (Despite the French Laundry scandal, Newsom won the recall election handily.)

THE QUICK AND THE QUEUED

Explaining how a first-come, first-served allocation system is easy to use — until excess demand makes it go haywire

Restaurants, spas, doctors' offices, performance venues, and stores regularly use first-come, first-served rules to dole out in-demand reservations, appointments, tickets, and products.

When there is enough to go around, this system makes allocation easy. When you're buying online, you simply go to an app or website, see what options are available, then book or buy the one you want. When you're shopping in person, you walk into the store, grab a good off the shelf, pay, and walk out with your purchase.

However, when there are more people who want a reservation than there are reservations available or more people who want to buy a product than products in stock, things get more complicated. In the presence of such excess demand, first-come, first-served rules take one of three forms. One is a race, which we will talk about in this chapter. The other two are lists and lines, which we will discuss in chapter 3.

The French Laundry reservation system is a race. The starting gun goes off at 10:00 a.m. on the first of the month. Whoever clicks the button for a particular reservation first ends up the winner. Those who are too slow — like me that fateful June — end up with nothing.

THE RACE IS ON!

You need to recognize you are in a race to have any chance of winning it

Possibly the most important thing you need to do to succeed in a race is recognize that you are in one. I started clicking frantically for a French Laundry reservation at 10:00 a.m. on June 1 because I knew, based on my online research, that I would be running in a race.

But sometimes you can get a head start over other participants by inferring that a race is likely, even without being told.

For example, every semester I participate in a race for afterschool activities in the 87 Afterschool program. PS 87, our local public elementary school, is a crown jewel of New York City's Upper West Side. It counts among its alumni Henry Winkler, Jordan Peele, and Timothée Chalamet.

The 87 Afterschool program offers enrichment classes every day from dismissal, around 2:30 p.m., until 6:00 p.m., which is great for working parents like us who need a convenient and affordable childcare option that lasts until work ends.

Isla's favorite afterschool class is Rainbow Stages: Movie Lab, in which students film a movie in front of a green screen. The movie is shot and edited by a dedicated instructor who also hosts a premiere for the kids and their parents during the last week of the program. The kids are ecstatic to see themselves on a big screen in the school auditorium saying their lines in front of a superimposed background made possible by movie magic.

Securing a set of good afterschool classes like Rainbow Stages, which meets each Tuesday, is a big win for parents. Isla spends each weekday morning either looking forward to an afterschool class she likes or dreading one she doesn't. Getting a first-choice class rather than a second-, third-, or fourth-choice class makes for a happier kid (and easier mornings).

When I first signed Isla up for afterschool classes at PS 87, I didn't anticipate having to run a race. As a new parent to the school, I did not know that there was excess demand for afterschool classes. In my prior experiences signing up Cass—who did not go to PS 87—for afterschool programs, the good classes always had plenty of slots available.

But the wording of the emails announcing registration for the PS 87 afterschool program had triggered my market designer's intuition that a race might be afoot. An email for the afterschool program at Cass's school typically announced the opening and closing dates of registration. In contrast, the email from PS 87 announced the opening date and the start time of afterschool-class registration—June 21 at 10:00 a.m.—and did not specify an end date.

That was the first clue. Presumably the PS 87 program also had a cutoff day for registration, but the email had omitted it. That suggested to me that most people registered soon after the window opened, so the date of its closing was all but irrelevant. Even more telling was that the PS 87 email mentioned the time—not just the date—that registration opened. This was a clear sign that parents trying to register their children later in the afternoon on June 21 would likely find their options more limited.

My suspicions were confirmed by an email I received in mid-June informing me that, "due to a conflict with the pre-K graduation ceremony," online registration would begin at 10:30 rather than 10:00.

It was official—there was going to be a mad dash for afterschool classes. The fact that they had moved the time back thirty minutes to accommodate the small number of parents (eighteen families out of hundreds) whose children attended the school's prekindergarten program had confirmed it. Clearly, those spots filled up so fast that a mere thirty minutes mattered, and the school wanted to eliminate a conflict that would unfairly make a subset of parents unavailable when the starting gun went off.

When there is not a race to sign up for afterschool classes, we do not care about the exact time online registration opens; we can register our kids whenever it is convenient for us to do so. But when there is excess demand, minutes—and sometimes seconds—matter. This means that when you see both a date and a specific time posted for something being offered on a first-come, first-served basis, you can typically infer that a race is on.

WHEN MILLISECONDS MATTER

An example emphasizing the importance of speed in first-come, first-served races

When you are in a first-come, first-served race, the difference between winning and falling short can come down to something as simple as your internet speed.

In 2005, I was enrolled in a yearlong master's program in economics at Trinity College at the University of Cambridge. Trinity College, founded in 1546, boasts a rich history and many illustrious alumni, including Charles III, the current king of England, and, perhaps most famously, Sir Isaac Newton. (Sadly, the story that Newton first conceptualized gravity as a student at the college when an apple fell from a tree and landed on his head is apocryphal.)

The Trinity campus, with buildings dating from the sixteenth and seventeenth centuries, felt old in a way that I had never experienced before. Whenever I walked out of the dining hall and toward my dorm, I stepped on a stone slab that had been worn down many inches in its middle by hundreds of years of footsteps (perhaps including those of Isaac Newton).

Unfortunately, when I was a student there in 2004 and 2005, the school's old-world charm appeared to extend to the college's information-technology infrastructure. As it turns out, it is difficult to wire ancient buildings for high-speed internet and to create a reliable Wi-Fi network when so many walls are made of stone, so connectivity was spotty. If walking around campus transported me back to the sixteenth century, trying to use the internet at Cambridge transported me back to the twentieth.

I was able to tolerate the slow internet connection because I knew my time at Trinity College was going to be short. After my yearlong program, I was headed back to the States for my PhD. But moving from Cambridge, England, to Cambridge, Massachusetts, turned out to be logistically difficult, particularly when it came to housing.

• The Need for Speed •

At that time, Harvard's real estate services, which leased residences close to campus, had a program that allowed incoming graduate students like me—people who were looking for a lease for the upcoming school year—to view and select from the available housing options remotely. After applying for the program, I was told that my window to lock in the apartment I wanted would open at 6:15 a.m. on May 18. The specificity of this start time (down to the quarter of the hour) was a clear sign that a race would be on.

The stakes for securing one of these apartments were high. The housing options offered through this service were both cheaper and closer to campus than most of the housing available on the private market. In advance of my race, I scoured the website for suitable apartments, and I found a great one: a one-bedroom with a large study that could easily be a second bedroom. It even had a balcony. As one of the most desirable apartments on offer, it would be in high demand, but I decided to go for it anyway, assuming I had just as good a chance as anyone. This assumption turned out to be wrong.

When May 18 rolled around, I was ready to go at 6:15 a.m. eastern time on the dot. I logged in, navigated to the apartment I wanted, and clicked to select it. It was already taken. I then looked at some of the other, smaller apartments I had considered; they were gone too.

At first, I couldn't understand how this had happened. But eventually it dawned on me that the speed (or lack thereof) of my connection—which had to travel through the slow internet infrastructure at Trinity College and make its way across the ocean to the servers hosting the housing website—had me lagging behind students who had better internet service closer to campus. (My future classmate and friend Sam was living in Brooklyn with high-speed internet at the time, and he had no problem snagging the housing he wanted.)

Losing this race was costly; I ended up moving into an apartment that was 25 percent more expensive and farther from campus. But the extra $4,200 a year I paid in rent was nothing compared to the vast sums of money riding on one's internet speed when trading in global financial markets.

Stock markets used to operate in person. Once upon a time, there were five thousand people on the floor of the New York Stock Exchange, running around shouting orders, essentially desires to buy or sell a certain number of shares of stock at a certain price. The first person to fill an order—such as by agreeing to sell shares at that price—got to make the trade.

When these markets went electronic, the computer servers implementing the transactions retained the first-come, first-served market rules for executing trades. The incentives to be the first one to make a desirable trade didn't go away, and the internet era opened the door for certain firms—called high-frequency trading firms—to make boatloads of money by figuring out how to make trades faster than everyone else.

Imagine that you are selling shares of a stock, say, IBM, that can be traded on multiple exchanges in the United States, including the major national stock exchanges (NYSE and Nasdaq) and over seventy-five additional trading venues regulated by the SEC. A buyer has just purchased a bunch of shares of IBM on the NYSE at above the current price, driving the price of IBM on the NYSE slightly higher than it is on all the other exchanges and trading venues. If you have been offering to sell the now-more-valuable shares of IBM at their old price, you might want to refresh your quote to ask for a higher price (to reflect the higher value of IBM following the trade).

But here is where the race comes in. Everyone has learned at the same time that shares of IBM are now more valuable, and everyone knows that you are currently offering to sell IBM shares for a below-market price. You want to refresh your stale quote, but everyone else wants to buy those shares at your below-market price before you get a chance to do so.

Because the exchanges process messages in the order that they are received, whichever message gets there first is the one that is executed—either your request to change your price or, perhaps more likely, one of the many requests made by buyers hoping to buy your shares at the old price.

Faster communication with the exchanges therefore allows firms to effectively buy low and sell high simultaneously, what's known as *latency arbitrage*. The amount of money made by winning the race on any given trade might be small, since the price difference between exchanges can be as little as a penny. But a penny here and a penny there can add up quickly because of the massive volume being traded.

My coauthor and former classmate Eric Budish along with economists Matteo Aquilina and Peter O'Neill estimate that five billion dollars a year is at stake in these races in global equities markets alone (and that over 20 percent of all trading volume takes place in latency arbitrage races). Add in the commodity, currency, treasury, bond, and all the other financial markets that are facilitated by electronic trading, and there are even more billions of dollars to be made.

Because being even a little bit faster matters tremendously in these races (and there is no prize for second place), firms are happy to invest in faster and faster communications. Shortly after the financial crisis of 2008, a company called Spread Networks spent an estimated three hundred million dollars to build a fiber-optic cable line between the Chicago Mercantile Exchange and Carteret, New Jersey, where the Nasdaq's primary data center is located. The cable line decreased the round-trip time to get data between the two sites by three milliseconds. Three milliseconds might seem like nothing, but in these races, it can be worth billions.

Investments in speed did not stop with new fiber-optic lines. Since data travels faster through the air than through glass, some financial firms started using microwave technology to transfer data over long distances, lowering the round-trip speed from Chicago to New York and back from 13.3 milliseconds to 8.5 milliseconds (approaching the theoretical minimum set by the speed of light in a vacuum, which is 7.96 milliseconds).

Firms have even invested in lasers, which can work more reliably than microwaves in bad weather, to transmit data between the Nasdaq's data centers in Carteret and the NYSE data centers thirty-five miles away, and there are plans to connect data centers across continents using a network of satellites, speeding up transmission beyond what can be achieved using fiber-optic cables run across oceans. As data transmission approaches the speed of light, races are now won by microseconds and nanoseconds.

Of course, the average person does not have hundreds of millions of dollars to invest in fiber-optic cables and satellite networks, but regular people don't need to. We can increase our speed in the races that matter to us by purchasing gigabit internet services (offered by most providers) or upgrading our cell phones to secure faster data transmission. We can run our races while plugged directly into an Ethernet cable on a high-speed network at home or at the office, which can give us an advantage over using the coffee-shop Wi-Fi.

In the case of my Cambridge housing, I could have flown to Boston beforehand to sit in a computer lab on campus to race for my preferred housing. It may sound extreme, but if a few seconds made the difference between getting the apartment and not, the $4,200 in rent savings would have easily been worth the trip. In these kinds of races, reaching the server first might give you the edge you need to win.

KNOW THYSELF (OR LEARN THYSELF QUICKLY)

Explaining why it pays to make your decisions in advance

One reason the high-frequency trading transactions can be executed on the order of milliseconds is that there is no need for a human to think or decide about any given transaction; the trades are all automated by algorithms.

While we might not have algorithms to make our decisions for us when we play in first-come, first-served races, we can do prep work to make sure we do not waste precious time contemplating when we should be clicking.

At the schools that my kids attend, the availability of parent-teacher conference slots is usually announced unceremoniously in an email sent to parents by the teacher or school principal at a seemingly random day and time each semester. Once that email is sent, the race begins. Since most parents check their email at different times throughout the day, the race for the best slots is won on the order of minutes rather than seconds, but I do not like to take any chances; as soon as I see that email come in, I drop whatever I am doing and click on the link.

I used to scour the options and then call Ilana to try to find a time when neither of us had a conflict. But with the clock already ticking, even the briefest conversation could mean the difference between getting a convenient time slot and having to reshuffle an entire day's schedule to get a precious fifteen minutes of face time with one of our kids' teachers. Now we are in the habit of blocking off conflicts on a joint calendar ahead of time so either one of us can confidently book a time that will work well for both of us when we receive that email.

In cases like these, when you do not know when a race will start until it has begun, it is also useful to do some research. Now that our kids have been at their schools for a few years, Ilana and I can look back at prior parent-teacher conference sign-up emails to get a sense of when that starting gun might go off. Then we can pay extra attention to our inboxes when we expect the emails to be sent.

GO FOR GOLD OR SETTLE FOR SILVER?

Introducing a strategy for playing in first-come, first-served races when there are multiple options

A key feature of many first-come, first-served races like restaurant reservations and parent-teacher conference sign-ups is that they are not actually one race. They are multiple races happening simultaneously, one for each of the options from which you can select. In these cases, you need to develop a plan about what to go for. The first and most critical step is recognizing that each option represents a different race.

If there had been only one seating option available when I was trying to get Ilana her dream birthday dinner, all I could have done was click as fast as possible and hope for the best. But when the July reservations opened, each seating option was a different thing to which I might have raced. Which option should I have gone for?

This might seem like a simple decision: You might think you should race for the thing you want the most. But since there are always other people racing against you, this logic can lead you astray. You need to consider what your opponents are racing toward too.

For the French Laundry, certain reservation slots—certain days (Friday and Saturday) and times (7:00 or 7:30 p.m.)—are going to be more desirable than others. Even if you know nothing specific about the people you are racing against, it's safe to assume that there are going to be more people in the race for a 7:30 p.m. reservation on Saturday than for a 4:00 p.m. reservation the following Tuesday.

Another factor is party size. I had a bit of an advantage relative to others because I was trying to get a table for three, which is usually less popular than a table for two. This is especially true at a place like the French Laundry, where people often go to celebrate anniversaries, events where one is less tolerant of a third wheel. (Had I been trying to snag a Sunday reservation at a popular brunch spot where people are more likely to be eating with a group of friends, trying to get a table for three might have been a liability.) That said, since tables typically have either two or four seats rather than three, I was likely also competing against groups of four.

In first-come, first-served races where there are clearly more desirable and less desirable options and what you want is likely to be popular, you have two strategies to choose from.

One strategy, what I call the *go-for-gold* strategy, is to make a beeline for your first choice. This high-risk, high-reward strategy is the only way to go if you will be happy with nothing short of a dinner reservation on a weekend night at a desirable time. But with dozens if not hundreds of people clicking the same blue box as you at the same time, your odds of getting that desirable table are not great. That said, if you are willing to risk ending up with nothing for a shot at your first-choice option, or if it is the only feasible option for your schedule, racing for it might be your optimal strategy.

Going for gold might have been the optimal strategy for me in my quest for a French Laundry reservation. I was trying to book a surprise meal for which I would have to prepay an arm and a leg. To maximize the chance that my grand gesture was going to be viewed as the work of a considerate—nay, heroic!—husband, I wanted it to be perfect. I wanted it at the ideal time that worked seamlessly with her itinerary. It would be a much less desirable birthday surprise if, without discussing it with Ilana, I decided that an afternoon she had planned to spend biking country roads or relaxing by the pool would be spent eating a meal instead. So I decided to take a chance on winning the perfect reservation rather than winding up with one that forced her to change up her birthday-weekend plans.

But while I was going for the gold, those 4:00 and 4:30 p.m. reservations were being scooped up by those using the second, less aggressive approach, which I call the *settle-for-silver* strategy.

Settling for silver requires treating something less desirable as if it were your first choice. We might all want to stand at the top of the podium with the gold medal. But like a figure skater who finds herself somewhat behind a leading competitor, getting there might require making a risky move, like executing a triple Axel that she has never successfully landed in competition. A skater going for gold might take that chance despite the high probability of falling onto the ice and walking away without any medal at all. Or that skater could settle for silver by sticking with the tried-and-true routine.

In this scenario, she gives herself a higher chance of getting on the podium by giving up on her chance of securing the top spot. Clicking first for a 7:30 reservation is going for the gold; clicking first for a 4:00 reservation is settling for silver.

This settle-for-silver strategy is lower risk but lower reward. In a competitive situation where your preferences are similar to those of others—for example, most people would rather eat dinner at 7:30 than 4:00—going for a less desirable option can dramatically increase your odds. Put simply, you are more likely to win a race when fewer people are running in it.

CHANCE, PAIN, AND GAIN

Providing a framework to decide when to go for gold and when to settle for silver

When should you go for gold and when should you settle for silver? There are three factors to consider in deciding which strategy to play.

The first is your chance of succeeding in your quest for gold. If the figure skater had nailed the triple Axel during her last practice and knew that doing so again would secure her the gold, she might decide that she had a decent chance if she went for it.

The second is the pain of failure. If you go for gold but fail, how much worse off will you be than if you had settled for silver? If landing on her butt instead of on the podium costs the figure skater a lucrative endorsement deal, the pain of failure might be very high. In that case, she might decide to settle for silver by skating a safe, simple program.

The third factor is how much you gain from gold rather than silver. If the endorsement deal the skater would get as a gold medalist is only slightly better than the deal she'd get as a silver medalist, she might decide the risk of going for gold is not worth the reward.

Settling for silver might be optimal if you will be nearly as happy with your second choice as with your first.

It is possible that if I had asked my wife about the reservation rather than trying to secure it as a surprise, she might have told me that she would be nearly as happy with a 4:00 p.m. slot as with a 7:30 p.m. one. Maybe she and her friends would not want to be at the pool that long, and she would still be on East Coast time anyway. In that case, the value gained from getting 7:30 p.m. rather than 4:00 p.m. would be minimal, so I might have been better off going for the earlier reservation that fewer people wanted. Given that the slot for 4:00 p.m. on Saturday was still blue when the page refreshed and everything else had turned gray, if I had gone for it first, I very likely would have gotten it.

These three factors play out in countless first-come, first-served markets. I think about them whenever I'm looking for parking.

The allocation of parking spots is a classic case of a hidden market. There are better and worse spots in parking lots, but we do not pay more for the more desirable spots. The allocation mechanism is first come, first served, but the environment is fluid. The best spot in the lot — the spot closest to the Costco entrance or the main gate at the zoo — is usually the first one taken. But that spot will become available again when the car that took it leaves, so the top spot might be available when you arrive later in the day.

But there's a catch. When you pull into the Costco lot, it is typically impossible to see if there is a desirable spot all the way up at the store entrance. Rows of parked cars block your view. You start to drive toward the entrance, and when you come across an open spot — one that's still rather far from the store — you must make a choice. You can settle for silver by taking that far-from-the-entrance spot and resign yourself to a long walk. Or you can go for gold by driving closer to the entrance in the hope that a more desirable spot is available.

Some people feel so strongly about how to handle this parking problem that it is almost a matter of religion for them. Some are settle-for-silver people who always take the first decent spot they see. Others are go-for-gold people who always drive up to the front for a chance at the very best spot. But sticking to the same strategy no matter what is not the best way to play in this market. Instead, you should consider the three factors to determine which strategy is best.

When the lot is full enough that I cannot tell what spots are available near the entrance, I usually assume that it is unlikely I will get a spot right out front. The chance of succeeding in my quest for gold is small.

I then consider the cost of failing. In most cases, driving to the store entrance and finding no spots is unlikely to cost me the chance to park at all. It just means I spend a minute or two driving around the lot before I circle back to the spot I passed. So the pain of going for gold and failing is small. However, if the lot is almost totally full or if there are other cars circling for that silver-medal spot, someone might scoop it up in my absence. In those cases, the cost of going for gold is higher, and I take any spot I see.

So, unless the lot is packed when I am deciding which strategy to play, the key consideration is usually the third factor, the gain: How much better off will I be if I get the spot right in front of the entrance rather than the one farther away?

At Costco, this depends on whether it is just me or me with my kids. When I have three kids in tow, the benefit of getting the spot by the entrance is massive. It means no trudging through the parking lot with a four-year-old complaining she's tired of walking and less worrying about navigating back to the car with a cart full of seltzers and toilet paper and three kids distracting me as I desperately try to recall where we parked. Sure, there probably won't be a spot at the entrance, and I'll likely waste a few minutes circling the rows of cars and end up in the silver spot anyway, but it is worth it for a chance to hit the parking-lot jackpot.

When it's just me, the calculus works the other way. I'll feel a little silly in the unlikely event that I trek from my car to the entrance only to see an open spot right out front. But it's not that much of a burden for me to make the walk from a few rows away when I am alone, and I would rather just get the errand over with than risk having to spend a few extra minutes circling the lot.

THE OUTSIDE OPTION

Introducing an option that mitigates the pain of failure and can change your calculus

One of the disappointing features of the settle-for-silver strategy is right there in the name: You must settle. Even when you win your race for silver, you might end up a bit disappointed. So it would be nice if you could design circumstances that make it optimal for you to go for gold instead of settling for less than what you really want.

While you usually can't magically improve your chances of winning gold, you may be able to mitigate the pain you feel if you go for gold and fail. In our Olympic-medal metaphor, when the figure skater is deciding whether to go for gold, it might be important to know whether she already has (or is likely to get) a medal in another event, perhaps from the team competition. Knowing that she will still medal at these Olympics no matter what happens on the ice tonight might make her feel safe enough to go for gold.

Economists have a name for the backup prize that you can secure if you do not get what you want from a market. We call it your *outside option*, since it is something you can get outside the allocation mechanism: a plan B you can fall back on.

Sometimes there is no way to establish a desirable outside option. When I drive to Costco and am looking for a parking spot, I need to park somewhere; my outside option is deciding to go home empty-handed (not really an option at all if we are out of toilet paper).

But in other cases, like in the French Laundry example, all it takes is a little creativity to identify an appealing outside option.

Ilana's fortieth-birthday trip to Napa Valley was not her first time in Yountville. Her parents live in the East Bay of San Francisco, a little over an hour from the town. As a result, when Ilana and I had fewer kids, we used to take the whole family to California once a year, leave Cass (or Cass and Isla, depending on the year) with my in-laws, and sneak away for a night or two in Yountville.

On those trips, our best dinners were the ones we had at another Thomas Keller restaurant, Ad Hoc, which serves high-end comfort food. Ad Hoc is not nearly as expensive as its sister restaurant down the street, and it is relatively easy to get a suitable reservation. And unlike fancier restaurants, Ad Hoc doesn't charge a fee for last-minute cancellations; if you make a reservation and change your mind, they just ask you to call and tell them.

If sometime before 10:00 a.m. on June 1, I had secured a desirable Saturday-night reservation at Ad Hoc for my wife and her friends (easy to do, since I was planning more than a month in advance), I could have felt more confident about being aggressive when trying to get a French Laundry reservation. When a good outside option mitigates the pain of failing, going for gold can be optimal.

KNOW THY COMPETITORS

An example illustrating the importance of understanding how much excess demand there is for something that you want

The first time I signed Isla up for afterschool classes, I went to the afterschool registration website a few minutes before the newly appointed time of 10:30 a.m. At 10:29 a.m., I started refreshing the page repeatedly. Because clocks aren't always perfectly synced across different servers, I thought it might hit 10:30 on their clock a bit earlier than on mine; indeed, I was able to log into the registration system while my clock still said 10:29.

Following my own advice, I had researched my options and had a plan. I asked Isla for her first-, second-, and third-choice afterschool classes for each day of the week. Once I was in the registration system, I followed their day-of-the-week interface, booking the best thing I could get on Monday before moving to Tuesday and then Wednesday, through the end of the week.

That strategy served me well that day and for a few afterschool-registration days that followed; I got Isla into her first-choice classes (including Rainbow Stages) in each of her first three semesters at PS 87.

In her fourth semester, my luck ran out. I selected Isla's first choice for Monday and then scrolled to the Tuesday options.

Her first choice for Tuesday, Rainbow Stages, was already waiting-list only.

It had filled up in just a few seconds, presumably because parents who had also logged onto the registration page at the earliest possible moment had—unlike me—gone straight to Rainbow Stages to register for it before they did anything else.

It turned out that by Isla's fourth semester, Rainbow Stages was even more popular. Kids had been talking to each other about the class, and those who had taken it in prior semesters started lobbying their parents to take it again.

Not being privy to such conversations, I did not realize how much demand had shifted. If I had realized the most competitive race of all was going to be for Rainbow Stages, I would have ditched my day-of-the-week strategy and gone to Tuesday first. Instead, Isla ended up disappointed and in her second-choice class on Tuesdays.

My Rainbow Stages debacle reinforces a broader point: Knowing what your competitors want and inferring what strategy they are going to play can help ensure you get what you want from first-come, first-served races.

In many markets, there is a consensus about what is desirable and what is not. As noted earlier, it is probably safe to assume that 7:30 p.m. is a more popular dinnertime than 4:00 p.m. (except, perhaps, in certain retirement communities) and that parking spots near the entrance are almost universally preferred over ones on the far side of the lot.

In some of these cases, you might realize your top choice is *not* very popular with others — perhaps you prefer eating dinner early or like getting some steps in when parking at Costco — so you can safely go for gold. If your gold is other people's silver (or bronze, or brass), you might not be facing that much competition for your top choice.

But in other races, you might be unsure whether you will be facing stiff competition. In these cases, it makes sense to invest in learning about your competitors' preferences. For example, I probably could have learned what the most popular afterschool activities were by paying attention to some of the school's many WhatsApp groups, in which parents periodically complained about their kids not getting into certain afterschool classes, or by asking Isla what her friends' favorite classes were. In high-stakes first-come, first-served races, knowing what your opponents are going after can make all the difference, and research can give you important insight into their plans.

Once you identify the preferences of other market participants, you may want to consider their possible strategies. If everyone agrees on which option is the best and most people are going to go for gold, you'll have a better chance of getting something suitable if you settle for silver. In contrast, if many market participants are resigned to settling for silver, that might increase your chances of securing gold.

Though this calculus will vary by situation and you can never truly know what strategy another person is going to choose, economics can offer a hint. Academic research suggests that most people are more focused on themselves and their preferences than on the preferences of their competitors. This leads most people to go for gold, even when they might do better settling for silver. So in the absence of additional information, I usually assume that most other market participants are racing for gold, which often pushes me a bit more toward settling for silver.

GET ON THAT WAITING LIST!
What to do when you don't win your race

You will not always walk away from your races with something desirable. But first-come, first-served markets with excess demand will often have waiting lists to make sure they can replace anyone who wins a race but has to cancel. You can and should get on any relevant waiting lists—ideally, as soon as possible.

This may seem obvious, but many people don't do it; they assume their chance of getting off the waiting list and onto the actual list is infinitesimal, so why even try. But this is too pessimistic. Restaurant reservation cancellations are common (data suggests about 15 percent of reservations are canceled). Cancellations may happen less often at hot restaurants, but they do happen—people get sick at the last minute, sitters cancel, cars break down, and so on. Since putting your name on a waiting list typically costs just a few seconds of your time, it is well worth it for even a small chance of success.

In some cases, after a cancellation, the now-open reservation is offered to people in the order they joined the waiting list (the same rules that your doctor's office might use to allocate newly available, nonurgent medical appointments). If there is a chance the waiting list you're joining uses this policy, you should add yourself to it as quickly as possible.

Going through a list sequentially takes time, however, so some places with waiting lists do not bother. Instead, when there is a cancellation, they send out an alert to all the people on the waiting list, essentially firing the starting gun for a new first-come, first-served race for anyone who is interested in snagging the newly open slot.

Like the emails for parent-teacher conferences, these alerts should get your prompt attention.*

After I struck out getting a reservation for Ilana's birthday, I emailed my in-the-know San Francisco friends to ask whether they had heard of any tricks to get a French Laundry reservation outside of the usual channels. I was hoping for a secret telephone number or website. Their advice was to just show up to the French Laundry on the day I wanted to eat there and see if there were any spots open due to last-minute cancellations.

Their logic was sound. Yountville is an out-of-the-way destination. If someone cancels a 7:00 p.m. reservation at 6:00 p.m., that might not leave enough time for someone on the waiting list to get to the restaurant. If you're standing there dressed appropriately, you might just get lucky.

LOOK FOR LOOPHOLES

Some first-come, first-served races have back doors that enable you to get what you want without winning — or even running — the race

About a year after my wife's trip to Napa, one of her travel companions was eager to try a New York City salon called MASA.KANAI, which offered what was known as a Head Spa treatment. Massively popular around Asia and, more recently, massively popular to watch on TikTok, this treatment is described as a facial for your scalp. It is supposed to be incredibly relaxing, leaving your body calm, your hair shiny, and your scalp fresh.

---

* Some systems use a hybrid policy, reaching out to a small group of people (perhaps emailing the first five patients who added themselves to a waiting list to see a particular doctor) and offering them a newly available appointment slot in a first-come, first-served race. The slot goes to the first person who claims it; if no one claims it within a designated period, it will be offered to another set of people on the waiting list (the next five, perhaps), and so on. In these cases, it matters when you joined the waiting list but also how fast you respond when you get an invitation.

Despite the salon's high prices (three hundred dollars for sixty minutes, last I checked), it was still very hard for a new client—Ilana's bestie included—to get an appointment. Like the French Laundry, MASA.KANAI released a month's worth of Head Spa slots at 10:00 a.m. on the first of the month (or the second of the month if the first was a Monday, when the spa was closed). But unlike the French Laundry, the booking system was old-school.

Rather than doing things online, if you wanted to make an appointment, you had to either go to the salon in person or call. The website emphasized that the salon would disregard voicemails left before 10:00 a.m., which meant that to make an appointment, you needed to start calling at 10:00 and hope that you got through before all the slots were gone.

The other distinctive feature of this race was that MASA.KANAI released its slots for the month on the first of the *same* month. This slight difference introduced a trick for snagging a spot without the hassle of hitting redial on your phone all morning. If you showed up when the salon opened at 10:00 a.m. on the first of the month, you might be able to just walk right in and claim the first or second appointment of the day, spots that were more likely to be available (since new clients had not had a chance to book them yet). And even if you could not get treated that morning, you still had a much better chance of getting an appointment at some point because you were already physically in the salon. A phone line can be busy for hours, but you probably won't have to wait more than a few minutes if you're standing in front of the scheduler. Being there in person allows you to leapfrog ahead of everyone else in the race and maybe even avoid running the race altogether.

Best of all, once you were a customer at MASA.KANAI, you could make appointments in advance without the rigmarole—you were in the club. So a savvy customer who didn't want to have to show up in person at 10:00 a.m. on the first of the month could book a less in demand (and ideally less expensive) service by phone, thereby establishing herself as a client. Often, the best way to win the game is not to have to play, and getting into the booking system lets you sidestep this first-come, first-served allocation process in the future.

When the COVID-19 vaccines were first made available, states imposed strict rules about who could access them based on age and health status. But even with restrictions on who was eligible, there was still massive excess demand for available shots.

This excess demand created first-come, first-served races among groups of people who all had the same priority for available shots. While relatively efficient and equitable, the process I experienced in New York City was exceedingly difficult for market participants. Races would start at seemingly random times whenever appointments for shots were made available on one of the multiple online systems that were built to help distribute the vaccines—a complicated patchwork of websites run by different city and state agencies.

Then a software engineer named Huge Ma built a website called TurboVax to help residents find and sign up for vaccines; it compiled vaccine availability and sent the data to the website's Twitter account in real time. The TurboVax Twitter account let potential users know when slots were available and on which of the websites they could be found. Now, rather than repeatedly checking various city and state websites for news that additional slots had been made available, people simply had to log onto Twitter and wait for a push notification letting them know a race had begun.

Ma's website garnered two million views within four months, turning him into an instant celebrity. He was given the nickname Vax Daddy and became so popular in the city that he eventually ran for the New York State Assembly (though he dropped out of the race when the state's redistricting put his Queens home outside of the district he had hoped to represent).

Though TurboVax made the race for vaccines significantly easier to navigate, some people discovered an even easier way to secure early jabs.

Their strategy was elegant. They showed up at vaccine sites—like large retail pharmacies—at the end of the day and waited around to see if the pharmacies had any unused vaccines. Vaccines came in multi-dose vials that had to be completely used or disposed of once the first dose was drawn, and pharmacies often had doses left over at the end of the day. This was sometimes because there were cancellations, but it also happened when multi-dose vials were overfilled and unexpectedly contained extra doses (for example, some Moderna vials designed to hold ten doses actually held eleven). Since the pharmacies would rather give people the shots than waste them, some people were able to opt out of the race completely and secure early vaccines that way.

THE BOTTOM LINE

Takeaways from this chapter to help you succeed as a market participant

In short, the keys to prevailing in first-come, first-served races are to recognize that you are in a race and then be there, ready to sprint, when the starting gun goes off. You also want to eliminate any potential obstacles that might slow you down. A world-class runner trains, gets the best shoes, and might even go over the race's course and note any twists and turns before the race. You can do the same by being on your highest-speed internet connection and familiarizing yourself with the interface that you will be clicking through (perhaps even doing a practice run).

Things get more interesting when you are racing against many others for multiple options. In these cases, you should consider whether you are going to *go for gold* or *settle for silver*.

To make that decision, investigate your options in advance. Figure out what you want most but also evaluate other things you might get from the market. Then you can consider the chances of getting your favorite options, perhaps by researching the preferences of your competitors to help you guess whether they are likely to want what you do. Next, decide how much you gain from getting your top choice rather than your second choice and assess the pain you will feel if you go for gold and fail. To help mitigate the pain of failure, identify an *outside option* that you can fall back on.

When the time comes, trust your plan and go as fast as you can (and then get on any waiting lists if you don't win your race). When all else fails, you can always look for loopholes so you do not have to race at all.

COULD THE MARKET DESIGNERS DO BETTER?

Describing possible improvements to first-come, first-served races

Races are not particularly easy for market participants. If you need to run a race, you must make yourself available at a specific time, one that is not necessarily convenient. You might also spend time, money, and energy investing in speed and investigating the preferences and strategies of other market participants. You do all of this for an uncertain outcome.

In addition, these market rules are not always equitable. In some races, people with faster internet connections have an advantage over those with slower ones. And people who have the flexibility to show up whenever races are happening have a big advantage over those who do not. The kids of those PS 87 parents who could dedicate time to sit in front of their computers at 10:29 a.m. on that Tuesday in June got the best afterschool classes, whereas kids of parents who had jobs that did not allow them to take a break were left with the dregs. Market designers can take steps to address these inequities. For example, the afterschool program eventually switched the start of the registration race from a weekday morning to a Sunday afternoon, when the school expected more parents were likely to be available.

But while that change made the race more equitable, it also made running it a bit more of an ordeal. While many working parents are, by default, in front of computers on a random Tuesday morning, the same is not true for a Sunday afternoon, when families might be at the zoo or at Costco. Parents who wanted a crack at popular classes now had to arrange their Sundays to make sure someone could be in front of a computer with reliable internet at the start of the race.

But there are things that clever market designers can do to mitigate both the costs and the inequities that races create. The after-school registration system could be improved through a mechanism that allowed participants to rank their preferences at their leisure, a market design solution that I worked on (with my colleague Eric Budish) and implemented at Wharton to improve the market for assigning students to popular classes, discussed in more depth in chapter 5. And first-come, first-served races for certain products, like live-event tickets, might be improved with lotteries, which I propose and describe more fully in chapter 7.

These innovations can eliminate some of the downsides of first-come, first-served races. And they might have the upside of helping me finally get Ilana a French Laundry reservation for her next milestone birthday.

CHAPTER 3

The Waiting Game

First-Come, First-Served Lists and Lines

ON A BUSY DAY, OVER TWENTY-FIVE THOUSAND PEOPLE VISIT THE VATican Museum in Vatican City, the world's smallest country at 0.17 square miles, nestled in the middle of Rome. While the museum boasts one of the greatest collections of art in the world, the main attraction for many people (including me on my first-ever trip abroad) is the Sistine Chapel, with its massive ceiling frescoes painted by Michelangelo at the start of the sixteenth century.

Getting into the chapel, though, requires a substantial time commitment. The relatively low entrance price of twenty euros means that many more people want to see the chapel than the 5,800 square feet (or 540 square meters) of space can accommodate. If you have not prepurchased premium tickets to enter the museum, you must wait in a physical line to buy one. That wait time can be as long as three or four hours, particularly during the summer, when tourists flock to Rome. That line is followed by another to go through security to get into the museum. Lines can be even longer on the last Sunday of each month, when the chapel is free to the public.

The Vatican Museum is just one example of the many markets that resolve excess demand by having people wait around for a chance to get a scarce resource. Like races, these markets use first-come, first-served rules to allocate things. But they differ from races in how they handle participants who arrive *before* the resource becomes available.

With a race, like the one for French Laundry reservations, showing up early doesn't do you any good. There is a moment when the resources become available and all that matters is who claims them the fastest. Other first-come, first-served rules, in contrast, give you priority for arriving before the allocation gets doled out.

These allocation mechanisms come in two key varieties: lists and lines. The difference between the two is your physical presence. Joining a waiting list requires you to simply put your name down to secure your place on the list, a version of which we mentioned briefly in the last chapter. Standing in a line requires you to physically be there—think of going through airport security, getting your picture taken at the Department of Motor Vehicles, or securing a seat on a Disney World ride. If you leave the line, it usually means you lose your spot, and since keeping your place requires a constant devotion of your time, lines are more costly for market participants and require different strategies.

GOOD THINGS COME TO THOSE WHO WAIT-LIST

Explaining first-come, first-served waiting lists (and how the strategy to play in them is similar to the strategy for races)

The rules for most first-come, first-served waiting lists are straightforward: People join the list at various times and are added in the order they join. When a resource becomes available, whoever is at the top of the list—the person who has been waiting the longest—gets it.

Because the earlier you get on a waiting list, the sooner you are offered the resource, some strategies from the last chapter apply here as well. You need to know that there is a waiting list, just like you need to know a race is afoot, and you need to get on the list as soon as possible.*

But there are new strategies with first-come, first-served waiting lists. First, you can often be on multiple lists simultaneously, and joining multiple lists may be worth the costs of doing so. When there are limits to the number of lists you can put your name on, you need to be strategic about choosing which ones to join.

Second, depending on the waiting-list rules, you may reach the top and be offered one of your less preferred options; for instance, if your doctor's office calls and offers you a newly available appointment at a time when you are scheduled to be in a meeting with a client. In these cases, you need to decide whether to take what you are offered or keep waiting for a more attractive option to become available — hopefully before too long.

TENNESSEE IS FOR LIVERS

How multi-listing can save your life

My route from the Thirtieth Street train station in Philadelphia to my Wharton office takes me down Market Street and through University City, home of the University of Pennsylvania and neighboring Drexel University. Though it's a nice way to get to campus, each morning I make that walk, my heart drops slightly as I pass a nondescript, industrial-looking six-story building.

If you were not paying attention, the structure could easily pass for the offices of one of the many companies that call Philadelphia

---

* Otherwise, you might end up like Homer in a 1998 episode of *The Simpsons* in which he returned from the video-rental store and said one of my all-time favorite lines from the show: "Well, they put us on the *Waiting to Exhale* waiting list, but they said, 'Don't hold your breath.'"

home. But the blue logo on the glass door says different. It says DaVITA, followed by UNIVERSITY CITY DIALYSIS. It is one of nearly 2,700 dialysis centers DaVita operates in the United States, and it has hundreds more centers in countries around the world.

DaVita provides dialysis to over 250,000 patients worldwide, including a large fraction of the more than 550,000 people in the United States with end-stage renal disease, also known as kidney failure, who need the treatment. Dialysis requires patients to be connected to a machine for three to four hours a day, often at centers like the one I pass, at least three days a week.

In addition to the time and discomfort, dialysis is also expensive. Medicare covers costs related to end-stage renal disease for approximately 85 percent of dialysis patients in the United States, and the price tag of this care is roughly fifty billion dollars a year, nearly 1 percent of the entire federal budget. Put differently, of every dollar of taxes the United States collects, about a cent is used to pay for dialysis treatment.

As costly as it is, dialysis is desperately needed. When the kidneys cease doing their job of filtering the blood, a person needs either dialysis or a kidney transplant to stay alive. And there is massive excess demand for kidneys.

Roughly one hundred thousand people in the United States are currently waiting for a lifesaving organ transplant, and the vast majority—about ninety thousand—are waiting for a kidney. Only a little over half of those on the waiting list receive a kidney within five years.

The market rules determining who gets kidneys when they become available are complex and include various measures of a patient's health, the compatibility of a particular donor kidney and patient, and the geographic distance between the patient and the available kidney (organs must be kept on ice in transit, and a shorter time on ice increases the chance of transplant success). But another key component is how long the potential recipient has been on dialysis waiting for a transplant.

While it might seem more fair to rely exclusively on waiting time—or, put another way, it might seem unfair that someone waiting for a shorter time is offered a kidney before someone who has been waiting longer—the biological complexity of organ transplantation makes it sensible to offer organs only to people for whom the transplants are very likely to be successful. It would be wildly inefficient to give an organ to a biologically incompatible recipient (say, from a donor with blood type A to a recipient with blood type B) just because that recipient was at the top of the list. As a result, the time waiting for a kidney is a component of the allocation rules but not the only one.

Given the complexity of the market rules, you might reasonably assume that patients' outcome in this market—whether they make it to the top of the waiting list and whether compatible organs become available once they get there—is governed by luck or perhaps some higher power. But although you cannot control when a compatible organ becomes available, you may be able to increase your chances of being at the top of a waiting list when one does by using a strategy known as *multi-listing*.

The people in the United States waiting for a donor organ are registered through the nation's roughly two hundred fifty transplant centers. These transplant centers are organized into eleven regions. Because proximity to a deceased donor's organ enters the calculus of who gets offered it, organs recovered from a given region are typically distributed to patients at the transplant centers in that region. But potential recipients can multi-list—they can join waiting lists in more than one region. Since an ideal match for a patient might become available in a different part of the country, multi-listing can decrease the geographic distance between a donor organ and the closest transplant center, putting a patient higher on the list for that organ. Multi-listing can literally save a patient's life.

This strategy is not without its costs. Patients need to be evaluated by a transplant center before they join its waiting list, and evaluations at more than one transplant center may not be covered by insurance. Depending on the rules of the transplant center, patients may need to establish a residence in the region or confirm they have a place to stay nearby during their recovery. Transplant centers may also require that the patient be able to get to the center on short notice if an organ becomes available.

While onerous, these conditions can be met, particularly by people with means. When former Apple CEO Steve Jobs received a liver transplant in 2009, he got it about two thousand miles from his home in Palo Alto, California. That's because he was on the waiting list in Memphis, Tennessee, where wait times for a liver were substantially shorter (48 days) than the national average (306 days).

Around the time of this highly publicized transplant, some people criticized the policy of letting people multi-list because it created inequities based on wealth and income. Jobs could afford to buy a mansion near the transplant center in Memphis to stay in during his recovery, and he was also able to guarantee that he could get to the transplant center in a few hours—he could simply fly in on his private jet. (Concerns were raised again when it was reported that Jobs's transplant surgeon lived in Jobs's Memphis mansion for two years after the 2009 surgery and then bought it from him in 2011.)

Despite these inequities, given that it is allowed, multi-listing at transplant centers in as many regions as you can is clearly the right strategy when your life is on the line.

TO HAVE AND TO HOLD

In some cases, there are multiple lists to join but you cannot join them all

The United States boasts over seventeen thousand public libraries from which around one hundred seventy million library-card holders collectively borrow around two billion items—mostly books, but also magazines and movies—each year. With many titles to choose from, a library patron can generally find a great read among the available options. But often, readers want a particular book—a page-turner recommended by a friend, a bestseller that everyone is talking about, or whatever their book club has decided to read that month.

While libraries can purchase multiple physical copies of each book from publishers, they might not purchase enough to meet the demand for a particularly popular title. In these cases, many libraries use first-come, first-served waiting lists to decide who should get to borrow that book next when its current reader returns it to a branch.

Say I wanted to borrow *The Snowy Day*, the award-winning children's book by Ezra Jack Keats, the most borrowed book in the first one hundred twenty-five years of the New York Public Library system's history (with *The Cat in the Hat* by Dr. Seuss a close second). If it was not available, I could put it on hold, essentially adding myself to a first-come, first-served waiting list for the book. Once it was my turn for the book, I would have seven days to pick it up from the branch before it went to the next person on the list.

Because there is a natural limit to the number of physical books any one person can carry back and forth, the New York Public Library was historically happy to let readers borrow basically as many books as they wanted, up to fifty at a time. This logic extended to waiting lists, and readers could have holds on up to fifteen books at once. If your goal was to maximize the number of books you got to borrow, your optimal strategy might be to add yourself to the maximum number of lists. But if your goal was to have a good book or two to read each week, and you wanted to avoid carting a dozen books back and forth between the library and your home each visit, you could put just a few books on hold. Demand was low enough that even if you used only a few holds, you would likely get your hands on some good books.

The system worked well. Then two things happened.

The first was the proliferation of ebooks and e-readers like the Kindle. The virtual nature of the books meant that people could borrow them without coming to the library, eliminating the constraints about how many books they could carry home. Many libraries — happy to increase their circulation and readership — embraced the opportunity to make borrowing books easier. But publishers worried that ebooks would be too easy to borrow, read, and return for the next reader, cutting into book sales. So publishers set the price for a library ebook much higher than the price you and I would pay if we bought a personal copy. And even though an ebook could theoretically be duplicated for free and given to whoever wanted to read it, eliminating the scarcity that leads to excess demand, publishers imposed rules about borrowing library ebooks. Like a physical book, each library ebook could be shared with only one patron at a time.

The second thing was the COVID-19 pandemic. The physical libraries shut their doors and lockdown orders kept people at home, often with nothing to do. Demand for ebooks skyrocketed. New patrons joined the library, and regular patrons, no longer able to come in to borrow physical books, switched over to ebooks (Ilana and I included).

The New York Public Library's rules allowed each patron to borrow fifteen ebooks and join fifteen waiting lists at a time. This led the number of people on ebook waiting lists to skyrocket. For popular books, there could be hundreds of people ahead of you, meaning a book you were excited to read today might not be available for months or years. Suddenly, it was sensible for eager homebound readers to use all their holds, which further increased wait times. The library encouraged people to return books faster, but excess demand persisted.

This system might have been equitable — everyone could have fifteen books and put holds on fifteen books at a time — but it was far from efficient. Because you could put a hold on any book with a few clicks and without a library visit, being willing to join a list was not a great measure of how much you valued reading that book. Moreover, it is hard to predict what books you'll want to read in a few months. You might get a lot of value out of reading a particular book now while all your friends are reading it but get much less value out of the same title when it becomes available in six months and finally hits your Kindle.

In the face of this inefficiency and increasingly frustrated patrons, the New York Public Library did something counterintuitive: They cut down on their users' options. The library decreased the number of ebooks patrons could borrow and the number of waiting lists they could join from fifteen to three.

There were complaints—particularly by the library's heaviest users—about having fewer options to secure a book when it was already taking so long to get a good one. But the change worked exactly as the library had hoped: Its tweak to the market rules dramatically improved efficiency. With fewer people eligible to have a given book and fewer people putting that book on hold, books suddenly had much shorter waiting lists. Patrons started getting the books they wanted faster.

In addition, by restricting the number of holds, the library effectively made holding a book more costly—using one of your three holds on this title meant you could not use it for another. Customers now needed to think more carefully about their preferences and be more selective, perhaps using their holds only on books that they really wanted to read. And as waiting lists got shorter, patrons did not have to predict their own preferences far into the future, so people were more excited to have the books they borrowed when they finally reached their e-readers.

Thanks to this clever market design tweak, the library was able to increase its circulation and the number of satisfied customers throughout the pandemic without exploding its budget for ebooks by buying more digital copies.

TAKE IT OR LEAVE IT (AND KEEP WAITING)
The important strategic decision at the end of the waiting list

When you get to the top of the waiting list for *1984* by George Orwell (number three on the New York Public Library's most-borrowed list), there is no strategic decision to make. If you still want to read it, you borrow it; if not, it goes to the next person on the list.

But other lists are for things that are less precise than a specific book, and you might not be particularly happy with what you are offered when you reach the top of the queue. This happens in markets for public housing where there is a single waiting list for housing options in multiple buildings, and the unit you are offered when you get to the top might be in a less-than-ideal neighborhood. It happens with spots in nursing homes—when a room becomes available, it might be more expensive or smaller than your most preferred choice. It happens with day care, where a chain with multiple locations might have a spot for your little one in a less desirable center. It also happens with organ donations: Since no two donor organs are alike, a patient may be offered one that is a less-than-ideal match or is just less desirable overall, like one from a less healthy donor.

In these cases, you must decide whether to take the thing that's offered or turn it down and hold out for something better. Your strategy should depend on the market rules associated with the waiting list.

Some waiting lists offer little flexibility—if you do not take this option, you get bumped back to the very end of the list and must start over. These rules usually push you toward taking whatever you are offered as long as it is better than your outside option (what you already have or what you can get from outside the market). For example, if you are offered an apartment that is not perfect but is better than your current housing situation and the costs of moving are not too onerous, you might as well take it and then put yourself back on the list. Whether you take the apartment or not, you will be way down at the end of the list. If you take it, at least you will spend the time waiting in slightly nicer digs.

In other cases, taking something offered on a waiting list might prevent you from rejoining the waiting list immediately or might change the process you go through next time. The Chicago Housing Authority has rules like these, requiring families to live in a unit and remain in good standing for a year before they can apply for a transfer. In these cases, you might be less likely to take a mediocre apartment if it causes a delay in applying again or more likely to take it if it is a shorter wait to get a transfer than to get a unit as a new resident. Identifying the optimal strategy here may require research and will depend on the specifics of the market.

Other rules offer more flexibility—they do not require you to give up your spot at the top of the queue when you turn something down. If a day-care center says it has a spot for your tot at a less preferred location, you may be able to say, "No, thank you," but keep your place in the queue for your preferred center. These are also the rules for organ lists. If you do not accept a particular transplant, you are not penalized when the next organ comes along.

This strategic decision is similar to the one we just discussed, but since declining an option does not send you back to the bottom of the list, the cost of waiting is typically smaller. You still need to compare the value of what is being offered (such as the less ideal kidney available today) with what you expect to get if you wait (a better kidney) while considering any costs associated with waiting (continuing to be on dialysis and an increased risk of getting too sick to receive a transplant).

In the case of organ donations, the patient does not make this decision alone. Transplant patients have surgeons who understand the compatibility of a given organ and have the experience to predict the quality of organs that will become available and with what frequency. They might also be able to assess whether the patient's condition is likely to deteriorate in the meantime.

It might seem preferable to let market participants stay at the top of a waiting list if they are unhappy with what is offered to them, but this policy is not without its costs. For example, as patients rise toward the top of the kidney waiting list, they get offered many more organs, and so they can become pickier about which one to take. As a result, most kidney offers are rejected, and the same organ typically gets offered to many, many people on the waiting list.

Unfortunately, this process takes time. Some decisions can be made in advance—a surgeon can rule out low-quality or bad-match organs automatically. Others can be made before an organ is removed from a donor's body. But some information might be revealed after an organ is removed, perhaps when a tissue sample is tested against a particular recipient to see if it is compatible. And while people are deciding whether to accept this organ, it is spending time outside of the donor's body and becoming less desirable. If a match is not found fast, the organ may not get used, even if there is someone at the bottom of the list who would have taken it.

Because of this dynamic, over 20 percent of kidneys available for transplant are not taken by anyone and discarded. If a kidney might be viable for some patients, discarding it is a clear waste, but each patient might be better off rejecting a mediocre-quality organ than taking it, given what they expect to get if they keep waiting. While we could minimize waste by forcing patients to take any viable organ offered to them or face returning to the bottom of the list, this would worsen allocative efficiency, since many people would end up taking organs that were worse matches for them than what might come along later.

Given these tensions, researchers are working on ways to allocate kidneys more efficiently, such as by creating smaller, more targeted lists of patients based on various compatibility factors. This means each patient gets offered fewer kidneys, but each kidney that is offered is more likely to be accepted. The researchers estimate that these improvements could increase patient welfare to the same degree that an 18 percent increase in the supply of available kidneys would while also reducing the discard rate by more than 7 percent.

FALLING IN LINE

Explaining the costs associated with first-come, first-served lines and how to lower them

Unlike waiting lists, where you can add yourself to a list and walk away, first-come, first-served lines are commonly used when someone's presence is required to access a scarce resource.

This investment of time is how lines help achieve allocative efficiency: Those who are willing to wait hours to get their driver's licenses renewed, experience the thrill of Space Mountain, or view the ceiling of the Sistine Chapel likely value those things more than people who aren't willing to wait.

Economists have a name for what you must give up while you wait. We call this your *opportunity cost*. In the case of lines, your opportunity cost is the lost enjoyment or productivity or earnings from whatever you would have been doing if you were not waiting in line.

The advice you can find on the internet for beating the lines at the Sistine Chapel often involves going early, perhaps before the museum opens, to secure a spot toward the front of the line. The economist in me is not sure about this advice. If I arrive an hour before tickets go on sale to be first in line, but the wait would be only forty minutes long if I arrived when the museum opened, I would end up waiting longer, not less. Whether arriving early shortens my wait depends on when others choose to arrive, and if all tourists follow the same internet advice and arrive an hour early, the lines at opening may be the longest of the day. It is hard to predict when the wait will actually be the shortest.

This is why you are better off considering opportunity cost rather than just waiting time. Rather than going when you think the line might be shortest, you can go when your opportunity cost is the smallest—for example, when you have nothing (or little) better to do. Thinking about opportunity cost can make arriving an hour early seem sensible, even if it increases the total amount of time you wait. By arriving before opening, you get your waiting out of the way when other activities are not yet open. Sure, you might give up an hour of sleep or the chance to have a leisurely breakfast, but assuming you value those things less than your other planned activities, queuing up early is probably a good choice. If you're first in line at the museum, you can see the chapel and still enjoy a packed day visiting other sites in Rome.

MY LINE OR YOURS?

Describing when a single line is more equitable and efficient than multiple lines

When I was growing up, the large grocery stores at which my family shopped became the training ground for me to master an important life skill: how to pick the fastest line. At these grocery stores, each cash register had its own line. This meant that before you decided which register to queue at, you needed to guess which line would move fastest.

As a novice, I would usually pick the line with the fewest people in it. But as I honed my craft, I quickly learned that the shortest line was not always the fastest. One line might have more people, but each of them might have fewer products to scan. Some lines were shorter, but their cashiers were working slower, stopping to look up the produce code for apples or (gasp!) chatting up each customer.

But even when I was strategic about which line I chose, I could still get unlucky. There might be a price check, a customer with lots of coupons to scan, or a shift change, each of which could increase the wait. In addition to being highly annoying when I was in a hurry, this created inequity. My line might get hit with an extra wait while other lines did not.

When I was old enough, I would split off from the parent who'd brought me to the store and stand in a different line. In that case, we had options. If my line moved more quickly than my mom's, she could roll our cart over to me and we could check out faster. Like multi-listing, this multi-line strategy improved our chances of getting in the fastest line (as well as our chances of getting dirty looks from other customers).

Thankfully, in the main grocery store I shop at now, lines are structured differently. All shoppers wait in a single line until they get called to the next available cashier. This is a far better way to manage the line from a market perspective.

First, it is easier. As a shopper, you no longer need to strategize about which line to stand in, and there is no longer any benefit of playing a multi-line strategy. You just get at the back of the one long line. It is also more equitable, since the cost of any of the issues described above (like the price check or the slow cashier) gets shared equally by everyone in line, not just the few people who were unlucky enough to pick that lane.*

Despite the clear superiority of the single-line system, not all grocery stores have adopted it. When Ilana and I were dating, we periodically went shopping together and encountered that one-line-per-register structure. But I stopped playing my multi-line strategy once I realized that while Ilana and I standing in different lines

---

* Having a one-line-for-all system is not always optimal. It may be more efficient and equitable to have a special line for complicated cases, as the New York Passport Agency office on Hudson Street was known to do, so as not to slow down people with easy cases. The fewer people who are kept waiting by an officer handling a complicated case, the more efficient the system will be, and it may be more fair to have the burden of waiting for complicated cases borne primarily by people with their own complicated cases. (This same logic is why supermarkets have dedicated lanes for customers with ten or fewer items—it gives shoppers with fewer items a faster checkout.)

might have made our time waiting a little shorter, it also made the experience worse.

Like minimizing opportunity cost, making my time waiting in line more pleasant can mitigate my costs. Now instead of trying to pick the fastest line, I think more carefully about how to improve my wait. Spending time with Ilana is one way. Shooting off a few emails or reading a few news headlines while waiting is another.

When playing in markets with first-come, first-served lines, even when you cannot do much to reduce your waiting time, there are plenty of ways to reduce the cost of waiting.

ESTIMATED TIME OF ARRIVAL

How to decide when to join a line

Everyone who waits in line for the Sistine Chapel eventually gets to see the ceiling, and everyone who waits in line at the grocery store eventually gets to pay for groceries.

The strategy for first-come, first-served lines gets more complex when you must stand in line for a limited resource that might run out.

In the early years of the iPhone, lines of devotees would form outside of Apple stores hours before they opened on days a new version hit the shelves. Some eager buyers would even camp out in front of their local Apple store overnight. Being closer to the front of the line made it more likely that you could buy a new iPhone in the model, configuration, and color that you wanted before they sold out at that location. Those who joined the line later had a more limited selection to choose from, and those who showed up too late ended up empty-handed.

In cases like this, you must weigh the opportunity cost associated with waiting in line longer against what you expect to gain by getting in line earlier. But assessing what you expect to gain isn't easy, especially when resources are limited. It's impossible to know for sure if arriving at 6:00 a.m. will guarantee you your pick of phone colors or if arriving at 10:00 a.m. will guarantee that you get a phone at all. When you're making this calculation, it pays to know as much as you can about the strategies of other people, a lesson I learned firsthand back in high school.

When *Star Wars: Episode I—The Phantom Menace*, the first new movie in the franchise in sixteen years, hit theaters in May 1999, my best friend Dean and I were determined to see it on the very first day it was released. Our tickets, procured in a first-come, first-served race, were for the 5:00 a.m. show. We had opted for that absurdly early hour not just because it was easier to get tickets for a time when most reasonable people were still asleep but also because it allowed us to convince our parents to let us see the movie on a weekday. Even with its over-two-hour run time, we could see it and still not be late for school.

In those days, you didn't get assigned to or get to choose your seat when you bought your ticket. Instead, you lined up outside the theater, and you were let in once the doors opened for your showtime. What this meant, of course, was that the earlier you arrived, the better your chances of snagging your desired seat.

For me and Dean, however, the opportunity cost of arriving early was high, since each hour spent waiting in line for a 5:00 a.m. movie was an hour of lost sleep. But the potential gain was high too: We wanted to see the movie from the perfect seats. So we got up extra early (as early as I could remember waking up for anything). As it turned out, it was not early enough. We arrived at the theater only to find that a long line had already formed for our showtime. We ended up toward the back of that line and were relegated to the front left of the theater in some of the least desirable seats.

Our mistake had been underestimating the intensity of the other fans who had bought tickets for the 5:00 a.m. show. These fans were so eager to see the movie from good seats that many of them had arrived insanely early. Given the enthusiasm around the movie's release, we should have known better. As disappointed as we were, we learned an important lesson about the importance of estimating the demand you will face in a first-come, first-served line. Had we known how aggressive other people would be, we might have woken up even earlier (or, more likely, just stayed up all night).

While it might be difficult to guess when others will join a line, it is not impossible. In the case of movie tickets, it's easy to find out whether it is opening weekend, whether the movie has sold out in the time since you bought your ticket, and whether other showings have sold out. The more excited people are for the movie, the more likely people will want to get there early to snag the best seats.

First-come, first-served lines can achieve allocative efficiency — how many hours of sleep you are willing to give up is a pretty good measure of how badly you want to get good seats for *Star Wars: Episode I — The Phantom Menace*. And although some seats are better than others, most people have an equal opportunity to wake up at 2:00 a.m. to queue up for seats, so the policy scores well on equity. But participating is far from easy for customers (think of all the hours of lost sleep for just our single 5:00 a.m. showtime), which is why some markets have introduced rules to make waiting in line less costly.

Shakespeare in the Park is a series of free summer performances for fans of the Immortal Bard (and of theater in general; it's not all Shakespeare) held in the Delacorte Theater in New York City's Central Park. The outdoor venue, adjacent to the park's Great Lawn and below the looming Belvedere Castle, can seat over eighteen hundred people.[*]

---

[*] Belvedere Castle was built in the late 1800s, around the time Central Park was established, as a place to enjoy views of the park and the city (*belvedere* means "beautiful view" in Italian). The castle is famous in our household as a target for walks through the park and, most notably, as the spot where I proposed to Ilana (and she said yes!).

New York is known for its excellent theater productions, and Shakespeare in the Park is no exception. The performances, which have fixed runs of just a month or so each, often receive rave reviews. And the tickets are free, which means demand regularly outstrips supply.

There are a few ways to secure tickets for Shakespeare in the Park that combine a mix of allocation methods. But the traditional way is with a first-come, first-served line. Tickets are released at noon on the day of the performance, and a line sometimes begins to form outside the park even before it opens, at 6:00 a.m. But thanks to a clever design feature of the market rules for tickets, on a typical day, most people don't line up until around 8:00 or 9:00 in the morning.

That feature is that being closer to the front of the line does not give you access to better seats. Seats are randomly assigned, which means that you have an equal chance of getting primo seats whether you are at the head of the line at 6:00 a.m. or you show up at 10:00 a.m. and end up being the last person to get tickets before they run out. So, while you need to arrive early enough to get one of the theater's eighteen hundred seats, you have no extra incentive to show up earlier.

These rules may reduce allocative efficiency. If I really want a certain seat, I cannot increase my chances of getting it by waking up earlier. I have just as much chance to get it as you, even if you are close to agnostic about where you sit. But the increase in ease for market participants is likely worth it.

Shakespeare in the Park has one other innovation that makes waiting for tickets less costly, at least for those in their golden years. While the (relatively) young have to wait in the hot summer sun, those sixty-five and older get to enjoy a special line where they can sit on park benches in the shade as they wait for the box office to open. They also get access to seats in the theater that do not require taking stairs, which includes the desirable first ten rows. This separate-line policy reduces the costs of waiting (and, for those with limited mobility, of seeing the show itself) for the over-sixty-five group, advantaging them over everyone else.

At first blush, this might seem unfair or inequitable. Up until now, I have talked about equity as treating everyone equally, achieving what economists call *equality*. Doing that makes sense if you do not know much about market participants. A market designer who does not know anything about participants would not want to generate unequal opportunities or outcomes between them. However, if a market designer knows a certain group of participants is disadvantaged relative to another—in this case, it is harder for older people to stand in line for a long time (especially under the hot summer sun) and they might not be able to enjoy the show if their seats require taking stairs—it might be more equitable to improve things for the disadvantaged group so that their costs of participating in the market and their outcomes are more equal to the costs and outcomes of the advantaged group. Achieving equity this way is a major benefit of the line rules for Shakespeare in the Park.

NO BACK CUTS!

There are loopholes with lines, and they are all essentially ways to cut the line

I have many memories of lining up for things as a kid: for food in the school cafeteria, for a chance to swing at a piñata at a friend's birthday party, for showers at sleepaway camp. There was rarely an adult present to enforce the sanctity of the line, leaving that task to the kids themselves. As you might imagine, things could devolve quickly (the book *Lord of the Flies* comes to mind).

In the absence of a rule-enforcing adult (and sometimes even in the presence of one), kids regularly went up to friends near the front of the line and asked to cut. No one liked to let someone cut in front of them, so the answer was almost always no. But an alternative was to ask for a back cut, a request to slip in right *behind* that person in line.

Because the person being back-cut would incur no extra waiting time—only the people behind them in line would—this request was regularly granted.

As market designs go, allowing back cuts is not very equitable. In addition to providing some people with much shorter waiting times than others, it gives too much control to whoever is at the front of the line. If I am first in line for cafeteria food and you are second, I have the power to move you from second in line to last by giving the entire rest of the third-grade class back cuts.

Nor is it particularly efficient. The kid who asks to back-cut doesn't necessarily value faster access to the pizza slice, piñata swing, or shower than any other kid in line. He or she might just have more social capital or more chutzpah than the other kids.

At some point, there was an innovation in line maintenance. Kids farther back in the line—who were at risk of being cut in front of—would yell, "No back cuts!" Enough people yelling could force a potential back-cutter to the end of the line.

When you are a market participant, it is in your interest to help enforce lines to prevent people from coming in ahead of you. But enforcing the line takes work. If you are conflict-averse, you might prefer someone else stand up to the line-cutter. As a result, when the task is left to market participants, enforcement is sometimes lax.

In the absence of obvious enforcement, you might find cutting the line a tempting strategy. You are more likely to get the thing you want and you also reduce your waiting time. That said, cutting is risky, thanks to people like me who are sticklers for enforcing lines.

In my younger days, I would get so incensed about line-cutting that I regularly jumped in to prevent someone from doing it. Once, as a young teenager, I got into a heated argument with a kid at camp when he cut the line at a cookout. Things were about to escalate to blows when my friend Aaron talked me down (thank you, Aaron). And lest you think that line-cutting happens only among kids, about a decade later, while I was waiting in a line of cars queued up to board a ferry, I put my car in park, got out of the vehicle, and—with the demeanor of a sheriff of the old West—approached the middle-aged driver of an SUV who was trying to cut a line of cars. (She pretended she had not seen the line and grudgingly drove to the back.) This raises an additional risk of cutting the line: While you're attempting to sneak ahead, the line might be growing behind you, so if you are forced to the back, you have longer to wait.

Thankfully, market designers often take it upon themselves to enforce first-come, first-served lines. This could be as simple as using stanchions (like those retractable lane dividers used to direct the flow of traffic in airport security lines) to make it harder for someone to maneuver to the front of the line, or it could involve hiring staff to prevent people from trying to cut in.

My favorite enforcement method is a new policy—initially piloted by American Airlines and recently expanded to over one hundred airports—designed to discourage passengers from pretending they are in an earlier boarding group in order to get on the plane faster (a common form of line-cutting, often motivated by the desire to secure precious overhead space). The system detects when passengers scan their boarding passes before their designated group number has been called; these passengers are promptly removed from the line and forced to enter with their group. This eliminates the potential gains to be had from cutting and further disincentivizes the behavior with some good old-fashioned embarrassment.

Reports from travelers say some gate agents go further (perhaps even against the policies of their airlines) to discourage these types of cutters by threatening to force customers to board in the last group and automatically gate-check any of their luggage if they are caught trying to board early.

TIP YOUR WAIT-ER

How money can sometimes be used to avoid waiting in first-come, first-served lines

Each year between October and April, the US Supreme Court hears oral arguments on cases that can be of massive social, political, and financial importance to our country.

There is no video taken of the oral arguments. And while the court does live stream the audio and post same-day transcripts, the justices' facial expressions and body language can offer clues as to how they might rule, so if you are a journalist, a lobbyist, or any other interested party, there is no substitute for attending in person.

Technically, the Supreme Court oral arguments are open to the public and free to enter, but the courtroom has only 439 seats. To resolve the massive excess demand (especially for high-profile cases), the court gives out tickets for at least 50 seats to members of the public each morning, starting around 7:30 a.m., for arguments being heard at 10:00 that day. Because these seats are allocated on a first-come, first-served basis, lines tend to form hours — and sometimes days — before tickets are given out.

If you do not want to wait in the line yourself, for around forty to sixty dollars an hour, various companies — with names like Skip The Line and Washington Express — will send someone to wait in your place. These companies offer similar services for hearings and other events around town where spots are allocated using first-come, first-served lines.

Paid line standers bring money into a market designed to allocate things without it, allowing financial resources to determine access to something that is supposed to be widely available. This strikes many as unfair.

But proponents of paid line standing argue that basing access on time waiting in line is unfair because it disadvantages those with demanding jobs (like lobbyists). Why, they ask, should people who have nothing better to do than spend hours and hours waiting in line get to see the Supreme Court in session while those with time-intensive jobs cannot? If these same busy people get a lot out of attending, there might also be an allocative efficiency argument for letting them in. But even if these arguments make sense, allowing people to buy their way into the hallowed halls of our democracy is not a good look.

BUYING TIME

All the ways you can pay to cut first-come, first-served lines and lists

Paying to avoid standing in line is not unique to our highest court. You can pay line standers to make reservations at popular restaurants, get you into sample sales, or buy in-person tickets at a box office.

This same principle is at play (although the recipient of the funds is different) in lightning lanes or fast lanes at amusement parks, which allow patrons to pay for faster access to rides, and so-called Lexus lanes on highways, which offer drivers the opportunity to buy access to special lanes that have less traffic than the free ones. You can also pay extra for online tickets to reduce your time waiting in line at many tourist attractions, including the Sistine Chapel.

I think about paying to avoid time in line whenever I travel. At some airports, a first-class ticket not only gets you on and off the plane faster but also gives you access to special lanes—with substantially shorter lines—at passport control. Global Entry status allows you to speed through passport control into the United States, but it costs $120 (at the time of this writing) just to apply. If you are flying out of a US airport, you can pay for TSA PreCheck, which gives you access to separate, usually shorter and faster, security lines. A more expensive service ($199 a year) called CLEAR Plus lets you cut to the front of the regular and the PreCheck security lines.

Renewing your US passport normally costs $130, but you can pay the State Department an extra $60 to expedite the process. Other services charge you even more—on the order of hundreds of dollars—to further accelerate getting or renewing a passport or visa.

When deciding whether to avail yourself of innovations like TSA PreCheck and CLEAR, you should consider the opportunity cost of the time you could save to determine if the shorter wait is worth the money to you.

But no matter what you decide to do, it may be worth considering whether these services are good or bad for the market as a whole. Do these services improve things for just a few market participants— those who can afford it—or for everyone?

One factor to consider is whether total waiting time decreases when you use the service. Compare, for example, the aforementioned Lexus lane with a high-occupancy vehicle (HOV) lane. In both cases, we have granted certain drivers access to special, faster travel. But the latter, which gives access to drivers with multiple people in their car, rewards carpooling, an activity that (at least theoretically) can decrease traffic for everyone on the road. The former, which gives access to only those with the ability and willingness to pay, decreases traffic for some but not all.

TSA PreCheck, Global Entry, and CLEAR have elements of both HOV lanes and Lexus lanes. You do pay for access—as you would for a Lexus lane—but each of these in some way expedites the security screening process. Going through the prescreening to qualify for each of the services means you require less attention from security personnel and passport control agents. So, at least theoretically, using these services makes the line move faster overall. Similarly, if the Lexus lane revenue is used to fund a highway expansion (creating a new lane for those drivers willing to pay), it could speed up travel for everyone.

If paying to cut down on time appeals to you, it makes good sense for you to take advantage of any opportunities to do so. But whether these innovations are positive for society depends on whether they improve things for everyone or just a select few.

THE BOTTOM LINE

Takeaways from this chapter to help you succeed as a market participant

The strategies for succeeding on a first-come, first-served waiting list are the same as those for races: know that there is one and get on it quickly.

In addition, you should look for opportunities to *multi-list*. Putting your name on multiple lists is typically low cost. If there are limits to how many lists you can join, putting your name on one list might come at the expense of another, so you need to be a bit selective.

If you don't like what you are offered once you reach the top of the list, consider whether turning down an option means you must go to the bottom of the list or if you can keep your spot at the top. Regardless, think about how taking the option offered to you compares with what you expect to get if you continue waiting and how long it'll be before your next option comes along.

Unlike lists, first-come, first-served lines require your physical presence, which means that you incur a higher cost the longer you are in the line. To mitigate the pain of waiting, try to time joining the line when you expect to have the lowest *opportunity cost* of waiting. This might be when you expect the wait to be short—which depends on when other people join the line—but it's also about what you could otherwise be doing in the time spent waiting. You should also take advantage of ways to make standing in line less unpleasant or, perhaps, consider paying to cut down on your waiting time if the market provides an option to do so.

Finally, when standing in line earlier gets you better options or gives you access to a limited resource and you need to decide how early to arrive, consider how much you value the most desirable outcome over the least desirable one as well as when others are likely to arrive to strategically time when you should join the line.

COULD THE MARKET DESIGNERS DO BETTER?

Describing possible improvements to markets with first-come, first-served lists and lines

First-come, first-served lines are costly. Bringing down the costs to market participants without sacrificing efficiency or equity can improve the market. Thanks to technological innovations, we have seen efficiency and equity gains in many markets where lines have been replaced by less costly lists or races.

To reduce the costs of waiting on hold, for example, many customer-service centers offer to call you back, replacing a line (in which you lose your place if you hang up) with a list (in which you call in to secure your place on the waiting list and then are called back).

Credit cards, which allow people to pay for things without being physically present with cash in hand, have turned many lines—like those for theater or movie tickets—into races. Computerized ticketing systems have enabled additional innovations, like assigning seats in movie theaters, which eliminates the opportunity cost associated with arriving early to the theater for better seats. Instead, you race for the seats you want at the time of purchase and then roll into the theater at your leisure.

But beyond just reducing costs and making the market easier for participants, more creative rules governing lists and lines can open up other opportunities to improve efficiency and equity.

As one example, the first research project that I did with my adviser, Alvin Roth—the project that led me to join the ranks of market designers—looked at how to improve the market rules for allocating kidneys to those who need them.

About half of Americans (among whom I proudly count myself) are registered as organ donors. Upon death, these donors provide the organs to the patients on the organ waiting lists discussed earlier. There are many good reasons to become an organ donor. I signed up because, while I would like to live a long, full life, if I end up going prematurely, I want my organs to be put to their best possible use. Others agree to donate the organs of a recently deceased loved one because they want to find a silver lining in what is often a horrific tragedy.

And yet, while there are many people registered as organ donors and many next of kin who consent to donation, it is far from universal. To increase the supply of viable organs available to those who need them in the United States and around the world, we need to encourage more people to become donors.

While it is nice to believe in the generosity of the human spirit, economists typically do not expect people to do things for others if there is not something in it for themselves. Perhaps the most famous quote from Adam Smith's *The Wealth of Nations* reads, "It is not from the benevolence of the butcher, the brewer, or the baker that we expect our dinner, but from their regard to their own interest." It stands to reason that more people would register as organ donors if given a financial incentive to do so, but because payment for organ donation has been deemed illegal in the United States, we need another way to motivate donors.

A little over a decade ago, inspired by policies that had been implemented in Singapore and passed in Israel, Al and I decided to investigate what would happen if we gave priority on organ waiting lists to people who had previously agreed to register as donors themselves.

Our hypothesis was that if people knew that signing up to be organ donors today would give them preferential treatment if they needed a kidney down the road, it would incentivize more people to do so, thereby increasing the number of organs that became available. That seemed like a win-win.

Since we were not able to experiment with the way that organs were allocated in practice, we ran an experiment with undergraduate students that modeled the organ-donor registration decision. We compared registration rates when organs were allocated according to a first-come, first-served waiting list to rates under new market rules in which registered donors were moved to the front of the line if they needed an organ. The results were staggering. Only 36 percent of subjects agreed to donation under the first-come, first-served system; this shot up to 74 percent when registered donors got priority.

This priority policy clearly improves efficiency. By boosting registration rates, it makes more organs available for transplant. And people who register as donors when they are young and healthy to ensure they have priority later in life increase the supply of high-quality organs that are more likely to be transplanted successfully.

At first blush, it might seem like these rules introduce inequity, since those who register are more likely to get organs than those who do not. But while giving everyone the same access to organs might treat everyone more equally, it also seems quite fair — and perhaps even more so — to allocate scarce resources like donor organs to those who are more willing to contribute to making that resource available.

A few weeks after our paper about this experiment was published in a top economics journal, the Royal Swedish Academy of Sciences awarded Al a Nobel Prize in Economics, elevating the subfield of market design and solidifying Al's stature as one of its founders.*　In the years that followed, together with coauthors Avraham Stoler, Tamar Ashkenazi, and Jacob Lavee, Al and I were able to analyze data on the rollout of the actual priority policy in Israel.

---

* While Al had over a hundred and fifty papers and books in his oeuvre already, I like to say ours was the straw that broke the camel's back for the Nobel Committee.

The Israeli policy gave priority for organs to individuals who had signed donor cards at least three years prior (a rule designed to prevent individuals from gaming the system by signing donor cards only after they realized they needed a kidney). The policy also gave priority to the immediate family members of people whose organs were donated, creating an added incentive for family members to agree to donate the organs of a deceased loved one.

The Israeli policy increased registration and donation rates, just as we'd expected. A campaign alerting Israelis to the policy led to a surge of individuals signing donor cards. Our estimates suggested an increase of nearly a hundred thousand signed donor cards (above what would have been collected otherwise) in the seventeen months between when the law was publicized and when it went into effect. In addition, next of kin became over 20 percent more likely to consent to donation.

Since the successful rollout in Israel, similar policies have been implemented in Chile and China, and I remain hopeful that the United States will eventually adjust its market rules as well.

CHAPTER 4

That's So Random!

TWICE A WEEK WHEN I WAS GROWING UP — WEDNESDAYS AND SATURdays — I would watch as my mother filled in bubbles on the long pink slip of the New York State lottery. She got two plays for one dollar in each drawing, and with one play she would always select the same set of six numbers. All of the numbers were meaningful. They included the day of the month that various family members had been born and the number 18, which Jews consider lucky.

I thought it was strange that the highest number we played was 30 — the day in April that my father was born — even though the possible numbers to pick from went up to 54. Not yet fully understanding the rules of probability, I thought our odds would improve if we distributed our numbers more evenly like the people in the television ads for the New York Lotto did.

The ads, which played regularly, showed a series of close-ups of quintessential New Yorkers. Each would look at the camera and say what they would do with the jackpot.

An older mustached man with a taxi driver's cap said: "I'd keep my job...but I'd hire somebody to do it for me."

An attractive young woman with big '90s hair said: "When I bring home doggie bags, I really would give them to the dog."

The ads would freeze on the person's face and show six numbers in a row at the bottom of the screen, presumably the numbers they played in the hope of winning the jackpot. The ads would end with a deep voice delivering the state lottery's tagline: "All you need is a dollar and a dream."

A close family friend named Gary, a man who was equipped to teach a precocious kid a bit of probability theory, explained that the numbers we played did not affect our chances of winning the jackpot. Since each number was equally likely to be picked, any set of numbers was just as likely to be picked as any other. (Ironically, my instinct that we shouldn't play just our birth dates was technically right but not for the reason I thought. Since many people play birth dates, our numbers were more likely than a random set of six to be played. Choosing those numbers didn't affect our chances of winning, but if we ever did win the jackpot, we had an increased chance of having to share it with the holders of other winning tickets.)

Because there were so many possible combinations, Gary explained, the chance of matching all six numbers was infinitesimal—nearly one in twenty-six million. He thought people who played the lotto were throwing money away, and he would drive that point home with his own version of the state lotto tagline: "A dollar and a dream... two dollars and a delusion."

One afternoon, I asked my father why we played the lottery each week when the odds were stacked so high against us. "Doesn't it bother you that we never win?" I asked.

He expressed no angst over squandering a dollar two times a week.

"I won the only lottery that ever mattered," he replied.

THE ONLY LOTTERY THAT EVER MATTERED

An example of a high-stakes randomized allocation

On December 1, 1969, millions of Americans sat anxiously around their televisions.

Unlike a few months earlier, in July of 1969, when they had gathered around their televisions waiting to witness Neil Armstrong take his triumphant first steps on the moon, the mood that December was somber. CBS was broadcasting the first ever national lottery for the draft to fight in Vietnam.

America had started sending active combat troops to Vietnam in 1965, and the war had continued to rage throughout the latter part of the decade. By 1969, there were over five hundred thousand US military personnel stationed in Vietnam, many of whom had been drafted into service.

For the first few years of the war, the draft had been implemented through local boards that called up eligible men and determined whether they were fit to serve. These boards—staffed by military veterans and older, educated, and almost exclusively white members of the community—had discretion to grant exemptions and deferments to individuals for medical or academic reasons.

The draft constituted a hidden market.

You could not directly pay to avoid being called into service in Vietnam. Paying to get out of military service had been possible a hundred years earlier, during the Civil War, when with three hundred dollars—ostensibly to pay someone to fill in for you—you could buy your way out of service. Due to the obvious inequities, the US military had ended this practice. But while you could not pay directly to get out of serving in Vietnam, you *could* find a loophole to avoid being sent to war. You could join the National Guard, enroll in college, get a letter from a doctor that stated you were unfit, or, perhaps the most direct loophole, have people in your community lobby members of the local draft board on your behalf so they would grant you a deferment.

These loopholes favored the white, wealthy, and well connected—those who could afford to pay college tuition, who knew a doctor who would write a letter, or who knew someone on the draft board (like the "millionaire's son" or the "senator's son," as Creedence

Clearwater Revival put it in "Fortunate Son," their famous protest song about the war). As a result, men who were poorer, less well connected, and Black were much more likely to serve on the front lines. According to a 1967 report by the National Advisory Commission on Selective Service entitled *In Pursuit of Equity: Who Serves When Not All Serve?*, while Black men made up about 11 percent of the US population in the 1960s, they made up "22.8 percent of the enlisted men in combat units" in late 1965 (and roughly the same percentage of "all Army troops killed in action" the following year). The report also documented wide variability across the thousands of local draft boards in how they handled particular deferment cases (such as vocational-school students, workers in certain professions, and conscientious objectors), which also contributed to unfair outcomes.

The lottery that was televised on December 1, 1969, was an attempt to create a more equitable allocation of the undesirable job of serving in Vietnam. Rather than have the local boards identify eligible men born between 1944 and 1950 to send overseas, the draft was designed to make the selection randomly.

Each month and day of birth—from January 1 through December 31—was printed on a piece of paper and put inside a blue capsule. As young American men and their families watched anxiously at home, capsules were dumped from a black bin into a large glass container. One at a time, the capsules were pulled out, the date inside read aloud, and the paper placed on a large bulletin board.

Those born on the first dates to be picked would be the first called into service in 1970. The longer it took to pull the blue capsule containing your birthday out of the glass jar, the less likely you were to see the battlefield.

The first date selected was September 14. Next came April 24. Then December 30. The lottery proceeded until all 366 days of the year (including February 29) had been picked.

In 1970, the highest lottery number that got called for service was 195. My father said he'd won the only lottery that ever mattered because his birthday, April 30, was lottery number 208.

Given that some people were called to serve while others were not, the draft system had real ex-post inequity. There is no way around that type of inequity when a system must pick a hundred thousand men out of a million. But the lottery was ex-ante equitable, giving everyone an equal chance of being in the first group called to serve, the last group called to serve, or anywhere in between. Even though the rules still allowed for the education deferrals and medical exemptions that benefited more well-off citizens, the use of a lottery took discretion away from the local draft board and demonstrated an attempt to share the burden more evenly across the nation.*

Because they achieve ex-ante equity, lotteries are regularly used to allocate not just undesirable outcomes, like being shipped off to war, but also desirable ones.

Each spring, young people ages fourteen through twenty-four apply for the New York City Summer Youth Employment Program, which offers paid summer jobs—a hundred and fifty hours spread over six weeks—typically at nonprofits, for-profit businesses, or government agencies. The New York City summer program is the largest in the country, but most major US cities have something like it. In New York, kids earn the city's minimum wage, over sixteen dollars an hour, which means getting a slot in the program can be quite lucrative—very appealing for a teenager or young adult who might not be able to find a summer job otherwise.

Because summer programs like this one are so popular, many are perennially oversubscribed. In a typical summer, there might be nearly two hundred thousand New Yorkers hoping for the nearly one hundred thousand jobs available. The constraints on the number of

---

* It also may have helped accelerate the anti-war movement that eventually pulled the US out of Southeast Asia. As more advantaged households faced the burden of sending their sons to Vietnam, the political pressure against the war grew. America started winding down its operations in the region, and by early 1973, America had left Vietnam.

available jobs come from both the limited funding—the programs are expensive—and the limited number of employers who can take on the young workers. Even in a city as big as New York, there are only so many jobs that sixteen-year-olds can do.

To distribute available jobs to eligible youth, the New York City program could use a first-come, first-served rule, as some programs (like the one in Washington, DC) do. But first-come, first-served favors youth who are aware of the program, perhaps because they participated in a prior year, have a family member who works for the city, or are encouraged by an adult in their life to apply on the day the program starts accepting applications.

To avoid such inequities, New York City runs a computerized lottery. When not everyone is equally aware that the program exists, let alone aware of the date it starts accepting applications, it can be fairer to open an application window, leave it open for several weeks while the city advertises the program, then select from the pool of applicants at random.

In addition to achieving ex-ante equity, the lottery has other three-*E* advantages. It is easy: It does not require people to show up at five in the morning to stand in line or toil over applications trying to stand out from the others who might apply. It also achieves Pareto efficiency, because it gives out all the available jobs each year.

However, lotteries can fall short on allocative efficiency. Random allocation methods that treat everyone equally are mechanically agnostic to how much an individual values winning. As a result, they may not always allocate things to those who value them the most.

Nonetheless, lotteries like the one for summer jobs in New York City are used to determine who gets seats in charter schools, who gets a visa to come to America, who gets to run in popular marathons, who gets to hunt big game, and much more.

And even though lotteries allocate resources at random, it is often possible to improve your chances of winning the ones in which you participate: You can make yourself lucky.

DOUBLE-DIPPING

*One strategy for succeeding in lottery allocations
is simply to enter more times*

The first strategy to improve your chances of success in these markets is reminiscent of the strategy to enter multiple waiting lists: If the market rules allow it, you want to enter the lottery as many times as possible.

We can call this strategy *double-dipping*.

For example, many Broadway shows that want to expand access to dedicated fans offer a limited number of tickets for low prices, a practice popularized by the musical *Rent*, which in 1996 started offering twenty-dollar rush tickets for prime seats. These tickets were initially first-come, first-served at the box office. They went on sale two hours before showtime and were available until they sold out. But *Rent* was a huge hit, and lines started to form the day before the tickets went on sale; fans camped outside overnight for a chance to get those twenty-dollar seats.

The producers realized that their first-come, first-served market rules were far from easy for participants, and they started to worry about the safety of the fans who were sleeping on the street in Times Square, so in 1997, they switched from a line to a ticket lottery. A few hours before showtime, people who wanted to participate could enter their names for a chance at winning up to two twenty-dollar tickets to that night's performance. Since your chance of winning did not depend on how long you had been waiting around, entering the lottery was a lot easier than standing in line.

And by eliminating the incentive to camp out, the ticket lottery also helped on the equity dimension by giving equal opportunity to people who could not—or were afraid to—spend the night on the street.

The switch to the lottery, however, also created an opportunity for double-dipping. Since going to the theater is often a social experience, if you're given a chance to buy low-price tickets, you're usually allowed to buy a pair. Under the rush-ticket market rules, if you and I wanted tickets to see a show together, there was no reason for us both to spend the night on the street. If I arrived at 2:00 a.m. the day the rush tickets went on sale, your showing up at 3:00 a.m. did nothing to increase our chances of getting to see a Broadway show for off-off-Broadway prices. With the randomness of the lottery, however, we could double our chances of winning if we both entered the lottery angling for a pair of tickets.

By allowing fans to buy tickets in pairs, the Broadway ticket lottery favors those who plan to see the show with a companion; someone who is looking to buy a single ticket can't take advantage of this double-dipping strategy (unless he can find another singleton milling around outside the theater who is willing to double-dip with him). A similar dynamic plays out in other lotteries in which benefits accrue to groups or families even if only one member wins.

At the time of this writing, the Diversity Visa Lottery allocates access to the United States to people from nations that do not typically send a lot of immigrants our way. The program requires applicants to have a high-school degree or equivalent or work experience in certain professions, but it is designed to ensure the United States receives a diversity of immigrants of various backgrounds each year.

Winning the visa lottery means you — and your family, including a spouse and any unmarried children under twenty-one — can move to the United States and have the opportunity to get a green card. Since each individual has an independent chance of being picked by the lottery, if your family wants to come to the United States, both you and your spouse should apply to the Diversity Visa Lottery to double the family's chances of winning.

From the perspective of the US government, which may assume that families who settle together are more stable than those coming as individuals, this opportunity to double-dip might be a feature rather than a bug because it increases the chances that families get selected.

Sometimes organizations allow certain groups or individuals to double- or even triple-dip to achieve social goals within their own lottery systems. When New York State legalized marijuana, for example, legislators expected that many new businesses would crop up to cultivate, process, distribute, and sell marijuana within the state. Since marijuana markets are tightly regulated, these new businesses would all need to get licenses. The state decided to give priority to certain disadvantaged groups, including those who had been disproportionately targeted by law enforcement during the prior decades of cannabis prohibition.

The order in which the state agency processes license applications is still determined by lottery. But if you are an applicant who can demonstrate that you qualify for extra priority, you get three entries in the lottery instead of one, thereby tripling your chances of being high on the list to be considered for a license.

In lotteries you enter where the stakes are high, it makes sense to investigate the rules to see if you are allowed to double-dip (such as by submitting multiple entries for the same lottery) or if you can somehow indicate that you are eligible for extra priority.

BENDING THE RULES
Sneakier ways to double-dip

Though both the rush-ticket and green-card lotteries allow double-dipping within groups and families, they have safeguards—box office representatives check IDs and the US State Department monitors applications—that prevent any *individual* from entering in the same lottery multiple times. Since duplicate entries will be thrown out, improving your odds requires that multiple people enter the lottery to win the desired theater tickets or immigration visas.

Other lotteries are less strict about multiple entries, allowing shrewd participants to enter multiple times using different email addresses. While this is perhaps against the spirit of the lottery (especially in cases where multiple entries from the same email address are rejected), markets that neither explicitly state that this is against the rules nor monitor or enforce restrictions on multiple entries invite this kind of manipulation.

Since Broadway ticket lotteries have mostly moved online and entering no longer requires showing up in person, you can more easily double-dip by asking friends—even those who are not interested in seeing the show with you—to enter the online lottery on your behalf and give you the tickets if they win.

Asking a friend to show up at the theater in person to enter a lottery with a small chance of winning is a big request that is unlikely to be fulfilled by busy people who reap no benefit from winning (unless your friends are nicer or have less to do than mine). But asking someone to enter an online lottery is a small, reasonable request that might take less than a minute of your friend's time. If she wins, she will have to go to the theater to pick up the tickets in person and then hand them off to you. In this scenario, she's being asked to come to the theater only when she has already won a lottery and is guaranteed to get tickets for you. Even my friends would (probably) do that for me.

While one might feel apprehensive about this kind of double-dipping, there is a three-*E* logic to allowing, or at least tolerating, sneaky double-dipping. People who are willing to go the extra mile to increase their chances of winning a lottery, whether by creating email accounts or by recruiting their friends to enter a lottery on their behalf, may value the prize of that lottery more than those who don't bother to find creative ways to enter more than once.

If people willing to go the extra mile indeed value winning more, then these tricks can help improve the allocative efficiency of the lottery. So while we might not want to reward people who *break* the rules, we might feel okay about giving an increased chance of success to those who bend over backward to bend them.

EARLY AND OFTEN

How to take advantage of the fact that many lotteries reward repeat entries

Even when a lottery prohibits multiple entries, many are repeated, so participants can choose to enter again later for a shot at essentially the same prize. Your family might not be selected for the visa lottery this year, but you can try again next year. If you do not win rush tickets for tonight's performance, tomorrow is another day.

These rules invite you to enter a lottery repeatedly. Like bending the rules to enter multiple times, entering repeatedly requires dedication; those who do so probably value the prize more than people who enter the lottery only once. So allowing repeated entry can improve the efficiency of a lottery.

While entering repeatedly—what we can call an *early-and-often* strategy—is useful for any lottery, it can be particularly useful for lotteries designed to improve ex-post equity. While lotteries that are run only once are ex-ante equitable (everyone has an equal chance of winning), they do not eliminate the ex-post inequity that comes from picking winners and losers. But when lotteries are run multiple times, they can be designed to achieve more ex-post equity by giving those who have been unlucky in the past a higher chance of success in the future.

I am reminded of these market rules whenever I enter the American Museum of Natural History, one of my favorite places to go as a kid and, if I'm honest, also as an adult (I take my kids there so regularly that they have started to complain about it).

On the ground floor of the museum is a bronze statue of Theodore Roosevelt. He is seated on a bench just past the membership entrance, and I regularly sit beside him while I wait for my kids to take off their mittens and jackets (so we can finally get to the fun of exploring the museum).

While I am keeping an eye on my kids, Roosevelt is forever staring into the distance. The statue is meant to depict Roosevelt on a camping trip that he took to Yosemite National Park with naturalist John Muir during the first few years of his presidency.

Teddy Roosevelt is famous for many things. He was forty-two when he became the twenty-sixth president of the United States and remains the youngest person ever to fill that role. Before that, he was a hero in the Spanish-American War and the thirty-third governor of New York. As president, he broke up large corporations, built the Panama Canal, and became the first American to win a Nobel Prize (he won the Nobel Peace Prize for negotiating an end to the Russo-Japanese War). But in the Theodore Roosevelt Memorial Hall at the Museum of Natural History, where his statue sits, he is honored for his dedication to environmental conservation.

Teddy was a New York City kid—born around the corner from where I grew up—but he had dreams of living the frontier life in the West. When he finally made it to the Dakotas in the 1880s, he was struck by the notable absence of bison. The majestic creatures had widely and freely roamed the plains in the preceding decades, but by the time Teddy arrived in what is now North Dakota, they had been hunted nearly to extinction.

Those of us who grew up in the 1980s and 1990s got to experience the overhunting of the bison (kind of) firsthand by playing the (allowed at school!) video game the Oregon Trail. In the version I played, if you were low on food and had not yet died of a broken arm or dysentery, you could clumsily use the arrow keys to aim your rifle and, with a tap of the space bar, fire at a slow-moving bison. Killing a bison would yield meat for your entire wagon party. But a successful bison hunt was always wasteful. You might succeed at killing a thousand-pound bison, but you were able to carry only a hundred pounds of meat back to the wagon.

As president, Teddy wanted to protect the bison—among other species—from real-life overhunting. He put 230 million acres of land under federal protection and established what would later be called the National Wildlife Refuge System to protect our nation's rich ecology. The system still exists today and is run by the US Fish and Wildlife Service.

Each year, wildlife biologists assess various species and determine whether the population needs to grow or shrink. When animal populations need to shrink, perhaps because their numbers are threatening their habitat's ecology and therefore the other species that live alongside them, that is good news for fans of recreational fishing and hunting, of which Teddy himself was fond.

Because regulations around recreational hunting and fishing are designed with conservation in mind, there are strict rules about how many animals can be killed and when. This is why there are restricted hunting and fishing seasons and why hunting rules differ by species, with a distinction being drawn between small-game hunting (think pheasants, geese, squirrels, and rabbits) and big-game hunting (think deer, elk, bears, moose, and, of course, bison).

For big-game hunting, wildlife biologists are very precise about how many animals can be killed. To reach the population goals, the state agencies issue tags that grant a recreational hunter permission to kill a single animal. To avoid decimating certain herds in certain locations while other populations grow unabated, each tag may specify not only a certain species and a certain gender, say, a doe (a deer, a female deer) but also a certain area where it may be hunted.*

Because killing some types of big game is a particularly relished

---

* The benefits of this system are financial as well as ecological. Sales of these hunting tags and the associated hunting licenses raise significant funds for state agencies dedicated to conservation. Estimates suggest that in a typical year, they bring in one billion dollars from around fifteen million hunters in the United States.

challenge for recreational hunters, the demand can often far outstrip the number of available tags for those animals each hunting season. Some states might have only a few dozen tags available for a male elk, for example, while there are thousands or tens of thousands of hunters who are interested in securing a tag to hunt them.

In the presence of this excess demand, the states set market rules to determine how these tags are allocated. While some tags in some states are auctioned off to the highest bidders,* the vast majority are distributed by lotteries.

The rules governing these lotteries can vary significantly depending on the state, the species and gender of the animal, and whether a hunter is a resident or nonresident of that state. As a result, hunters can apply for multiple tag lotteries in multiple states—a kind of double-dipping across different lotteries—but face a complicated patchwork of market rules to navigate.

If you want to hunt one of Alaska's Roosevelt elks (named after—you guessed it), you can enter a tag lottery for five dollars per entry. Participants can enter up to six times in a year across regions within Alaska, though to help achieve ex-post equity, Alaska laws dictate that if you win multiple lotteries in the same year, you do not get multiple tags; you must pick a single tag, and the others get redistributed.

But while Alaska's rules let you win only one tag a year, they have very limited memory. You cannot win the exact same drawing two years in a row, but otherwise having won or lost in prior years has no bearing on whether you win or lose this year. So, while the one-tag-per-year rule may give everyone an equal chance of winning in a given year, there is no rule preventing one hunter from winning or, perhaps more likely, losing tag lotteries for ten years in a row.

To prevent such outcomes and improve ex-post equity across time, many states use lotteries that have more memory built in.

---

* In 2023, Jimmy John Liautaud, the billionaire founder of the sandwich chain Jimmy John's, paid $500,000 to hunt a single mule deer in Utah's Antelope Island State Park.

These systems—often called bonus-point systems—give hunters higher chances of winning based on how many years they have entered a tag lottery and lost. For example, they may give hunters one extra entry for every previous, consecutive loss. If you fail to win the lottery for a female-mule-deer tag this year, you'll get two entries instead of one for that lottery next year. If you fail to win the next year, you'll get three entries the year after that, and so on.

But even if multiple previous entries give you a better chance of winning the lottery, they don't guarantee it. And given the popularity of hunting as a sport and the limited number of big-game tags available in certain regions of the country, there are still hunters who lose the lottery year after year, sometimes to lucky newcomers or to hunters who have won in prior years. Attempts to mitigate this inequity have pushed many states to make these rules more extreme.

South Dakota, for example, recently switched from a standard bonus-point system to a cubed bonus-point system for big-game hunting. Under the regular bonus-point system, someone who failed to secure a tag in the past nine years would have ten entries this year, making his chances of winning ten times higher than a newcomer's. Under the cubed bonus-point system, he would have ten cubed—one thousand—entries in the lottery, making his chance of winning a thousand times that of a new hunter.

Other states go even further to give prior losers a leg up in the lottery. For example, for bear tags, Michigan prioritizes waiting time—the number of years you have been applying to hunt a bear—over everything else. This is essentially a first-come, first-served system that plays out on the order of years or even decades. Those who have been waiting the longest get first dibs on tags, and the lottery enters the equation only if there are more people who have waited the same number of years than there are tags available.

Some hunters say these priority-based systems go too far, making it all but impossible for new hunters to secure the highest-demand tags. They fear that these rules will discourage the next generation from joining the sport, since the newbies might be hesitant to apply for a tag when they know they will have to wait at least a decade before they have a shot (pun intended) at the most exciting hunts. But if a goal is to spread the scarce resource—in this case, the chance to hunt an animal in one's lifetime—across as many people as possible, it makes sense to design market rules in which participants who have lost in the past get an advantage in the future.

Given their equity benefits, these types of market rules are not unique to big-game hunting.

The city of San Francisco is known for having particularly strong protections for renters and very high housing prices. As a result, many landlords in the city would like to convert their small rental buildings—six units or fewer—into condominiums, then sell the individual units to new owners at the city's high prices. But just as states regulate the number of tags available to hunters, San Francisco regulates the number of conversions allowed each year and allocates those permits via a lottery system that rewards prior losers.

While a building's place in the lottery also depends on its ownership and eviction history, building owners who have applied and lost at least three times are placed in a special pool where permits are allocated according to the number of years that owner has participated in the lottery (for example, owners who have participated for seven years or more are selected to receive permits first, followed by those who have participated for six years, and so on). Once all these participants have received permits, owners who applied fewer than three times get their shot at winning a permit through the lottery.

Rules like these create an incentive to play an early-and-often strategy. In any lottery system that increases your probability of success with each prior loss or with time spent waiting, you want to enter as early as possible to secure your place in line and then keep entering each chance you get. It might take time before you win, but participating now sets you up for better odds later in your lifetime.

BANK YOUR WINS (OR LOSSES)

Why playing early and often can be useful in settings where you can postpone using something you win today

Early-and-often strategies suggest that you should enter a lottery whenever you can. But what if you do not actually want to win the lottery when you have a chance to enter? Say you are a big-game hunter who has a family trip planned for the upcoming hunting season or you have a health issue that precludes your going on a hunt that year. Surely that would be a year to sit out the lottery, right? Not necessarily.

Depending on the market rules, you may want to enter even when you do not want to win. In the case of hunting lotteries, some states have programs that let you pay an entry fee just to build up your bonus points. You pay as if you were entering the lottery, but they do not actually enter you. Instead, they treat you as if you entered the lottery and lost.

Many states also have programs that allow hunters to keep their points if they win a tag but are unable to use it. In these cases, you can often return the tag and get back your bonus or priority points as though you had lost, which means you'll still have a chance at that dream hunt in a different year.

Intentionally or not, these return policies also incentivize double-dipping. Though many hunters will enter lotteries in multiple states to increase their chances of winning, those who win tags in more than one state may not be able to use all of them in a given year. If Colorado has a return policy and Michigan does not, the lucky hunter can hunt in Michigan this season without sacrificing his accumulated points in Colorado.

For those who prefer running to hunting, the London Marathon is another example of a hidden market that invites playing an early-and-often strategy and allows some participants to bank their wins.

There are more people who want to run the London Marathon than the race can accommodate, so, like in Tokyo, New York, Berlin, and Chicago (all the other World Marathon Majors except Boston), runners enter a lottery—the London one is called the ballot—for a chance to run.

Because running in the London Marathon is a dream for many racers, the odds of getting a spot are slim. In 2024, over 840,000 people applied for around 17,000 spots, giving each entrant about a one-in-fifty chance of winning one. The marathon previously had a priority system that gave a spot to anyone who had lost the lottery five times in a row, but that list grew too long for administrators to continue offering entry that way.

Even though the odds of winning the lottery no longer improve with repeated entry, the London Marathon lets you defer a win, giving folks an incentive to enter the lottery (which costs nothing unless you win, in which case you pay to run in the race) even in years they know they cannot run. If they cannot run this year but expect to be able to run next year, the option to defer allows for a form of double-dipping. You can enter this year and, if you lose, enter again next year, in both cases for a chance to run in next year's race. It's even better to apply if you're pregnant or planning to be; lottery winners can defer for up to three years if they are pregnant or have just given birth. So an expectant mother hoping to run a few years after she gives birth could start applying now, getting four chances for the same year's race.

LOOK FOR LOOPHOLES
Advice on how to find a way around the rules in lottery markets

The lottery is not the only way to get a chance to run in the London Marathon or the other World Marathon Majors. Those other ways onto the course serve as useful reminders that loopholes can be found even in allocations determined by chance.

Serious runners who want to run in the World Marathon Majors can circumvent the lottery simply by being fast enough. This is the primary way to get a spot in the Boston Marathon, which does not have a lottery.

But slower runners are not entirely out of options. To avoid introducing inequities based on biological sex or age (since, on average, younger runners are faster than older ones and men are faster than women), UK residents who meet the qualifying time for any marathon within the prior year are eligible to apply for one of the London Marathon's six thousand "good for age" slots. For eighteen-to-thirty-nine-year-olds, a woman must have a time under three hours forty minutes (about 8:24 per mile); a man must have a time under two hours fifty-five minutes (about 6:40 per mile). The qualifying times are longer for older runners—you get about an extra hour if you're sixty-five to sixty-nine. That said, if there are more than six thousand applicants who qualify on time, they give the slots away based on speed. So you might need to be ten or more minutes faster than the qualifying times listed above if you want to ensure a spot this way.

If these speeds are out of reach (no judgment; I will consider it "good for age" if I am even thinking about going for a jog in my late sixties), all the major marathons, including the Boston Marathon, have programs that guarantee spots to runners who raise enough money—usually on the order of a few thousand dollars—for one of the charities that partners with the marathon. While most people raise this money from their friends and coworkers, these policies mean that you can buy your way into the marathon by making a sizable donation to one of the affiliated charities yourself (as you may be noticing, using money to circumvent market rules that are designed to avoid money is a common theme).

In a similar vein, the London Marathon has a charity program that allows you to essentially buy extra entries into the ballot if you are willing to donate to the London Marathon Foundation. Going this route (stuffing the ballot box, one might say) requires donating 49.99 pounds at the time of applying. This donation is nonrefundable but comes with a few perks. If you are lucky and win a spot, you get a twenty-pound discount on your entry fee. But even more compelling is the promise that if you lose the first lottery, you will be entered into a second lottery that guarantees to at least double your chances of winning. For those who really want to run, this extra probability might be worth the fifty quid.

SETTLE FOR SILVER

How to choose the best strategies in lotteries that let you select from a set of options

Perhaps you want to appreciate the splendor of the American West without shooting anything. In that case, you might find yourself a few hours outside of San Francisco at another one of Teddy Roosevelt's old haunts: Yosemite National Park. If you are more adventurous than me, you might decide to spend your time at the park doing the notoriously strenuous Half Dome hike.

The hike is at least fourteen miles round trip and requires climbing up and then back down nearly five thousand feet. The very last stretch of the hike, near the summit, is known as the Cable Route. Thick metal cords are affixed into the rock face — they look like metal banisters sticking out of the rock — and enable hikers to ascend the last four hundred feet, basically walking up the side of a rock, without any special equipment. That final stretch, let alone the whole twelve- to sixteen-hour round trip, is not for the faint of heart.

I can only imagine that completing this difficult hike gives one an incredible sense of accomplishment. And the views from the peak supposedly leave you breathless (although any stretch of the hike would leave me that way). As a result, the daylong trek is extremely popular. But in the interest of hikers' safety and serenity, the park allows only three hundred trips up Half Dome a day. Those who plan far enough in advance can enter the preseason permit lottery, which takes place in March.

If you are hiking with a group, the permit lottery for the Half Dome hike allows for serious double-dipping. Because you can ask for six permits in a single application, six hikers could theoretically submit six separate applications for six permits each, one application under each hiker's name. They would need only one to win for all six to get to hike together.

But the catch is that the set of permits is valid only if the named applicant is physically present at the start of the hike. That means that if your friend who won the permits needs to cancel her trip to Yosemite, the other five will also be out of luck. Each application can list an alternate who is allowed to take over the permits if the primary applicant cannot be there on the morning of the hike. If someone is listed as an alternate on an application, however, he cannot submit his own application that year (doing so will get all the applications on which his name appears thrown out). So if your hiking sextet wants to have a backup on each application, you can file a maximum of three applications listing each hiker once as either an applicant or an alternate (but not both).

Regardless of how many applications you file, on each you can list up to seven dates you want—in order of preference—between late May and mid-October, when the cables are up. If your application is selected via the lottery, the system will check to see if there are enough permits to accommodate your group on your first-choice day. If there are not, it will try your second-choice day, then your third-choice day, and so on, down your list of seven options.

Listing seven different dates is a different form of double-dipping. Each date that you list is another chance to win permits. But like reservations at a hot restaurant, some dates are more competitive than others.

Perhaps unsurprisingly, there are more requests for Saturday permits than for any other day of the week (50 percent more requests than for either Tuesday or Wednesday), and equally unsurprisingly, Fridays and Sundays are also relatively high-request days.

You might *really* want to hike on the weekend and be tempted to list seven Saturdays on your application. But while that go-for-gold strategy *might* get you a Saturday hike, your odds of getting a hike at all will increase substantially if you list at least a few weekdays.

Because the lottery will check your preferences in order, it certainly makes sense to list a few top-choice days first; if you are one of the first applicants selected, you could end up with one of those top choices. But with the application success rate for Half Dome just 22 percent in 2023, many people increase their odds by listing weekdays among their seven options. If your application is randomly selected after all the desirable weekend dates are taken, you might still get a chance to hike this year if you settle for silver with, say, your fifth through seventh slots, by listing some weekdays when you think you could get away.

MAKE YOUR OWN LUCK

In some cases, you can control how likely you are to win a lottery by controlling who else enters

When Ilana and I first started living together in New York City, we went to a fundraiser for a charity that connected tutors with underperforming elementary- and middle-school students at local public schools. I remember the event vividly because it was the first time I had seen a raffle that allowed you to decide how to distribute your raffle tickets across multiple possible prizes.

I had participated in raffles with a single big prize. I had a childhood memory of my grandmother winning a fifty-fifty raffle to raise money for the firehouse in her town (I was visiting and answered the phone call delivering the news she had won).

In fifty-fifty raffles, the prize is 50 percent of the money collected from selling the tickets; the other 50 percent goes to the charity. The more tickets you buy, the higher your chances of winning the money.

I had also seen raffles with multiple prizes in which the prizes were announced one at a time and a random ticket was selected to win each one. But that type of multi-prize raffle is inefficient, because it can allocate certain prizes to winners who would far prefer a different one. Each ticket you buy is just as likely to win you the bottle of wine you are hoping for as it is to win you the pair of hideous decorative throw pillows that you would not let into your home under any circumstance.

So at this fundraiser, I was very excited to see a multi-prize raffle that was structured differently. I was even more excited when I realized that, unlike more traditional raffles, it would allow me to strategize.

Around the room were various prizes on display, a small fishbowl next to each one. Any raffle ticket I purchased could be placed in any bowl. At the end of the night, the organizers would draw a winning ticket from each bowl to determine who won the associated prize.

This structure was much more efficient than the typical multi-prize raffle. If you hated the throw pillows, you simply would not put any tickets into that bowl and instead devote your tickets to the bottle of wine, the autographed baseball, or anything else that appealed to you. It also had another helpful feature: The fact that the tickets were deposited in clear glass fishbowls meant that it was easy to see how many tickets were in each bowl and thus which prizes were the most popular.

Once I clocked the rules of the raffle, I immediately started thinking about what the optimal strategy might be. For each prize, there were two considerations: How much I wanted it and how many tickets were in the bowl. The first determined how happy I would be if I won. The second suggested how likely I would be to do so.

In a situation like this, the prize that appeals to you the most may also be highly appealing to other people and might already have a lot of tickets in its bowl. So you have to decide whether to go for gold, with a small chance of getting an awesome prize, or settle for silver, by finding a prize that you like less but have a higher chance of winning.

That night, I saw an almost empty bowl of tickets next to a five-piece Le Creuset cookware set. While it would not have been my top choice, I knew Ilana had been eyeing something similar for our kitchen and that it cost a few hundred dollars when sold retail. I figured it was a good prize to go for.

But I faced one more dilemma. I had bought a pack of twenty tickets, so now I had to decide: Should I go all in on the cookware or should I hedge my bets and put some of those twenty tickets toward other prizes that I wanted?

There were only about ten tickets in the bowl next to the kitchen set, so the first ticket I put in gave me a roughly 10 percent chance of winning the prize. But if I dropped all twenty into the bowl, there would be thirty tickets in the bowl, which meant that the last ticket I put in would have only about a 3 percent chance of being the winning ticket.

Worse still, by the time I put in my last ticket, most of the tickets in the bowl would be mine. Each ticket I put in would make my other tickets less likely to be selected. That dynamic meant that the last ticket I dropped in would increase my chances of winning the prize by only about one in a hundred—even less than its 3 percent chance of being selected.

Despite these diminishing returns, I still decided to make an aggressive play for the Le Creuset set and put all twenty of my tickets into that bowl. Why do this instead of spreading my tickets around multiple prizes? Because I wanted to make my own luck.

If I had put only ten tickets into that bowl, I would have given myself a decent chance of winning the kitchen set: fifty-fifty, the same as a coin flip. But those odds could change if more people decided to make a play for the set. The only way to discourage them from doing so—besides standing next to the bowl with a scowl on my face—was by filling the bowl with extra raffle tickets. If the ticket receptacle had been an opaque box that no one could see inside, this tactic would not have worked. But because people who came along later could see roughly how many tickets they'd have to compete with to win the set, my extra raffle tickets in the bowl made the Le Creuset set seem like more of a long shot and therefore less appealing. (This logic is also why I put my tickets into the bowl earlier in the evening rather than later.)

The strategy worked. By the end of the night, mine were still the majority of tickets in the bowl, and we won the set, which we use to this day. And everything we cook in it seems to taste just a little bit better because it includes a hint of sweet victory.

THE BOTTOM LINE

Takeaways from this chapter to help you succeed as a market participant

We tend to think that winning a lottery is all about luck. But even though market designers often choose lotteries to give everyone an equal chance of winning, there are still plenty of strategies you can play to improve your odds.

The first thing to look for is an opportunity to *double-dip*. If the lottery allows for multiple entries or if you can enter with groups of friends or family members, you can increase the chance of at least one of you winning. Sometimes that is all it takes. If you are really motivated, you might try to bend the rules to get more entries; you can look into entering from multiple email addresses or paying for extra entries if the market rules allow that.

Another thing to consider is whether the rules of the lottery reward prior losses in subsequent lottery draws. If so, you might want to play an *early-and-often* strategy, where you start entering now to increase your chances in the future. This strategy works particularly well when you can *bank your wins* by deferring your prize if you are not able to enjoy it immediately; in those cases, it sometimes makes sense to enter the lottery even for draws that you do not want to win.

Finally, your chances of winning a lottery increase not only when you enter more times but also when others enter less, so scaring people off can help you *make your own luck*. For the lotteries that really matter, it pays to do everything in your power to increase your chances of a win.

COULD THE MARKET DESIGNERS DO BETTER?
Describing possible improvements to markets with randomization

We've seen how simple lotteries can achieve ex-ante equity by giving everyone an equal chance of winning. We have also seen how lotteries with memory can improve on ex-post equity by rewarding past losers with a higher chance of winning. Lotteries that do this—like those that offer bonus points to participants who have lost in prior years—are more technically complex to orchestrate, since those who are running the lottery need to keep track of entrants and past outcomes. But because these investments help distribute winnings more equitably across people and because the cost of keeping track of prior winners and losers is shrinking as technology improves, I expect these lottery rules to become more common over time.

One limitation of randomization is that it typically does not do great on allocative efficiency. Since lotteries without memory treat everyone equally, they are agnostic to how much an individual values winning and so can end up allocating things to those who value them less than others who walk away empty-handed. But doing better on allocative efficiency requires market designers to work against the instincts we have developed in the prior chapters. We need to make the lotteries *harder* to enter, not easier.

The easier a lottery is to enter, the more people who will throw their hats in the ring. This means that the winners may include people who were not willing to enter when the costs were higher but who became willing to enter when it was easier to do so. Economists would say they were originally "on the margin" (regular people would say they were "on the fence") between entering and not entering. Since they chose to enter only when it got easier to do, they must value the prize less. On the flip side, when a lottery gets harder to enter, the winners will be people who value the prize enough to incur those higher costs of entry.

One might worry about making costs higher, but since the increase in costs discourages people from entering, doing so might not actually increase the *total* costs incurred by market participants by that much. Even though the costs go up per person, fewer people will suffer them.

To achieve the optimal lottery design, market designers need to find a balance between ease and allocative efficiency. And in doing so, they must ensure the costs do not introduce inequity by making it disproportionately harder for specific groups to enter.

This is the challenge for US charter schools, which receive public funding but are not run by public-school districts and so have more autonomy when it comes to curriculum and staffing. Because they receive public funds, when there are more applicants who want to attend a particular charter school than there are seats available, charter schools in almost all states are required to hold a lottery to determine who gets in. The rules governing those lotteries, however, are left to each school to determine. If a charter school decides that entering the lottery requires parents and children to show up at the school on a weekday, this might exclude parents who cannot afford to miss work, thereby favoring certain families even when the school picks among its applicants randomly. By running the lottery this way, the charter school might be screening out a subset of parents and students who particularly value the opportunity to attend and cannot afford a private-school education. In this case, moving the lottery online or extending the days and hours in which parents can enter would make the lottery more efficient and more equitable.

Another way to increase lottery efficiency is to leverage what you know about entrants. If there is good reason to believe some people benefit more than others from a resource that is allocated by lottery, market designers can introduce rules that increase their probability of winning. This is why the New York City Summer Youth Employment Program that I described earlier has shifted to a lottery that gives a higher probability of winning to kids identified as being at heightened risk of contact with the criminal justice system or who live in the city's housing projects. In light of academic research—including mine—indicating that these youth benefit more from the program than the average applicant, by giving them increased access, the lottery is more efficient and could also be interpreted as more equitable (helping to level the playing field in some broader sense), even if the odds of winning are distributed less equally.

Finally, an obvious way to improve lotteries is to mitigate or eliminate cheating. We've discussed how it might be okay for people to bend the rules (for instance, by having friends enter ticket lotteries on their behalf) because allowing that sort of rule-bending makes the lottery more efficient, assuming it takes work for people to increase their number of entries. But we still do not want to reward people who break the rules.

In 2024, Bloomberg News uncovered a rampant case of cheating in the market for H-1B visas, which are allocated to certain highly skilled workers (like those with talents valuable for tech, finance, and research firms). The first step in that process is winning the H-1B visa lottery, which companies can enter on behalf of their workers.

In 2023, the lottery allocated 85,000 visas to nearly 450,000 applicants. But about one out of every six of these visas, Bloomberg reported, went to outsourcing or staffing companies that broke the rules to get them. Bloomberg discovered that some staffing firms entered the same employee in the lottery multiple times through multiple different companies (one offending staffing firm got hundreds of visas over four years by entering the same employees up to fifteen times).

Part of the reason that this fraud has ballooned since 2020 is that the lottery has gotten easier to enter. Rather than submitting a full application, which can be hundreds of pages, the firms enter the lottery online, pay a ten-dollar fee, and do the full paperwork only if they win. This reduced cost of entry allegedly increased fraudulent applications (while making it easier to apply legitimately). Thankfully, technological improvements can help catch cheats, and investing in enforcement is essential. When used properly, technology can improve both equity and efficiency, giving each worker an equal chance of being selected while also helping to ensure visas are fairly allocated to companies that get value from these workers' skills rather than to firms most willing to break the rules.

Market design improvements that mitigate or eliminate cheating will benefit you as a market participant, particularly now that you are armed with additional strategies for playing in these markets.

CHAPTER 5

Ranks a Bunch

BACK WHEN I WAS IN COLLEGE, STUDENTS GATHERED EACH SPRING IN the dining hall of their residence—in my case, Adams House—for the annual room-assignment lottery.

Adams House was one of Harvard's twelve residential houses that were open to sophomores, juniors, and seniors. The residential houses each had a dining hall, a hundred or so dorm rooms, and various other facilities, including libraries, computer labs, theaters, and game rooms (imagine a space the size of a large walk-in closet with a pool table or foosball table).

That I snagged a spot in Adams House had itself been determined by a housing lottery, a relatively new mechanism for allocating dorm rooms at Harvard. Before the lottery was implemented in 1995, Harvard had let groups of up to sixteen students rank which residential houses they wanted to live in and used those preferences to determine house assignments.

First-year students lived in dorms in Harvard Yard and then moved on to residential houses as sophomores. Groups of rising sophomores usually applied to residential houses where their upperclassmen friends already lived. For reasons that might be obvious (a phenomenon for which sociologists have a fancy name: *homophily*, Greek for "love of sameness"), friend groups within and across years of college typically had common interests, backgrounds, and demographics, which led to significant homogeneity within each residential house. There was the "Jock House," the "Arts House," and houses where Black students congregated (although, given the small percentage of Black students on campus, they were a small minority even in the residential houses where many of them lived).

Eventually, exposing students to diversity became a priority of Harvard administrators trying to mold the undergraduate experience. Dissatisfied with the outcome of the housing allocation process, university leaders decided to rethink their market rules for assigning students to the various houses.

By the time I arrived at Harvard, in the fall of 2000, they had implemented a random lottery. Students who wanted to live with their friends could still apply in groups (though the maximum size had been reduced from sixteen to eight, another helpful change for encouraging diversity), but instead of letting those groups pick which houses they wanted to live in, they were assigned to them at random. In doing this, Harvard prioritized diversity within each house over satisfying student preferences.

But being assigned to a house was just the first step in getting a room for the following year. That was determined by another market, an example of what economists refer to as a *serial dictatorship* but what regular people might call "picking in order." (Economists use *serial* in the sense of "taking part in a series," and *dictatorship* refers to the power to choose whatever you want when it's your turn.) The order was determined by two factors: the student's year in school and chance.

The selection process for rooms within a residential house proceeded in stages. Rising seniors got to pick their rooms before anyone else. To determine the order in which they could pick, rooming groups (students who had committed to living together) were randomly selected, one at a time—a theatrical ritual that involved a master of ceremonies pulling balls out of a bingo cage. Whatever group was selected first got their pick of all the available options, then, with that room or suite struck from the list, another group of students was selected and picked their room or suite, and so on down the line. Once the rising seniors had all picked rooms, the rising juniors got their turn.

Completing this process for each class took an entire evening, so rooming groups were given a limited amount of time (about a minute) to make their selection of available rooms. Since many rooming groups consisted of three or four people who didn't necessarily agree on which rooms were most desirable, selecting a room often required aggregating competing preferences.

Because failure to pick within the minute effectively meant giving up your place in line, rooming groups usually conducted these negotiations in advance (although this didn't entirely eliminate the drama of best friends audibly arguing over where to live, which sometimes added reality-TV-style entertainment to the proceedings). Many groups came with full ranked-preference lists: all available rooms in the house ranked in order from their favorite to their least favorite. As the night progressed, each group would cross off the rooms that were taken, so when it was their turn to pick, they would just select whichever of the available options was highest on their list. These housing groups might still have had arguments about whether the smaller rooms closer to the dining hall were preferable to the larger rooms a few minutes away, but those debates happened earlier, in private, without a master of ceremonies tapping his watch.

Given that most groups knew their preferences in advance, this lottery and selection process would have been incredibly easy to automate with a computer, even in 2001. What took two to three minutes in person—picking a ball out of a bingo cage, having a group select their favorite available room, making sure everyone heard what was selected, and striking that room from the available options—could have been done in milliseconds by a computer. Even if each class had included thousands of rooming groups rather than dozens, the computerized version would still have taken just a few seconds, whereas at that size, an in-person selection process would have been all but untenable.

As a result of these advantages, market designers regularly automate allocation processes through what economists call a *centralized clearinghouse*. Participants rank their preferences, then computer programs run algorithms on these ranked-preference lists, implementing market rules (like the serial dictatorship described above, although the rules are often more complicated) to determine who gets what. These systems can be highly efficient in the sense that they are both fast and can be designed to maximize people's preferences and achieve an outcome in which no participant can be made better off without making another participant worse off. As a result, ranked-preference systems are used to allocate scarce resources in a number of important markets.

SCHOOL CHOICE

Explaining school choice, a prime example of a setting that uses ranked-preference lists

Each year, nearly four million students enter publicly funded kindergarten in the United States. In many places, students do not have options; they simply attend the public school closest to where they live. But many large school districts, including those in big cities like New York, Boston, Los Angeles, and Chicago, allow parents to choose among different public schools within the district. Since some schools are better than others and some schools are better fits for certain students than others, districts can improve both equity and efficiency by expanding access to their best schools beyond those students who just live nearby.

I experienced such a school-choice market firsthand when Cass was entering kindergarten.

The New York City Department of Education (DOE) is the largest public-school system in the country, with over a thousand elementary schools and over eighteen hundred schools overall. The DOE guarantees a seat in a kindergarten class to every five-year-old living in New York City. While there was a dip in enrollment during the pandemic, each year, around sixty thousand incoming students apply for spots in the city's public kindergartens.

When I was applying for Cass, New York City allowed parents to submit a list of up to twelve elementary-school programs ranked from the most to least preferred option. (I say *programs* rather than *schools*, since some schools have multiple programs, so parents might list both the English-language elementary program and a Spanish-immersion program at the same school among their preferred options.)

The fall before Cass started kindergarten, a few months before the list was due, Ilana and I began researching the schools in our neighborhood so we could decide how to rank them. The rules allowed us to rank any of the city schools, even those far from where we lived, and the city would guarantee free transportation there and back each day. But, like many parents, Ilana and I wanted Cass to attend a school near where we lived. We wanted to spare him long bus rides, we liked the idea of him making friends in the neighborhood, and we figured Cass being closer would make it easier for us to become part of the school community.

Once we'd decided to focus on schools in our neighborhood, our investigations involved a combination of online research—such as scouring data on standardized-test performance and parents' responses to school-satisfaction surveys—and going to open houses, which gave parents of prospective students a chance to see the school buildings. These visits almost always involved a stint sitting in the school's auditorium (which was usually as uncomfortable as I remembered from my own childhood) to hear from the principal and some handpicked teachers.

It was clear from our research that some schools were more desirable than others. Some had nearly all students performing at state standards for math and reading. At others, only a small fraction of students reached those benchmarks. Some school-leadership teams received great ratings from parents; others got lackluster reviews. At some schools, the work displayed on classroom walls was impressive for the students' grade levels. At others, not so much.

And while the facilities at New York City public schools are rarely up to the standards that children deserve, some schools had better technology in their classrooms, nicer gyms, and more recently renovated cafeterias, auditoriums, and playgrounds than the other schools nearby.

Unsurprisingly, the more desirable schools also had more parents at their open houses and more oohing and aahing at the school facilities and the student work on the walls. Many more parents wanted to send their rising kindergartners to these schools than there were seats available in the schools' programs.

To secure Cass a spot in one of the most popular elementary-school programs, we needed to identify the optimal strategy to play in this hidden market. That strategy would be determined by the following rules for allocating the kindergarten seats.

PRIORITIES, LOTTERY NUMBERS, AND PREFERENCES

Explaining a multipronged rule for the allocation of seats

To determine which students would get access to which schools, the DOE designed an allocation mechanism with three components: each student's level of priority at each school (determined by the DOE's sense of who should have first dibs at an available seat in each school), a random lottery number given to each student, and each student's preferences (the list of up to twelve schools that parents or guardians could submit for their kid).

A key component of priority was proximity. For most elementary schools, the DOE gives priority to students who live close by. There are many reasons why the DOE might do this. Living closer to the school might improve attendance and parental involvement in a student's education. The DOE might also want to minimize the number of kids who need to be bused and the amount of time kids spend on school buses, both for the kids' sake and because the city is on the hook to pay for the busing.

To quantify proximity, the DOE uses school zones. A typical zone comprises a few dozen city blocks, and there are many zones within each of the city's thirty-two districts. Children who live in the zone designated to a school get higher priority at that school than students who live outside it. And students who live outside the zone for a school but within that school's district have lower priority than students in the zone but higher priority than those outside the district.

Another way to get priority status is by having a sibling at the school (or at another school in the same building, since schools are sometimes co-located). This rule is designed to make life easier for families; as a parent who has, at times, had kids at three different schools simultaneously, I can attest firsthand to the logistical complexities of schlepping kids to so many drop-offs and retrieving them all at pickup time. Having multiple kids at the same school or school facility may also increase family involvement in school communities and in their kids' educations.

The final factor in priority status is whether a rising kindergartner is currently in that school's prekindergarten program; it makes sense to give those kids priority because switching to a new school can be disruptive to young children and their families.

DOE then stacks these criteria to determine a child's full priority status. And the decision of how to stack each factor is not trivial. Top priority goes to students who live in the zone *and* have a sibling enrolled in the school. The next priority group is students who live in the zone without a sibling at the school. The next priority level is students who live outside the zone but in the district and who have a sibling at the school. And so on.

But in many cases, schools will have to choose among students who all have the same priority level. What if they can accommodate some but not all of the students who live in the zone and have a sibling at the school? Which ones should they accept?

That is where the lottery comes into play. Each student receives a lottery number that is used to break ties within a priority group, allowing each school to construct a full priority ranking for all the students who apply.

While schools are ranking students by priority and lottery number, parents are ranking schools. Each time one of our kids has applied to DOE schools, Ilana and I have constructed a list of twelve schools and—just as I ranked rooms in Adams House a few decades earlier—ordered them from our favorite to our least favorite.

Once the DOE administrators know every student's preferences and that student's priority status at each of the schools on the preference list, they endeavor to assign each student to the school as close to the top of the list as possible while still honoring the school's priority rankings. But how, exactly?

JANE AUSTEN VERSUS EDITH WHARTON

Explaining the difference between two commonly used school-choice algorithms

If all parents had identical preferences, it would be easy to combine those preferences and schools' priority rankings—we would simply start with the school everyone liked best and admit the kids with the highest priority there, then repeat the process at everyone's second-favorite school, and so on.

But parents have wildly diverse preferences because of where families live and what they value in a school. Your first-choice school might be my fourth choice or might not be on my list at all. This makes combining the schools' priority rankings and the students' preference lists much more complex. Market designers now need to decide what matters more, the students' preferences or the schools' priority rankings.

Imagine two different ways, which I'll discuss below, that the DOE could combine student preferences with the schools' priority rankings. In both systems, the parents submit a list of preferences starting with their first-choice school, then their second choice, and so on. The DOE then puts the preference rankings into a computerized algorithm that allows many, many rounds of selections and rejections to be done nearly instantaneously.

In both systems, everyone initially and automatically applies to their first-choice school. Each school ranks everyone who applies, combining priority status and lottery number, as described above, and takes as many students as it can. If a school reaches capacity, it rejects the rest of the applicants. Then students who are rejected by their first-choice school automatically apply to the second-choice school on their preference lists.

The two systems differ in how they handle applications after that first round.

In one system, when I apply to my second-choice school, seats at that school that have been allocated to students who applied in the first round are not available to my child, even if he has a higher priority ranking. In other words, even if my child has a higher priority ranking than yours at a school, if you ranked it higher than I did on your list, your child is more likely to be admitted. For example, if you ranked PS 87 as your first choice while I ranked it as my second, it is possible for your child to get in while mine does not (even if you don't have another kid enrolled there or live in the PS 87 school zone like I do).

This can happen if the school admits your child in the first application round and there are no more spots available when mine applies in the second round (which might happen if she does not get into her first-choice school). That's because, in this system, when a school allocates a seat to a student, that child is immediately admitted. If my second-choice school is already filled up with people who ranked it as their first choice, then I am out of luck there and am pushed to apply to my third-choice school, and so on down my list of twelve.

My brother, Ryder, did four years of a PhD in English literature and was particularly enamored with British and American novels from the nineteenth and early twentieth centuries. He might call this first system the *Pride and Prejudice* system. In that Jane Austen novel, the protagonist, Elizabeth Bennet, has two suitors propose to her but can accept only one. Once she (finally) accepts Mr. Darcy's proposal, the book ends.

In this *immediate-acceptance* system, once a school admits a student, it has committed to that student (just as Elizabeth Bennet does with Mr. Darcy), regardless of who might apply later.

The second system works *almost* the same way, except that when the school picks students from its list of applicants, it does not immediately admit them. Instead, it holds them temporarily and waits to see what other applicants come along before deciding whom to admit.

While market designers refer to this as *deferred acceptance*, Ryder might call it the *Custom of the Country* system. In that Edith Wharton novel, written a century later, the main character, Undine Spragg, marries one man and then trades up for a better match each time the opportunity arises. The book ends only after Undine marries a rich businessman and concludes she can do no better—though not for lack of desire (her unfulfilled dream is becoming an ambassador's wife).[*]

---

[*] For Ryder, the unfinished English PhD was the first step in his Undine Spragg–like career, while I was Elizabeth Bennet marrying right into economics.

With the *Custom of the Country* system, if I have a higher priority ranking than you at PS 87, I will get prioritized over you even if PS 87 is your first choice and my second. This means that if someone with higher priority than you or with the same priority and a better lottery number applies to a school that is "holding" you, that student can bump you out of that school even if that school is low on his preference list and high on yours.

In this system, any student who is rejected by a school at any stage in the process automatically applies to the next school on his preference list, then the next, until everyone is being held by a school or is in the unenviable position of being unmatched, having been rejected by all the schools on their preference list. Only once the process is done — and the schools, like Undine Spragg, have determined they can do no better — are students who are being held by schools finally admitted there.

If you could choose between these two systems, you might be tempted to go for the first (immediate acceptance) rather than the second (deferred acceptance). For one thing, because the first system rewards preference more highly, it can more efficiently allocate spots in any school to the students (or parents) who value them more. You might also find it a bit unfair that in the second system, a school might bump a student who *really* wants to go there (or whose parents really want their child to go there) for another who seems less enthusiastic and just happens to come along later with higher priority or a better lottery number.

You may like Elizabeth Bennet, who falls in love and commits to Mr. Darcy, more than you do Undine Spragg, who is very willing to ditch her current husband for a shinier model. It is not a coincidence that *Pride and Prejudice* has been adapted for the silver screen over a dozen times, while *Custom of the Country* has never been turned into a movie. (Sofia Coppola once attempted to make a miniseries based on it, but she said the project was killed because Undine Spragg was deemed too unlikable.) It is understandable that you may not want to put your child's educational future in the hands of a system that behaves the way Undine does.

But it turns out that the *Custom of the Country* system has some very desirable properties.

First, and perhaps most important, it allows market participants to report their preferences honestly, without worrying about what priority status they have at which schools or what other parents are ranking. Market designers call this type of deferred-acceptance mechanism *strategy-proof*, because there is *no need* to strategize when participating in it.

In a strategy-proof mechanism, your priority ranking at a school does not change based on where you rank it, so you can honestly say which school is your favorite, second favorite, and so on. For example, if I do not love my zoned school, I can put it toward the end of my preference list (essentially as a safety school, since I am almost certain to get in based on my priority) without having to fear ending up unmatched. (In most school districts, being unmatched means you will be assigned by an administrator to whatever school has available seats, often without consideration of your preferences.) I can honestly list schools I prefer higher on my list, and if it doesn't work out at those places, I have not sacrificed my priority status at my zoned school.

In the immediate-acceptance mechanism, however, some strategy is necessary, and that strategy likely includes being dishonest about your preferences. If I rank my preferences honestly, say, putting my zoned school low on my preference list, I risk losing it as a safety school, since it might get filled up by parents who rank it higher than I do. The immediate-acceptance system, in other words, incentivizes ranking my safety school higher on my preference list than a school I really want my child to attend.

In addition, what you rank at the very top of your list is particularly important in immediate-acceptance mechanisms. If you list popular schools in your first few slots, you might find that your second-choice school has been filled by people who listed it first, your third-choice school has been filled by people who listed it first or second, and so on down your list. In these cases, failing to get into your first- or second-choice school could make you much more likely to be unmatched.

These dynamics mean it is not safe to report honestly in the immediate-acceptance mechanism; instead, you must lie about your preferences when ranking schools. For example, I might decide to list a school to which my child has a good chance of being accepted — like my zoned school or a different school that I believe will be less popular among other parents — as my first choice even though it is not actually my favorite option. The result is that I might end up with my sixth- or seventh-favorite school (that I strategically ranked high on my list) when I might have been able to secure a spot at my second- or third-favorite school if I had been able to safely rank my preferences honestly.

Immediate acceptance forces you to decide whether to go for gold (ranking your real first choice first but risking getting nothing) or settle for silver (ranking a less desirable school first because you think you have a good chance of being admitted there if it is at the top of your preference list).

When you're making these calculations, it's useful to have information about other parents' preferences to get a sense of what the demand is for various schools. This could mean paying extra attention to how many *ooh*s and *aah*s you hear from other parents at the open houses. Are they impressed? Indifferent? Put off by what they hear from school administrators? It could mean casually asking other parents in the neighborhood what schools they are planning to rank and what they will rank first (and second).

This strategizing can get tricky, but it is necessary for you to succeed when playing in a market with an immediate-acceptance mechanism.

WHEN HONESTY IS THE BEST POLICY

Explaining the benefits of a strategy-proof system in the three-E framework

Thankfully, when designing its mechanism, the New York City DOE called my adviser, Alvin Roth, to help them. Excellent work done by academic market designers had highlighted the weaknesses of immediate acceptance and the benefits of deferred acceptance for solving the school-choice problem. And Al and his research team were able to convince the DOE to adopt deferred acceptance for its admissions process.

Al and the other market designers who work on these problems understand the advantages of strategy-proof mechanisms like deferred acceptance in the context of the three-*E* framework.

The first advantage of strategy-proof mechanisms is that, because they don't require the kind of strategizing described above, they make the application process easier for students and their families. With a deferred-acceptance system, you don't have to worry about other families' preferences for schools, how many seats each school has available, or how your lottery number compares to the lottery numbers of other families who might like the same schools as you. You can simply rank the schools in order of your preference and be done with it.

The second advantage is that strategy-proof mechanisms can be more equitable. When Boston's public schools used immediate acceptance, it was clear that some parents—better-informed, typically more affluent parents—understood the system and how to strategize within it better than others. These parents knew that rather than rank their true favorite first, they needed to consider which schools might actually admit their kid if they ranked the school first. These parents also knew that for their second choice, they should list a school that was unlikely to be filled up in the first round (since they would have a chance of being admitted to their second-choice school only if it did not get filled up in the first round). Parents with this strategy-savvy had better outcomes than the—typically less affluent or less well connected—parents without it. That was unfair.

Given that the way you rank preferences differs dramatically depending on whether a market is strategy-proof or not, it pays to know whether you are facing a mechanism where it is safe to tell the truth. How can you tell?

Sometimes it is obvious that a mechanism does not require strategizing. That was true of the process used by Adams House to assign rooms. If all you care about is getting the room you like best, then when it is your turn to pick, you should pick the best room available from what remains.

But sometimes it is not obvious to market participants whether an allocation is strategy-proof. For example, if Adams House were to ask students to list room preferences in advance, students might mistakenly think they need to rank backup options among their first few choices. But in reality, students can do no better than rank the rooms in order of their preference.

In an experiment on the topic, Harvard economist Shengwu Li had undergraduates at the Ohio State University play a version of the Adams House dorm-assignment process using amounts of money (from zero to fifteen dollars) rather than rooms. Since receiving more money is clearly better than receiving less money, the undergraduate subjects were expected to prefer fifteen dollars to twelve dollars and so on down the list.

When groups of four students were randomly selected to pick which monetary prize they wanted, students almost never lost money by mistake. Ninety-two percent of the time, the student picking first selected the highest prize, the student picking second picked the second-highest prize, and so on down the list. That number dropped to 60 percent when students in the group had to submit preferences in advance. In that scenario, a third of the students submitted a preference list that did not rank the monetary prizes in order from highest to lowest.

The problem gets harder when the algorithm gets more complex. To know for certain that you should tell the truth to a school-choice system would require looking at the computer code that the organization uses to implement its mechanism and subjecting it to the type of proofs that Al teaches in his PhD class on market design. Thankfully, there are various ways to infer whether a market is strategy-proof.

When the stakes are high and the market is not strategy-proof, you are likely to see consultants popping up offering to help you figure out how to optimize your chances of success. So the presence of market shamans means it's a good bet that you can't safely tell the truth, and their absence suggests the opposite. (While there are consultants for public-elementary-school admission in New York City, they typically help you decide on your preferences—such as which schools are better than others—rather than how to rank them. When it comes to private schools, for which the market is far from strategy-proof, the consultants spend a lot more time helping you figure out how to navigate the market—but more on that in the next chapter.)

You can and should identify trusted sources, such as industry experts, who may emphasize whether a particular mechanism requires gaming or is strategy-proof (although they may not use that technical term when discussing it).

Perhaps most directly, you can ask past market participants. A telltale sign that a market design is strategy-proof is reporting from past market participants—in this case, parents in the school system who have used the mechanism before—that there is no way to game the system.

I would like to tell you that you can always trust what organizations say about their own mechanisms, but that is sadly not always the case. Back when Boston's public schools were still using immediate acceptance, administrators saw that most families were getting matched to their first-choice schools, and they took that as a sign that everything was going splendidly. How can you improve on most people getting their first choice?

What they did not quite internalize was that parents might be misrepresenting their first choice because of the market rules. Of course, the market participants, past and present, knew better. They were the ones surveying other parents at the playground and thinking carefully about what to rank, and they were the ones who might have learned the hard way the cost of failing to be strategic.

A TWELVE-OPTION CAVEAT

Emphasizing that deferred acceptance might not always be strategy-proof

I implied above that the DOE's version of deferred acceptance was strategy-proof. But there is one caveat to that claim that is worth highlighting.

A deferred-acceptance mechanism is truly strategy-proof only when it allows you to list as many options as you want. New York City and many other school districts have historically limited the number of schools you can include on a preference list; in New York City, for example, the DOE capped preference lists at a maximum of twelve schools until the 2025–2026 admissions cycle, when they finally made it unlimited, and the mechanism became fully strategy-proof.

When there is a cap, this creates a wrinkle when you think about ranking schools honestly. While you should still rank the twelve schools on your list in order of your true preference, it behooves you to include one or two options that you have a decent chance of getting matched to. This way, if things go badly, you still have a safety school to fall back on.

This caveat becomes more important when you are limited to even fewer options, an issue I return to later.

BITE THE BULLET

Emphasizing the importance of ranking preferences sooner rather than later

One critique of market designs like the Harvard housing lottery and the New York City school-choice program is that it is not easy for participants to determine and rank their preferences over so many different options in advance of the market running. With dozens of dorm rooms or elementary schools to choose from, you might indeed find it hard to determine what you like more and what you like less.

Moreover, some of this work will inevitably be wasted. If parents do rank all twelve schools and end up with something toward the bottom of their list, they will have wasted effort ranking schools that were out of reach (based on priorities, lottery numbers, and others' preferences). If they end up with one of their top choices, they wasted effort ranking schools that were relatively undesirable. But, to paraphrase the famous quip attributed to nineteenth-century businessman and postmaster general John Wanamaker, while they know they are wasting some of their effort, they do not know which schools they are wasting it on. (Wanamaker supposedly said: "Half the money I spend on advertising is wasted; the trouble is I don't know which half.")

Market designers could eliminate some of this wasted effort by allowing participants to wait to submit their preferences until later in the process. Unfortunately, this introduces even more problems.

Before the New York City DOE administrators partnered with Al and his team to help improve their school-choice mechanism, their market for high-school admission (which also factored in grades and test scores for admission to certain schools) allowed students to wait and see where they had been admitted before choosing which school to attend.

In that paper-based system, students first submitted a list of five schools that they would be interested in attending. They then received a letter from the DOE telling them which, if any, had offered them a seat. If it was more than one, they were able to consider their options and decide which one they wanted to accept.

So students had to develop only vague preferences; they had to choose five schools they liked, but they could avoid the hard work of deciding which they liked best, second best, and so on until they knew which schools had actually admitted them.

The problem was that while they were deciding, other students—those who had not been admitted to any of their top five schools—needed to apply to a second batch of schools. In order to do so, they needed to know which schools still had spots available, but schools did not know if they had spots until the students who had received multiple offers finally made up their minds.

Because this process took so much time, the city could do only three rounds of applications before the school year began, which left about 30 percent of students without a placement as school was about to start. They ended up administratively assigned, typically without any accounting for their preferences. This was very inefficient.

In addition to slowing things down for the entire system, market rules that allow you to defer thinking about your preferences until a later stage can also introduce inequity. You might end up as a lucky applicant deciding between multiple options or an unlucky one forced to wait for the lucky ones to decide what they want. And since lottery numbers often play a role in admissions decisions, you might not know which group you will be in until the first round of offers gets made. From behind this veil of uncertainty, you might prefer a system that makes everyone do a little bit of legwork in advance to improve overall outcomes.

And in some markets, you can at least figure out where to best focus your effort simply by finding out your priority status or lottery number in advance.

While students vying for the best dorm rooms in Adams House all learned their lottery numbers in real time over the course of the evening (at least back when I was there), housing lotteries at other colleges report lottery numbers beforehand. This helps set expectations and allows students to think more carefully about their preferences for rooms that might be attainable and avoid wasting too much time deliberating on rooms that they are very unlikely to get; after all, why bother to research and compare a Porsche 911 to a Maserati GranTurismo if all you can afford is a Toyota Corolla?

Similarly, to help parents focus their efforts on schools that are worth seriously considering, the New York City DOE is transparent about priorities (it also recently started showing parents their lottery numbers). But even if you have a good sense of your priority status and know your lottery number, you should still take the time to research which schools might be better than others. Ongoing work by a team of economists exploring how parents develop preferences for primary schools in Santiago, Chile, has found that parents systematically overestimate the quality of familiar schools and—relatedly—overestimate the quality of the schools they rank highly on their preference lists.

But the academics also found that when parents did their research, the preferences they reported changed. Paying extra attention to a handful of initially unfamiliar schools can go a long way to help you make more informed, better decisions.

THE RISKS OF MISREPORTING

Explaining how trying to strategize in strategy-proof mechanisms can backfire

We've established that in strategy-proof mechanisms, you should tell the truth. This advice should be easy to follow. Most of us have been encouraged to be honest since we were old enough to know what that meant. But people still manage to struggle with this instruction, and they pay the price.

If you know people who completed medical school in the United States, they almost certainly participated in the National Resident Matching Program (NRMP), which assigns medical school graduates to residencies in hospitals and other health-care institutions where they complete their training. Each year, nearly forty-five thousand soon-to-be doctors submit preferences for residency programs. They are each trying to secure one of the roughly forty thousand spots in one of over six thousand residency programs participating in the match—programs that differ in prestige, pay, and location—and a binding commitment occurs if there is a match. The algorithm that the NRMP uses is strategy-proof, so new doctors cannot do better than ranking their preferences honestly. (The NRMP technically has a cap on the number of programs you can rank, but it is usually above the number of programs where med students interviewed, so it is unlikely to be a real constraint.)

The stakes of this process are high. Doctors will spend at least the next three or four years in this residency program, so where they match will determine what city they live in, what faculty they train with, and who their coworkers are for a large chunk of time. Ranking these residency programs honestly to increase their chances of getting the best possible match seems like it would be a top priority for participants.

But research done by my Wharton colleague Alex Rees-Jones suggests that even well-informed, highly motivated applicants might not rank honestly and might make mistakes that cost them dearly.

In one study, Alex and Samuel Skowronek asked med students who had recently participated in the NRMP to play in an identical mechanism in which residency programs were replaced with various sums of money that they could receive based on where they matched; participants would earn fifty dollars if they matched to the best program, twenty-five to the second best, and so on down to five dollars in the event of no match. In their instructions, Alex and Sam made clear that their study used the same mechanism as the NRMP did.

Since — as the medical students had been told — the best you could do in the NRMP was report honestly, Alex and Sam figured they should report honestly in their game as well.

What Alex and Sam found surprised me and many other market designers. Almost a quarter of the over seventeen hundred med students in their study did not rank the programs from best to worst, and their mistakes were costly. Those who misreported earned over 20 percent less from the game.

The misreporting in Alex and Sam's game suggested the participants had probably also misreported in the NRMP. Alex and Sam concluded that many doctors who had just participated in the NRMP had not understood or internalized that the market was strategy-proof.

Other researchers have found similar patterns in different strategy-proof matching mechanisms. Students interested in getting a psychology graduate degree in Israel, for example, can submit a preference list for programs they would like to attend. On that list they can rank the same program two different ways: one way with a prestigious fellowship — free money, on the order of thousands of dollars, with no strings attached — and one way without it. Since it is safe to assume that students prefer getting the fellowship to not getting it, we would expect the students to always rank a program with the fellowship before they ranked the program without the fellowship. And yet the researchers found high numbers of prospective students who did not. As a result, some students ended up being admitted to the program without the fellowship even though they would have received the fellowship too had they simply ranked it higher.

Unfortunately, this type of misreporting is surprisingly common around the globe. In Hungary, many college applicants fail to appropriately rank undergraduate programs that include a tuition waiver above the very same programs without the waiver, even though the waiver could save them $6,600 on average.

Researchers are still trying to understand why people do this. Perhaps people are confused about how these markets work, believing that settling for silver is the best strategy when in fact they risk nothing by going for gold. Perhaps they don't want to be honest with themselves about their preferences; maybe on some level they're worried they would feel worse if they listed something as their true first choice and didn't get it and feel less bad if they convinced themselves they didn't really want it that much in the first place. Or maybe all of us are simply conditioned to think we should be trying to game any market we are in, even when it works against our interests.

SWAPPING AND SHORT-LISTING
Explaining two types of misreporting

There are two main types of misreporting. One is ranking things in the wrong order (*wrong* in the sense that it doesn't accurately reflect your preferences, such as inverting your first and second choices). We call this *swapping*. The other is failing to list the maximum allowable number of preferences (ranking only three schools when the application allows you to rank up to twelve, for example). We call this *short-listing*.

Both swapping and short-listing are common mistakes that can be costly for market participants.

When one of my best friends from high school, Marion, was completing medical school, her father hosted a party for Match Day, the day soon-to-be MDs receive their residency placements for the following year. At many medical schools, Match Day comes with pomp and circumstance. The students dress up, congregate, and are handed their match results in physical envelopes. They open these letters with their fate printed on them, often surrounded by their entire medical school class. (To me, that sounds like a nightmare, particularly since there is a chance of learning, in a very public and potentially embarrassing fashion, that you were unmatched.)

At Marion's party, we learned that she had gotten her first-choice placement. But not everyone at the party was quite so ecstatic about the contents of the envelope they had received.

While celebrating Marion (or Dr. Marion, as our kids now call her; she became a pediatrician and is our first call when our kids' pediatrician's office is closed), I ended up in a conversation with one of her classmates. She had gotten her second choice, and despite having been matched with a prestigious hospital affiliated with Yale University, she seemed all but devastated. Now facing the prospect of moving to a new city, she regretted having ranked Yale second when she truly preferred the program she had ranked third.

It was initially unclear to me whether her mistake stemmed from a failure to realize her true preferences early enough or from misunderstanding the mechanism and incorrectly thinking that listing Yale second would help her get her top choice. But regardless of the reason, her experience highlights that when you engage in swapping, you risk getting something you like less rather than something you like more.

Failing to list the maximum number of preferences—short-listing—can also have major consequences. Even if you think that only your top three choices are acceptable, it's likely that you would prefer to end up with a just-okay option that might be your fourth or fifth choice than with nothing. The only time it makes sense to omit options from your list is if you *really* would be happier with nothing or with whatever you might get from administrative assignment.

As with swapping, the reason people engage in short-listing is often a misunderstanding or a mistrust of ranked-preference mechanisms. Researchers who surveyed parents in Denver and New Orleans found that, in spite of messaging from the school districts, many parents incorrectly believed that listing more schools would make them less likely to receive a placement at one of their top choices. In reality, it had no impact on the likelihood of their getting a top choice and just made them more likely to get nothing.

RANKED-CHOICE VOTING
Explaining the perils of short-listing in ranked-choice voting

One of the best examples of the perils of short-listing came from the rollout of ranked-choice voting in the New York City mayoral election in 2021.

As in many cities that lean one way politically, all the action for the city's mayoral election was expected to be in the primary (the Democratic primary, in New York City's case). Historically, voting in the Democratic primary for mayor—and in all the city's elections—involved picking one candidate and giving that person your vote.

In those days, if the candidate with the most votes got less than 40 percent (often the case when more than two people were running), there would be a runoff election between the top two candidates. The problem was that holding these additional runoff elections was costly, and voter turnout in the runoffs was generally dismal.

Enter ranked-choice voting, which had been adopted statewide in Maine and Alaska and in various municipalities in many other states, including in San Francisco and Minneapolis.

Ranked-choice voting gives people the opportunity to vote for multiple candidates in the order of their preference. New York City allowed voters to rank up to five candidates. And while five might be enough slots to rank all or most of the candidates in a typical election, the 2021 Democratic primary for mayor had thirteen candidates on the ballot.

In advance of the election, advocacy organizations and news outlets tried to educate the public about how ranked-choice voting worked. The nonprofit Rank the Vote NYC, which had worked to get the new system passed, quickly transitioned to voter education; its website not only explained how this method of voting worked, it let folks practice by ranking their favorite bodega snacks. Similarly, the *Wall Street Journal* posted an interactive feature on its website that invited readers to rank their five favorite bagel-with-schmear combinations and then showed them how votes would get reassigned as certain candidates—including, to my dismay, the cinnamon raisin bagel with butter and jam—got eliminated.

These websites explained the market rules clearly: You could rank up to five candidates, in declining order of preference. Once votes were tallied, the candidate with the lowest number of first-choice votes would get dropped from the race. Any vote for a candidate who got dropped would then automatically go to the next person that voter had listed on the ballot. The process would then repeat, dropping the candidate with the second-lowest number of votes and reassigning those votes to whoever was next on those voters' ballots (if the next candidate a voter had chosen was already out of the race, the vote would go to the voter's highest-ranked candidate who was still in contention). Eventually, there would be only two candidates left. Whoever had the most votes at that stage would win.

This voting process is sometimes called instant-runoff voting because it eliminates the need for a runoff election between top candidates. Since voters have already ranked their preferences, we know who they would choose if forced to select between whichever two candidates got the most votes.

But we only *really* know this for voters who rank at least one of these top two candidates on their ballots. If voters do not rank either of the last two candidates left standing, then we say their ballot is "exhausted" (as though their ballot were too tired to make it all the way to the end of the election).

The 2021 mayoral primary had three front-runners. Polling suggested that Eric Adams, a former New York City police officer and Brooklyn borough president at the time, was likely to get the most first-choice votes. He was the most conservative of the candidates, running on a message that the city had gotten unsafe and needed a cop to clean it up. Another front-runner was Kathryn Garcia, the sanitation commissioner and go-to adviser to Bill de Blasio, the sitting mayor. Her supporters liked that she got things done and believed she would help the city get back on its feet after COVID. The *New York Times* agreed and endorsed her before the primary. The most liberal of the front-runners was Maya Wiley, former counsel to the mayor and former head of the Civilian Complaint Review Board; she received prominent endorsements from the liberal wing of the Democratic Party.

As expected, when the first-choice votes were counted, Adams was in the lead with almost 31 percent of the vote, Wiley had just over 21 percent, and Garcia had nearly 20 percent. As the other ten candidates began to be eliminated, Adams inched up, but so did Wiley and Garcia. When the fourth-place contender, entrepreneur and 2020 presidential candidate Andrew Yang, got knocked out, his votes went disproportionately to Garcia, with whom he had campaigned. (Cross endorsements are common in ranked-choice voting, since candidates can encourage their supporters to rank a particular ally second.)

With just the three front-runners left, Garcia had overtaken Wiley. Because of their political alignment—with Wiley more progressive, Garcia in the center, and Adams more conservative—when Wiley was eliminated, votes from people who ranked her highly were nearly three times more likely to go to Garcia than Adams.

When the dust settled, Garcia had nearly caught up with Adams but fell short by 7,197 votes, less than 0.8 percent of the primary votes that had been cast.

With a margin this narrow, every vote counts. And in this primary, over 140,000 voters had no say in the final contest between Adams and Garcia; 74,488 of the votes that had been cast for Wiley did not rank either Garcia or Adams, and nearly 66,000 voters—about

7 percent of those who cast a ballot—had not ranked even one of the three front-runners.

These voters likely had a preference between Adams and Garcia (and I would guess many of the 74,488 preferred Garcia, given how Wiley's other votes were split). But they failed to voice it, either because they ranked five candidates who were not those two front-runners or because they short-listed, failing to use all five of their votes. Data released by the New York City Board of Elections indicates that short-listing was mostly to blame. Only 46 percent of the ballots cast ranked five candidates, and roughly a hundred thousand of the ballots that were exhausted had room to rank one more.

After the election, many voters expressed regret for short-listing, but in my view, the voters themselves were not to blame. Much like Natalie playing her first-ever game of rock-paper-scissors, they had been taught the rules of ranked-choice voting but hadn't been given clear advice about what strategy to play. If they had, they would have had more of a say in the outcome of the election.

Ideally, they would have been told that they should use all five of their precious votes, even if that meant including candidates they felt were "just okay." They would have been told that they should rank candidates according to their true preferences but also that they should be sure to rank at least two of the three candidates who had already emerged as the clear front-runners, since it was very likely that two would be left standing at the end of the process. Just like you want to include at least one safety school on your preference list to ensure you get in somewhere, you want to make sure you list at least one of the candidates likely to be left standing in a final runoff election to ensure your vote gets counted.

Had voters gotten this advice, they might have felt better about the process, knowing their votes had been counted in the final tally. In addition, New York City might not have ended up with its first modern sitting mayor to be indicted (on charges of bribery, wire fraud, conspiracy, and soliciting campaign contributions from foreign nationals).

GET PRIORITY

Emphasizing one way to improve your outcome in strategy-proof mechanisms

In most cases, the best that you can do in a strategy-proof market is tell the truth and avoid short-listing. But sometimes, there are actions you can take to secure a priority position in these markets—you just have to plan ahead and take these actions *before* the market opens.

For school choice, getting priority status at desirable schools is generally assumed to require either moving to a new residence within that school zone or illegally registering your kid with an address at which they do not live (not recommended). But by fully researching the market rules, you might discover other opportunities available to you.

One such opportunity that Ilana and I attempted to use for our benefit was the DOE policy that gives priority to kindergarten applicants who attend a prekindergarten program at the same school.

The logic of providing priority to these students is about continuity and investment in a school community. Kids who attend the pre-K program at a school have a sense of the building and the teachers, which makes for an easier transition to kindergarten. And parents who know their child's pre-K year might turn into an entire elementary-school experience may get more involved with the school in that first year.

This rule gives parents an incentive to research elementary schools earlier than they might otherwise have and then try to get their kid into a pre-K program in whatever school they are excited about in the hope of also securing priority for elementary-school matching. (Once children are in a school for kindergarten, they get to stay for all six of those formative years.)

We tried to take advantage of this trick by sending Isla to the pre-K program at PS 84, an elementary school that we liked and that had a sizable pre-K program, which meant we were able to get Isla in even though we lived out of the zone. Her spot in the pre-K program gave her priority for elementary-school admissions there, which we expected to be much more competitive. (We ended up not needing it because we moved into the PS 87 zone before she started kindergarten, but it was a great backup I'm glad we had.)

As the city has expanded its programs for pre-K and even started offering 3-K (a free year of early childhood care and education when kids are three, the year before pre-K), a related attempt to game the priority rules for 3-K admission has begun to play out.

The 3-K program was proposed by former mayor Bill de Blasio, who rolled out the plan starting in lower-income neighborhoods and began to expand it across the city. As a result of the expansion, many private day cares now offer a 3-K program paid for by the DOE.

The application process for 3-K programs is similar to that of the pre-K and kindergarten programs in that it involves submitting a ranked-preference list. But an important difference is that being a paying member of a participating day-care center gives you priority when applying to 3-K at that center. Since there is no guarantee of getting a 3-K spot in a convenient day-care center, many parents find it beneficial to sign up their two-year-olds at a day-care center that participates in the 3-K program, increasing their chances of securing one of the center's coveted free 3-K spots when the time comes.

But registering your two-year-old for day care to get 3-K priority can come at a cost. It might mean an extra drop-off in the morning or parting ways with a beloved at-home caretaker before you are ready to say goodbye. Or it might mean moving from a more convenient day-care center that does not participate in the 3-K program to a less convenient one that does. And if you are giving up a more affordable childcare option, like leaving the little ones with their grandparents or other family members, the cost of private day care (which can be thousands of dollars a month) adds up fast.

So you would be fortunate even to be able to consider this trade-off—for many parents, enrolling their children in months of day care that isn't covered by the city isn't an option.

Given the growing demand for the day-care slots that put two-year-olds on the fast track for 3-K, unless the city expands the program so every day care guarantees a free 3-K slot, I would not be surprised to see day cares that offer the 3-K program raise their prices for two-year-olds (knowing that those slots are particularly valuable, given that they come with priority for 3-K). This would further disadvantage certain—namely, less wealthy—families.

PRIORITY BASED ON PERFORMANCE
Exploring performance-based priority in school-choice mechanisms

As students advance through school, admissions decisions begin to depend less on factors like residential address and prior school enrollment and more on student performance: attendance, grades, and test scores.

In some public-school systems, performance-based priority mechanisms don't kick in until high school, but in others they start much earlier. For example, when Cass was entering kindergarten, he got out of attending his less-than-stellar zoned school by qualifying for a Gifted and Talented (G&T) program based on his performance on an IQ-style test.

Tracking kids based on their test-taking ability in preschool might seem absurd, and there is a good deal of debate about its equity implications. I like to think that Cass was naturally proficient on the type of test given by the G&T program, but I also had the time and energy to go over practice problems with him using both the sample tests provided by the city and books I bought on Amazon. This gave him an advantage that isn't available to every child.

Parents who wanted (and could afford) to give their kids even more of an edge could enroll their little ones in test-prep classes for the city's G&T exam. These classes were offered primarily in the affluent neighborhoods on Manhattan's East and West Sides, and some of them paired each child with a one-on-one tutor and even modeled "testing conditions" so that children could get used to being taken into a classroom by a stranger to answer test questions. These classes (surprise, surprise) were not cheap.

The possibility of improving scores with this kind of preparation raises obvious questions about the equity of the testing system. As a result, many school districts have shifted admissions criteria away from tests, basing them instead on a combination of teacher recommendations and lotteries. New York City is part of that shift—its G&T program has stopped using a test to determine admissions.

The same shift is being made at the selective middle schools and high schools that have historically used test-based admissions and have also been plagued by a lack of diversity. Of course, this approach has its critics too, like the eighth-grader with perfect attendance and a perfect GPA whose lottery number was not good enough for her to get into her dream high school. These debates underscore the reality that whenever there is scarcity, there will be winners and losers, and no hidden market can always satisfy all three *E*s at the same time.

OPTIMIZING IN GAMEABLE MECHANISMS

Explaining scenarios where the best strategy is to lie (about your preferences)

In New York City, school-choice markets rely on a strategy-proof deferred-acceptance mechanism. But that isn't the case for schools everywhere.

In 2024, over thirteen million Chinese students took their version of the SAT—the Nationwide Unified Examination for Admissions to General Universities and Colleges (abbreviated as Gaokao)—in the hope of securing a seat in one of China's over three thousand universities.

With such massive numbers of students and colleges, this annual match is the largest centralized market of its kind in the world. Unlike the system for matching students with universities in the United States (which I discuss in more depth in the next chapter), in China's system, a student's priority status within each province is typically determined solely by his or her score on the Gaokao (although students from ethnic minorities can have points added to their scores to satisfy affirmative-action considerations; the number of extra points varies across provinces).

Students in each province must submit a ranked-preference list. For many years, most provinces used the immediate-acceptance algorithm, which meant that students who performed very well on the Gaokao could still end up unmatched if they failed to rank schools strategically.

But starting in 2001, provinces within this matching market made changes that helped improve outcomes for Chinese students. One important change was switching from immediate acceptance to a hybrid that combined elements of both immediate and deferred acceptance. This mechanism runs a version of deferred acceptance for the first few schools on a student's ranked-preference list. It then locks in those offers—as if it were immediate acceptance—before moving to the next set of schools on the ranked list for students who have not yet been accepted anywhere.

While this policy requires less strategizing than immediate acceptance, it does require some. If you can rank only a small number of schools in that first batch (say, four, which was the number Shanghai schools adopted in 2008 when they switched from immediate acceptance to the hybrid system), you may need to misrepresent your true preferences when deciding which four schools you will rank.

Although it might be tempting to list your four favorites, if they all require equally high test scores and you don't know how your score compares to those cutoffs, listing your preferences honestly is likely to be a mistake. That's because if your four favorite schools all have similar cutoffs, and your Gaokao score is not good enough to get you into your first-choice school, it is highly unlikely that it is good enough to get you into your second-, third-, or fourth-choice school either.

Yet people have trouble recognizing this fact, so they waste application slots on schools to which they have almost no chance of being admitted.

In this type of hybrid system, students should consider using one or two of their four slots on less desirable schools that they have a good chance of getting into even if they fail to get into the better schools on their lists. But they should rank the four schools in each batch in their true preference order. There is no benefit to ranking their safety schools anywhere other than last (assuming that it's the option they would least prefer); all that matters is that a safety school is included in the top four. This is the same logic that hikers who want to climb Half Dome use when they include less popular hiking days on their preference lists, although the stakes here are much higher.

In 2011, the large majority of provinces made this calculus much easier on students by informing them of their Gaokao scores before they submitted preference rankings. Students also learned their rankings within their provinces and what scores were needed to get into particular colleges over the previous few years. Like knowing your lottery number in the housing lottery, having this information allows students to use their preference rankings more strategically. For example, they may learn that their scores are high enough to put very desirable schools like Peking University and Tsinghua University in contention, though they can't know for sure if their scores are good enough this year until all preference lists are in and the market runs. Or they may learn that their scores are too low to waste even one preference slot on schools like that, so they can focus on less selective universities.

IMPROVE YOUR LOTTERY NUMBER

Illustrating how lottery numbers can sometimes be gameable

We have already talked about how to optimize your preference list and how to improve your priority status. But what about your lottery number? Surely you cannot improve that.

I would not have thought so. But occasionally, there are glitches or loopholes in the market design that make it possible. This was the case for a time with the DOE system when they started displaying students' lottery numbers on applications. An attentive parent who canceled and then restarted her child's application realized that her kid's lottery number had changed. When she canceled and restarted the application again, the lottery number changed again.

Had she kept quiet about this bug, she might have restarted her application repeatedly until she got a phenomenal lottery number for her child. Instead, she did the right thing and reported the bug to the DOE administrators, who fixed it.

THE BOTTOM LINE

Takeaways from this chapter to help you succeed as a market participant

Many markets attempt to balance efficiency and equity by inviting participants to submit ranked-preference lists that report which options (be they elementary schools, colleges, residency programs, candidates, or dorm rooms) they like better than others.

When you are making these lists, however, you may not always want to be honest about your true preferences. A key consideration is whether the allocation mechanism is *strategy-proof*. If it is, the best thing you can do is tell the truth without *swapping* any of your preferences and making sure to rank as many options as the market rules allow. (The only time it makes sense to list fewer options than are allowed—that is, to *short-list*—is if all the remaining available options are less desirable to you than getting nothing.)

If a mechanism restricts the number of options on your ranked list, you will want to make sure to include a safety option or two (such as a school to which you are likely to be admitted or a candidate who is likely to still be in the running at the end of ranked-choice voting).

When a mechanism is not strategy-proof, you want to be even more strategic by considering what options you can attain given the rules of the market and the preferences of other market participants. To decide whether such gaming is necessary, talk to people who have played in the market before, since they will have a good sense of what options are popular and whether honesty is the best policy.

Regardless of whether you are going to tell the truth, it behooves you to figure out what you really want and what you will tolerate to minimize regrets when the dust settles.

COULD THE MARKET DESIGNERS DO BETTER?
Describing possible improvements to markets with ranked preferences

Market designers generally strive to replace gameable mechanisms with strategy-proof ones because of the associated gains in ease and equity; these rules eliminate the need to strategize while putting more and less sophisticated market participants on more equal footing. Fortunately, this process of switching to strategy-proof mechanisms has been aided considerably by advances in technology.

One innovation made possible by improvements in computing power is a mechanism that we use at Wharton to assign students to classes.

The scheduling system, Course Match, assigns Wharton students to classes at the start of each semester. Arranging students' schedules is a complex issue known as a *combinatorial assignment problem* because there are many ways to combine individual courses to make a schedule—and it is particularly hard to make schedules for many students in a way that is both efficient and ex-post equitable.

Since students' preferences for certain courses depend on what else is in their schedule, the problem gets even harder. For example, a student might want to take only one accounting class, so getting into the class on financial-disclosure analytics means the class on accounting for complex financial structures is less desirable (although both classes taught by my distinguished colleagues are excellent). Or a student might want to take classes that are related to one another in some way. If she gets a seat in a venture-capital class, for example, she might be more excited about taking an entrepreneurship class that covers related material from a different angle.

When I first arrived at Wharton, the way MBA students got assigned to courses involved a complicated auction. Students had a fixed budget of fake Wharton auction currency that they used to place simultaneous bids on courses that interested them that semester. The logic of the Wharton auction mechanism, which was similar to mechanisms used at other business and law schools, was that it replicated the efficiency of using money to allocate things but without the inequity, since each student got the same amount of fake currency. Unfortunately, it had a major flaw.

With auctions using real money, if you don't bid enough to win something, you keep the money, which you can use to buy other things you want. In the Wharton course auction, students who did not bid enough to win a seat in a class ended up with a fake currency that had very little value (it could be used in subsequent semesters, but it was literally worthless when the MBA students graduated at the end of four semesters). This created problems for all three Es.

Participating in the auction was not easy. It required a lot of strategizing about how much to bid: If you bid a bit too low on all the classes you wanted, you'd end up with none of them. Nor was the system ex-post equitable. Some people bid slightly above the market-clearing prices and wound up with multiple highly popular classes, while others bid slightly below those prices and ended up with none. There were also speculators who as rising second-years would buy popular first-year classes before the incoming first-year class arrived on campus and then sell the classes to them at a profit. Because so much strategy, luck, and speculation were embedded in the system, the people who wanted classes the most did not always get them, which created inefficiency.

The year I arrived as a professor at Wharton, students had started to rebel against the auction system. I proposed using an alternative mechanism that a graduate-school classmate of mine, Eric Budish, whom we met in chapter 2, had developed in his dissertation. (Course Match is a much better name than what Eric bestowed on the mechanism when he conceptualized it in his dissertation. There, it was Approximate Competitive Equilibrium from Equal Incomes, which is a bit of a mouthful.) Students would be asked to provide ranked preferences in advance of the mechanism running, then the ranked preferences and the number of seats available in each class would be used to set a price for each course; the unpopular courses would cost less than the ones everyone wanted to take. The prices were determined by the mechanism so that if you gave everyone an approximately equal amount of fake currency, and everyone went out and bought the best schedule they could afford, all (or almost all) of the seats in the popular courses would be sold.

This system mitigated a problem with the fake currency described above. While it still used a fake currency, the way the mechanism set prices changed it from the equivalent of a single art auction (where you either get the painting or not) to the equivalent of shopping at a grocery store (where, if filet mignon and heirloom tomatoes are too expensive for dinner tonight, you can get ground beef and potatoes instead).

But to set these prices at levels that would allow the system to run optimally, Eric's mechanism needed a way to know each student's ranked preferences over *every possible schedule*. Given the many classes available in a semester and the various ways they could be combined to make a schedule, we estimated that there were hundreds of millions of feasible schedules that each student would need to rank. Obviously, people were not going to be able to rank them manually the way they might rank twelve elementary schools, five mayoral candidates, or even thirty residency programs. So we needed a way for students to provide a reasonable amount of information that could be used to infer their preferences for all possible combinations of classes.

Eric proposed asking students how much they wanted each course on a scale from 0 to 100 and which courses were substitutes (allowing them to indicate that they wanted only one accounting course) or complements (allowing them to say they liked the venture-capital course more if they also got the entrepreneurship course).

As elegant as this solution was, it would work only if it provided enough information for an algorithm to calculate a value for each schedule that accurately reflected students' preferences. With the help of my Wharton colleague Gérard Cachon, the head of the committee tasked with improving course allocation at the school, Eric and I decided to find out.

We brought real Wharton MBA students into a computer lab on campus and had them compete with one another for seats in courses while attempting to construct the best schedule possible for a hypothetical semester. They did this task once using the new Course Match mechanism and once using the familiar auction mechanism.

We then asked them a series of questions about which of two schedules they preferred. Then we compared their reports to the algorithm's predictions about which schedule they would like better (guesses based on the limited information we had from them). The algorithm turned out to be very good at predicting which of two schedules each one preferred.

As we had hoped, they were also somewhat happier, on average, with the schedules they got from Course Match than from the auction, suggesting the new mechanism was delivering efficiency gains.

And these improvements seemed more equally spread across the group of participants, suggesting that Course Match was delivering improvements in equity as well.

The test was so successful that Course Match was quickly rolled out for real at Wharton. After the first year of implementation, students reported higher satisfaction with the new mechanism than with the old course auction—more evidence that it was a big improvement on the three *E*s. It was so successful, Wharton spun off a company to license the software to other schools. At the time of this writing, the software has been used at Wharton for over a decade and is also being used by a dozen other professional schools to assign their students to courses.

Another problem market designers are actively working to solve is how to make it easy for participants to represent *interconnected preferences*, such as when one person's preferences are connected to another person's outcome.

With course matching, my desire for a seat in a financial accounting course is unlikely to change depending on whether you get a seat in that same course. But in many other markets, what one person wants can shift depending on what another person gets.

This phenomenon arises in the market for residency programs. Since doctors who meet in medical school sometimes partner up, two people who are married or in a romantic relationship sometimes apply for residency programs simultaneously. To accommodate their interconnected preferences, Alvin Roth worked with the NRMP to allow couples to submit preferences for pairs of jobs—one for each partner—so they could accurately rank job prospects (such as one person indicating that a job is more appealing if her partner secures a position across town).

Housing lotteries are another market where we see these kinds of interconnected preferences. In fact, this may be the reason that Adams House still uses a live, in-person process rather than having subjects submit full ranked preferences over dorm rooms in advance and running the mechanisms on a computer. If you want to live near your friends, it may be helpful to see where other rooming groups end up so you can adjust your preferences after they select their rooms.

As rising sophomores, my rooming group wanted to live next to our friends so we could open the fire door between our suites. This would allow us to share one common room, turn the other common room into a bedroom, and increase the portion of the year we each got a bedroom to ourselves rather than sharing (we switched things up at the semester break, for equity's sake). To implement that plan, we decided that whichever group got to pick first would select a suite located next to a suite that no other group would be likely to want. When our friends' lottery number got called, they chose something at the very top of the Adams C entry, five flights up. It was a trek, so no one wanted to take the suite next door, which was still available when my group got to pick. That's how we ended up in Adams House C-53 and C-57 in a large coed suite with six people and how I ended up with the strongest calves of my life.

CHAPTER 6

Choose-Me Markets

IN PRE-PANDEMIC TIMES, OVER A THOUSAND NEWLY MINTED AND soon-to-be-minted econ PhDs flocked to the annual American Economic Association (AEA) meeting to vie for coveted jobs at the hundred or so universities that were looking to hire new economics faculty that year.

In the winter of 2011, I was one of them.

I had flown to Denver, Colorado, to participate in both the annual multiday conference and the annual labor market for economics job candidates. The conference itself consisted of hundreds of sessions of academic talks held in various rooms at the conference hotels and punctuated by luncheons where high-profile academics were honored and gave speeches to hundreds of acolytes. At the end of each day, those halls would be partitioned into more intimate spaces for cocktail-hour events hosted by various university economics departments.

But while these events were happening on the lower floors of the conference hotels, hiring-committee members—whose ranks I would join after becoming a professor myself—spent nearly all day holed up in hotel rooms eating mediocre room-service food and interviewing a dozen or so job candidates back to back to back. If the committee members were lucky, they might have a break in their schedule to go see or give a talk at the conference. (If they had energy left at the end of a marathon day of interviewing, they might even attend one of the cocktail hours for a well-earned glass of wine.)

Meanwhile, job seekers like me were scurrying from hotel suite to hotel suite, interviewing with the hiring committees that had granted us audiences. My first interview, at 8:45 a.m. on Friday, had been a pleasant chat with two professors from the economics department at UC Irvine. Later on Friday, however, I had an interview with the Yale School of Management that did not go quite as smoothly—especially after I expressed an interest in teaching undergraduate business students, even though the school did not have any.

On Saturday, I interviewed with Princeton and Stanford, two of the top five econ departments. Both interviews involved a roomful of prominent economists (probably six to eight faculty attended each interview, but each group felt like a dozen) staring me down and grilling me on my dissertation work. They interrupted my answers with follow-up questions, asked me to defend decisions I had made in my research, and pushed me on how to interpret my findings, leaving me feeling like I had been hit in the head with a two-by-four.

But Sunday, as I trudged through the snow in my nicest suit to my twelfth and final interview of the weekend, my exhaustion was no match for my rush of adrenaline. I was interviewing with Columbia Business School. I was a native New Yorker with a soon-to-be fiancée (or so I hoped!) who had just passed the New York State bar examination and was already working in New York City, so Columbia was one of my top choices—and the roomful of economists whom I would be attempting to impress knew it.

They knew it because the AEA market gave candidates the opportunity to inform two schools that they were particularly interested in working for them. These email messages were sent to hiring committees around the time they were deciding who would be interviewed, a mechanism market designers refer to as *signaling*. Like many participants in this competitive labor market, I had applied for around one hundred positions and was initially a bit unsure which two schools I should send my signals of interest to, but my desire to work in or at least close to the Big Apple helped me narrow my options down to Columbia Business School and the Stern School of Business at New York University.

While the interview itself is a blur, it must have gone well. Columbia was one of the places that invited me for a second-round interview (I had not been so lucky at Stanford or—surprise, surprise—the Yale School of Management). The second stage is a day-long affair called a flyout, because the school will fly you out so you can give an in-person academic seminar (essentially an hour-and-a-half talk about your research) and sit through a series of one-on-one interviews with the school's professors, followed by an almost always awkward dinner with faculty from the department.

By the time my Columbia flyout wrapped up, I was confident that if they offered me a job, I would accept it. I had chosen them. But whether they would choose me was far from certain.

WHAT MAKES A CHOOSE-ME MARKET?
Describing the type of market where there are participants on the other side of the market selecting you (without a formula)

The labor market is what we might call a choose-me market. As in the other hidden markets we have discussed, in a choose-me market, you are doing your best to get an allocation that appeals to you, and there are decision-makers on the other side of the market who determine if you are successful.

But there is a key distinction. In the markets we have seen so far, the rules that determine allocation can be expressed algorithmically. When you are trying to secure a product, a reservation, a hiking slot, or a seat in a preschool, those making the decisions do not particularly care about you as an individual. Whether or not you get what you want is determined by a clear set of rules. And because the allocations follow those market rules, all that matters is when you clicked, your lottery number, or your priority status.

In the absence of such rules, choose-me markets are much more subjective. And those doing the choosing are also market participants, in that they are trying their best to get an outcome that satisfies their preferences. To do so, they will be particularly keen to know more about you.

They will be concerned about two things.

First, they will compare you to other options on the market to see if you are indeed among their top choices. Second, they will want to figure out whether you are interested in matching with *them*. If they think you might be interested in them, that will encourage them to spend more time, energy, and resources learning about you and deciding whether to choose you. If they think you will be unlikely to want to match with them, they might not bother.

Many of the markets that we participate in—indeed, some of the most important ones we participate in—are choose-me markets. Parents who consider private school for their kids enter a choose-me market. Unlike charter schools, which typically use lotteries, or traditional public schools, which combine priorities with lotteries, private schools can admit whichever students (or, perhaps more accurately, whichever families) they want using whatever criteria— usually criteria they do not share publicly—they want.

In the United States, the market for college admission is also a choose-me market. Unlike schools in China, where the majority of students gain admission based on Gaokao scores alone, US colleges and universities admit candidates based on a variety of characteristics. These schools are interested in admitting students who will make the academic and extracurricular life of the school vibrant. But the schools also care about their yield: the fraction of students they admit who end up matriculating.

Similarly, in labor markets, employers are trying to find the best employees they can. But they are also looking for candidates who are likely to accept the job offer and, ideally, stay at the firm for a while.

Perhaps the most classic example of a choose-me market is the market for romantic partners. For a match to work in the romantic sense, both participants must be interested in and choose each other (for the night or perhaps much longer). And with limited time each week to go on dates (and a limited number of years on biological clocks), they are also trying to gauge if their dating partner is interested in them as well. If not, they might decide their dating hours would be better spent with someone else.

While markets for private schools, jobs, and romance might seem very different, succeeding in each of them requires some strategy for signaling what it is that you want. To whom should you signal your strongest interest? What specifically should you signal about yourself when given the chance? This chapter will help you figure out how and what to signal to improve your chances of finding the perfect match in school, work, and love.

THE CURSE OF THE OVERQUALIFIED

Explaining why, when you have limited bandwidth, you may need to screen out the top as well as the bottom

In choose-me markets, you want to learn about potential options so you can go after something good. But learning requires time and effort. As a market participant, you should be wary of wasting your limited resources forming preferences about things you cannot get.

The hiring committees at the AEA meeting in Denver, for example, had a limited number of interviewees they could squeeze in that weekend. Out of hundreds of applications from potential professors, they could select between twenty and thirty to interview in person.

For second-round flyouts, committees need to winnow down the list further, often to about five to ten candidates. The constraint on the number of flyouts is about effort, cost, and timing—each flyout consumes a day for the entire department and requires paying for the applicant's travel and accommodations, and there are only so many days between the AEA meeting and the time that offers need to be made.

At the end of those flyouts, a department will typically make just one or two offers. Then they need to persuade those candidates to say yes—a potentially difficult task when candidates have competing offers. Because getting to this point is a large amount of work for an uncertain outcome, departments need to be thoughtful about whom they advance at each stage of the process.

In an ideal world, this might mean advancing only those candidates who they think would be the best additions to their faculty. But there is one complication. In the same way that you might hesitate to spend a Saturday night trying to get to know someone who seems "out of your league," if an applicant looks like a superstar destined to get a job offer from a top economics department, a low-ranked department might not want to waste an offer, a flyout, or even an interview slot on that person.

Screening out candidates who are out of your league, romantically or professionally, is sometimes called top-coding. This invokes the idea that you aren't rejecting them because they are not good enough but because they are too good.

When I was on the job market, I was obviously very excited whenever I got a call granting me an interview, but I was also very excited each day I was *not* offered interview slots from the lower-ranked schools to which I had applied. By not inviting me to an interview, those schools were top-coding me. If the schools had reached out to me in droves, it would have been an indication that they all thought the higher-ranked programs would be uninterested in me and that I would be very likely to end up at one of my safety schools.

The idea of top-coding goes by many names. Perhaps the most

common way to top-code people is to declare them *overqualified*. If this term was used to describe you when you were passed over for a job opportunity, you might have been frustrated by the idea of being denied something you wanted due to being overqualified. Rightfully so. When you are unemployed or looking for a new job, you are presumably applying only to jobs you would take. So why should employers rule you out based on the assumption that you are too good for them?

The issue is that employers need to worry about not just whether you will accept a job but also whether you will stay. If they hire you, they will likely train you for the job and integrate you into their team. Though a good investment for a worker who will stay awhile, it is a risky proposition if you might leave any minute for a better opportunity. If you are indeed overqualified, the future job offers you are likely to get might also pay substantially more money, making it harder and more costly for the firm to retain you.

These dynamics play out in the dating market as well. I once heard an anecdote about a friend of a friend who worked for a nuclear agency and periodically got sent abroad to countries like Russia to inspect nuclear facilities. Before one such trip, a colleague asked him how attractive he thought he was on a scale from one to ten. The guy rated himself as a five or a six. Then the colleague asked what he would think if a woman who was a nine or ten on that scale came over to him at a hotel bar and started flirting. The correct answer, from the perspective of the colleague, was that his guard should be up. He should be wondering whether this person was expressing genuine interest in him or trying to seduce him for nefarious reasons—like to get her hands on some nuclear secrets.

When it comes to being overqualified in an employment setting, you are the incredibly attractive woman at the hotel bar. Yes, there is a chance that you are applying for your dream job, but it is also reasonable for the firm to worry that you are interested in the job only to hold you over until you find something better.

GENERAL VERSUS IDIOSYNCRATIC PREFERENCES

Explaining two different places preferences can come from

To understand how best to play in choose-me markets, you need to have a framework for thinking about preferences, both yours and those of the people on the other side of the market.

Economists rely on a framework for thinking about preferences that splits each person's preferences into two parts: a *general* preference that most people agree on and an *idiosyncratic* preference unique to each individual.

When evaluating jobs, we generally prefer jobs that offer higher pay and better benefits. And on the flip side of the market, employers generally prefer candidates with higher grade point averages, good reviews from former employers, and more work experience (especially more prestigious work experience).

One day in graduate school, I mused about who would be best to play me in a movie about my life. I started to say Paul Rudd (who, about a decade later, was named Sexiest Man Alive by *People* magazine). After I said *Paul* but before I said *Rudd*, my quick-witted friend interrupted with "Giamatti?"

He was referencing the excellent actor of a similar age whom the *Independent* once quoted as saying, "Let's be honest about this. I'm limited by my looks so I'm a tough sell, but there's plenty of folk out there who look just like me, and someone has to play them."

The reason my friend's joke was funny (as harsh a burn as it might have been) is because of a general preference for Rudd's looks over Giamatti's.

If all any of us had were these general preferences, then choose-me markets would be simple to navigate. We would get what economists call *assortative matching*. If we all shared the same preferences, everyone and everything could be ranked from best to worst, and we all would agree on that ranking. For the labor market, the agreed-upon best employees would get the agreed-upon best jobs, the next-best employees would get the next-best jobs, and so on. The same pattern would arise in education markets and in romantic pairings. The best students would go to the best schools, and people who looked like Paul Rudd would marry people considered as attractive as Paul Rudd. There would be no surprises.

But even when people agree about general preferences, actual preferences are much more idiosyncratic.

You might prefer a liberal arts college while I prefer a research university. I might want to earn as much money as possible while you prefer a job working in a certain field even if it pays less. And when it comes to dating, you might find different people attractive than I do. The fact that we have different preferences is what makes markets—and life—more exciting. It's what makes a horse race, as the saying goes.

Eight years after participating in the economics job market as an applicant, I was a newly tenured professor at Wharton and chair of our junior recruiting committee, taking the reins of the recruiting process from the other side of the market. That year, one of our precious interviews, flyouts, and eventual offers went to a candidate I really liked—someone I thought would join our department for sure. We knew we were the highest-ranked school that had made her an offer and that we paid more than her other options. Based on general preferences, we were the obvious choice, so I assumed it was a done deal. I had overlooked, however, her strong idiosyncratic preferences. She was European, and when she received a job offer from a school in her home country—closer to family and friends—it turned out to be too tempting to turn down.

Had we anticipated that her strong idiosyncratic preferences trumped the general preference of working at a top US business school, we might not have invested so much time and effort in considering her for the job, even given how great a professor we expected her to be. Meanwhile, she might have needed to convince the faculty members in her home country that they should invest in making her an offer—that she would even turn down a great job from Wharton to take it. This is why identifying and signaling idiosyncratic—rather than general—preferences is often the best strategy for getting the things we want in choose-me markets.

MATCHMAKER, MATCHMAKER, MAKE ME A MATCH
Explaining the value of signaling, especially in crowded markets

Online dating is a multibillion-dollar-a-year industry. Countless apps and websites—including Tinder, Hinge, Bumble, Grindr, and OkCupid—exist to help people make a romantic match. Tinder, the most popular app by far, pulls in nearly a billion dollars a year in revenue and boasts approximately fifty million users each month.

The sheer volume of people with whom you might match seems like it would be an advantage for Tinder. And, yes, having a pool of people to search through is necessary (a dating app would not work if you were the only one on it). But the large number of potential matches poses its own problem.

Tinder, like many of the other online dating platforms, is designed to help you easily sort through the many possible matches available. You can set geographic, gender, and age filters that control which profiles you see. You can swipe right on profiles of people you want to connect with and left on those you do not. If you and a potential match both swipe right on each other, you get alerted and can start chatting—perhaps making plans to meet up in real life.

But while the system is supposed to help you find the proverbial needle in the haystack, the actions of certain market participants can complicate the process. Straight women looking for long-term dating partners on Tinder face a particular problem: They complain that at least some subset of straight men on Tinder swipe right on all profiles.

It might seem like a good problem, since it means more potential matches. But it also makes the needle-in-a-haystack search for the best matches way more difficult. If many men play this "it's a numbers game" strategy and swipe right on everyone, a woman who swipes right on a man who looks promising indeed has a higher chance of matching with him. But she does not know if this is someone who carefully looked at her profile and decided they might be truly compatible (the kind of man she might be looking for) or someone who swiped right on her merely because she was a woman on Tinder (the kind of man she might want to avoid).

Like the hiring committee with a limited number of interview slots, these women probably have a limited number of chats they can keep going at once and a limited number of dates they are able to go on each week. If these women want to find that special someone, they must become more selective in swiping right, and they might have to screen from both the bottom (swiping left on people they are not interested in) and the top (swiping left on people they might be interested in but might also be a waste of their time).

If men swiped more selectively, women could swipe more liberally. In that case, getting a match would be a good signal of true mutual interest. Instead, women need to do extra work to identify who might be a good match.

This outcome is less than ideal for women, who now must work harder to screen potential matches. This outcome is also problematic for the men who are carefully considering profiles rather than swiping right on everyone. Even if such a man finds someone whom he believes to be his soulmate, that potential soulmate has no way of distinguishing him and his true interest from the men who swipe right on everyone. This more discerning man has no way of expressing his strong preference.

This setting is one where increasing the cost of signaling interest in a match would be useful—the more costly the signal, the more confident a recipient can be that it's an expression of true interest.

The apps have obliged. Tinder now offers a Super Like; Bumble has a SuperSwipe; on Hinge you can send a Rose. But unlike regular right swipes, these signals cost money—on the order of three to five dollars a pop across the platforms (premium subscriptions typically come with a limited number of these special swipes to use each week, and Hinge gives users one free Rose a week).

By sending these signals to potential matches, market participants are indicating their extra-strong interest by putting their money where their mouth is.

These signals work. In one study, Seoul National University professor Soohyung (Soo) Lee and Stanford University professor Muriel Niederle partnered with a South Korean dating website that held short-term online-dating events. During these events, participants were allowed to make ten proposals to people they wanted to match with. If a proposal was accepted, the website shared each of their contact information with the other so they could begin chatting and potentially meet in person.

But there was a twist. Soo and Muriel gave participants a limited number of virtual roses that could be sent along with a subset of the proposals to indicate special interest.

Most participants were given two roses, meaning they could flag up to two of their ten proposals as special; others were given eight roses to send (whether someone got eight roses or two was random, and the rose recipients did not know how many roses the sender had). As they expected, Soo and Muriel found that proposals sent with a rose were 20 percent more likely to be accepted and that people who had more roses to send ended up with substantially more matches overall, around 40 percent more for men and over 80 percent more for women.

Soo and Muriel also found that when events included these virtual roses, participants accepted more proposals overall. People still valued proposals without roses to the same extent, but they placed extra value on proposals that had the additional signal of interest attached, which led to more total acceptances.

Based on these findings, the authors were convinced that the signal worked. But they were also convinced that people were not using the roses properly.

SIGNALING IDIOSYNCRATIC PREFERENCES
Explaining how to signal your idiosyncratic preferences

Say you had gone through the profiles of the people in the dating event that Soo and Muriel studied and decided to send proposals to ten people in the hope of making a few matches. To which proposals would you attach your roses?

Your instinct might be to send the two roses to your two favorites of the ten. But economic theory suggests that this strategy is not the most effective way to use your signals.

Signals can communicate that you find the recipients particularly attractive. This is valuable information for the recipients if they are unsure that you like them enough to be worth the investment in chatting and meeting up.

What this means is that you do not need to use a signal to express an interest in someone whom everyone finds desirable. (Paul Rudd already knows that you find him attractive—join the club.) So you are essentially wasting one of your roses by giving it to that person.

Signals are much more useful when you use them to communicate your idiosyncratic preferences, which might not be obvious to someone on the other side of the market.

Imagine that the obscure movie a potential match references in his bio happens to be your favorite film, that he lists hobbies that you also enjoy, or that he happens to be a physical type that is not conventionally attractive but appeals to you. When you are really excited by someone for reasons that they might not realize and send them a signal, you are giving them information they did not previously have.

Indeed, when Soo and Muriel considered the general desirability of dating partners, they found that a proposal sent by someone more desirable than the recipient (someone that the recipient might have believed was out of their league) was 50 percent more likely to be accepted with a rose than without one. But roses had no impact when they were sent to someone highly desirable. Highly desirable dating partners were not worried about someone being out of their league, so they did not need the rose to put their minds at ease.

And yet, many of the daters in their study were sending their signals to the people they liked the best when it would have been more effective to send them to people who might have been particularly surprised about the intensity of their interest.

In the academic job market too, signals are particularly valuable when used to express idiosyncratic preferences that might be a surprise to the recipients.

In the same way that people generally find Paul Rudd more attractive than Paul Giamatti, many candidates for academic economics jobs consider research universities, which typically give faculty more resources and more time to devote to research, more attractive than teaching colleges, which ask faculty to spend more time in the classroom. Knowing this, teaching colleges are often hesitant to make offers to candidates who they think might get jobs at good research universities and opt to work there instead. But while this preference for research universities exists on average, some new professors really love the teaching part of the job and would prefer to end up at a teaching college; sending their signals to teaching colleges is a good way of letting them know.

So, while signaling a school like Harvard or MIT is clearly a waste (I'm guessing very few people turn down a job offer from either of these schools), an aspiring professor would be smart to send signals to less prestigious schools for which she has strong idiosyncratic preferences.

TALK IS CHEAP
Emphasizing the value of limited and costly signals

As an adviser of PhD students who are going on the job market, I often email university hiring committees to tell them about graduating students and why they would be a good fit for their school. In these emails, I always try to emphasize a student's idiosyncratic preferences—like a strong desire to work with a particular researcher at that institution or a desire to live in a certain region. But it is easy for schools to ignore statements like that when they are made by me.

They know that part of my job as faculty is to help my PhD students get jobs, so they know I have an incentive to make the student sound more excited about the school than the student might be.

The hiring committees might decide to interpret my statements about the candidate as *cheap talk*, which is the term economists use to emphasize the fact that when a person can make a statement at little to no cost, he has no reason not to do so.

The beauty of the signaling systems used by the American Economic Association (AEA) and the similar systems implemented by residency specialties for medical school students trying to secure interviews with hospitals (in advance of the residency match described in the previous chapter) is that they make signals expensive. Not in actual money but in that the student has only a limited number to send.

A signal in the economics job market is an email sent by the AEA telling a school that a candidate has selected it as a recipient of one of that candidate's two signals. Since the AEA will send only two such emails per student, a signal a candidate sends to a particular teaching college near where her parents live costs her the opportunity to send a signal to another school.

So while I can, in theory, send effusive emails to colleagues at every school a student has applied to, signals that are more limited in number carry more weight.

While only a few job markets have official signaling systems like the ones used in academia, there are still many ways job applicants can use signaling to convey sincere interest in a position. Long and detailed cover letters—the type that take hours to compose and that someone could write only after researching a company and carefully thinking about what he might bring to that firm—were once particularly effective signals of interest. Sure, a candidate could technically spend days writing many detailed and well-researched cover letters, but because most people invested this kind of effort only for jobs they were very enthusiastic about, a detailed cover letter had the potential to send a strong signal of interest.

However, with the rise of large language models like ChatGPT, which can produce a very good cover letter in a matter of seconds, the cost of producing an excellent one is falling—and its signaling value is falling along with it.

Luckily, there are other ways to send costly signals of your interest in choose-me markets, and there are ways in which technology can make certain signals even stronger. In a world where most meetings are virtual, you can signal that you particularly care about a relationship—be it a business contact or a personal one—by going to a meeting in person.

As signaling goes, the farther you must travel to take the meeting, the stronger the signal will be. If an out-of-state firm is considering hiring you for a job, offering to fly there (perhaps on your own dime) signals a willingness to incur time and financial costs you might not be willing to accept for a job that interests you less.

Romantic partners who want to signal that they are serious might introduce their boyfriends or girlfriends to their friends or parents. (That you are willing to incur the cost of being embarrassed by your parents in front of someone you are dating highlights a true commitment.) Or you might invite the person to a wedding as your (one and only) plus-one.

Another way to send a costly signal is to move early and decisively, which signals both that you do not need to deliberate and that you do not need to hedge your bets. This is the move that many high-school students make when deciding to apply early decision or early action to college.

COLLEGE TOURS

Explaining why applying for college early is a particularly effective type of signaling

A classic choose-me market is the one for college admission in the United States. Each year, millions of American high-school students apply to two-year and four-year colleges.

Some popular colleges receive tens of thousands (sometimes over a hundred thousand) applications. And since even very large universities admit only several thousand students for each incoming class and smaller colleges admit only a few hundred, the top schools can be highly selective. Many of the country's most selective schools have acceptance rates in the mid–single digits.

But while these schools are being very selective, they want to maintain a high yield—in other words, they want to have a high percentage of students they accept say yes to their offer of admission. Back when I applied to college, this number factored into the *U.S. News & World Report* rankings of colleges and universities. While it is not used that way anymore, high yield is still a matter of pride and reputation. The good schools are perceived as good in part because so many of the people they admit end up attending.

Given that schools care about their yield, applicants who want to increase their chances of being accepted to a school have an incentive to signal their interest as particularly dedicated and likely to matriculate.

Most of the signals that students can send to a school are time-intensive, such as visiting the campus and taking a tour, actions some colleges track and use as a measure of "demonstrated interest." Some schools even allow prospective students to do informational interviews before they apply—a way to show extra drive and motivation. Students can also write tailored essays to emphasize why they believe a certain school is the right place for them (although large language models may be making this signal less useful as well).

But many schools do not measure demonstrated interest, because they do not have to. Instead, they use early decision and early action.

These policies allow students to signal strong interest by applying early to a school—often only one, making the signal more costly—and to receive the admissions decision a few months before everyone else. Schools incentivize sending this kind of strong signal by rewarding early applicants with a higher chance of acceptance.

Students who apply early decision can apply to only one school early, and acceptance is binding. If you apply to a school early decision, you are essentially committing to going there if it admits you. Schools that want to maintain high yield love early decision, since anyone they admit is more or less guaranteed to come. The policy also helps ensure the campus is full of people who are very excited about enrolling in the school. That school was their top choice—or at least they acted like it was.

Another way to signal interest is by applying early action. This also allows students to apply early, but acceptance is not binding; they are not committed to matriculating at that school if they get in. Many of the most prestigious schools offer a restricted version of early action, called single-choice early action, which allows applicants to apply early to only one private school. So students who apply to Harvard under single-choice early action cannot also apply to Princeton and Yale early, but they can apply to Princeton and Yale during the regular admissions period even if Harvard accepts them.

The policies and which schools adopt which policies vary from year to year as schools try to optimize their admissions and compete with their peer institutions. For example, certain colleges have introduced a second round of early decision (although *early* should probably be in quotation marks because the applications are submitted around the same time as the regular applications), which allows students to commit to attending a school, even though they can still simultaneously apply to many other schools during the regular admissions period. But schools can still use that second round of early decision to admit students who are sure to matriculate. This keeps their yield high but doesn't necessarily guarantee a cohort of students who have always dreamed of attending their institution, since, in this case, a student may be applying only because he struck out at his top-choice college in the true early-decision window.

What all the policies have in common is that they use some combination of moving early and restricting your choice set to signal what the colleges want to hear: that you will attend if admitted. Early decision is the most effective signal you can send to a school, because it comes at the highest cost. By applying early decision, you are forfeiting not only the opportunity to apply early to other schools but also the ability to keep your options open if you get in (a price that many are willing to pay, since it increases the odds of acceptance). Another cost involved in early decision is that you do not have the option to shop around for better financial aid offers if you are unhappy with the one you get from the school that admits you. As a result, critics of the policy say that it can harm low-income students.

Single-choice early action is not as costly because it is not binding, but it also sends a strong signal, since the school that receives an early-action application from you knows you are not applying early to one of its competitors.

BUT DO YOU *LIKE*-LIKE ME?

Explaining why grand romantic gestures are powerful signals, and not just in the dating market

It is not only elite colleges that care about whether a student will accept their offer of admission. Elite private preschools and elementary schools (the ones that some parents want their kids to attend to put them on a path to those elite colleges) also care about their yield, at least in part to maintain their good reputations within the community of parents who pay an arm and a leg for their kids to attend (and perhaps also to look good to their donors and boards of trustees).

Since private-elementary-school admissions markets do not have a mechanism for early decision (at least not yet), parents need some other way to signal their devotion and commitment to the schools. As a result, many motivated parents will send the schools what are colloquially—and perhaps appropriately—called love letters. These are letters to the admissions departments essentially stating in no uncertain terms *If we are admitted, we will certainly accept the offer.* (Schools that are high on parents' lists but not at the very top might receive what are called strong-like letters, which have more of a *We remain extremely enthusiastic* tone without making any promises.)

When I first heard about this practice, the love letters struck me as cheap talk. If I thought love letters would increase my kid's chances of admission, why not send them to multiple schools? Sure, if my kid gets admitted to more than one place, I will have to break some promises, but only to the schools my kid will not end up attending; I will have kept my promise to the one school that matters to me. And because love letters are not binding contracts, I don't face any direct consequences of breaking those promises. Wouldn't those dynamics give parents an incentive to spread the love, so to speak? And when admissions officers receive a love letter, wouldn't they think: *I bet you say that to all the deans of admissions?*

It turns out that the strength of these signals is boosted by the fact that many of these love-letter-writing parents are the same parents who enlist the services of high-priced consultants, who in turn are incentivized to discourage parents from sending letters to every dean of admissions in town—and that's a key to preventing cheap talk.

The consultants can charge a few thousand to tens of thousands of dollars to help a family get their little one into a private elementary school, and they offer a suite of services. They may guide parents toward schools that will be a good fit for their kids, help parents hone their application essays to play up how their family values dovetail with the mission and values of a particular school, and perhaps even back-channel with admissions officers, maybe to assure them that the tantrum a four-year-old applicant threw at a playdate interview (this is a thing) was a fluke.

But their involvement may also make the love (or strong-like) letter signals more credible. If admissions officers know that a consultant is working with a family, they may trust that the consultant is urging the family to send only one love letter (or they may call the consultant to confirm this is the case). That's because a consultant is playing what economists call a *repeated game*. Their reputations with the admissions committees are part of their currency, and they will not look good if their clients break their promises. So while a specific family might have an incentive to send multiple love letters, their consultant would strongly advise them against doing so, and the deans of admissions know that.

Whether they are sent to a potential romantic partner or a dean of an elementary school, love letters are relatively private statements, knowable only to the sender and recipient (and perhaps a hired consultant). But making such statements in public can be an even more powerful way to signal your intentions to other market participants, in part because public gestures of courtship assure a recipient that you are not actively pursuing other people. This is why, back when Facebook was our main social network, it was a big deal when someone changed their romantic status on Facebook from *Single* to *In a relationship*. That public declaration told the world that you were committed to the relationship in a way that whispered sweet nothings did not.

While you might not like the world to know your business, if private signals cease to be effective (for example, if deans of admission start treating the love letters as cheap talk after receiving too many from parents who renege), I suspect there will be a push to start making these statements in public, perhaps by pledging on social media to enroll at a school. Since I can make only one such statement (if I made a second, everyone would be able to see my duplicity), doing so would send an even more effective signal.

DOT YOUR I'S AND CROSS YOUR T'S

Explaining why sometimes the best signal is simply putting your best foot forward

Anyone who has ever applied for a job likely knows that typos in a résumé or cover letter are a huge red flag for potential employers. It may seem petty—after all, a typo is something minor that can be easily fixed—but the red flag isn't the typo itself. It's what the typo signals.

Beyond the obvious concern that someone who is sloppy with his own résumé might be sloppy with the work assigned to him, a typo in a résumé or cover letter sends a clear (if unintentional) signal to a potential employer that the person is not *that* interested in the job. Maybe he is shooting off so many applications that he didn't have time to proofread all his cover letters. Or maybe he wasn't excited enough about the job to spend an extra five minutes proofreading the letter before submitting it. In either case, it's a signal that the person's claims about having a strong interest in the position might not be sincere.

But signals of disinterest are not limited to typos in cover letters and résumés. Whether you realize it or not, you are sending and observing signals of interest or disinterest on a regular basis. When someone dresses less than professionally or shows up late for a job interview or business meeting, he is demonstrating that he does not actually care about the job or the meeting. If he cared, he would have bothered to iron his shirt or show up on time. Similarly, when a first date does not look her best or does not try to be interesting or charming, it's easy to infer she is not interested in pursuing the relationship further. When you care and when you want to impress, you bring your A game. When you fail to do so—even when your failure is subconscious—you send the signal that you are not particularly interested.

THAT WAS EASY (I MEAN, FOR ME)
Explaining why signaling can be particularly informative when signals are more costly for some people than others

In most of the signaling examples we have discussed so far, individuals expressed interest or enthusiasm via signals that either cost money, took extra effort, or required forfeiting a chance at something else they might want because of a limit on the number of signals that could be sent.

But signaling starts to get more complicated—and perhaps more useful—in cases when a signal is less costly for some people to send than for others. For example, if you are smart and highly dedicated, it may be easier for you to produce and send an eloquent, thoughtful, and typo-free cover letter than it is for someone less sharp.

In 2001, Michael Spence co-won the Nobel Prize in Economics for his work on markets. A paper he wrote—one of the most famous in economics—describes a certain type of signal that can be easier for some people to send than others.

Imagine that a firm is evaluating candidates for a job but is unsure about each worker's ability. Applicants know their ability, but until they are hired, there is no way for them to directly show it to the firm. If the firm asked them, everyone would say they were high ability, since they know it would help them get the job. Statements about ability would be cheap talk.

But there is a costly signal workers can invest in to more credibly demonstrate their ability to potential employers: graduating from college. According to Spence's model, graduating from college is easier if you have higher ability. And because the knowledge, skills, and talent that make it easier to get into college and succeed there are often the same ones required to perform well in one's job, companies could infer that college graduates are more valuable employees.

As in any model, these assumptions do not entirely map to reality. First, Spence published his paper in 1973, when college tuition was much more affordable. Today, many high-ability people choose not to attend or are unable to finish college because they cannot afford tuition or because they cannot afford to forgo earning an income when they are enrolled. Second, the model applies only to jobs for which being admitted to college and doing well enough to graduate are a good proxy for success, something that may not be true for many jobs (and may also depend on what you studied).

Another quirk of this model is that, in its simplest form, it is still valuable for students to attend college even if they do not learn anything there. It is enough that college is harder for some people than others; that alone can make it a valuable signal on the labor market. (As a college professor, I am confident that what we teach students makes them more productive, but even I must admit that this simplest version is quite elegant from a mathematical-modeling perspective.)

The key insight from Spence's model is that when taking an action is easier for one type of person (one who has a desirable trait) than another type of person (one who lacks that trait), taking the action can allow you to signal to others that you are in the first group.

Once you understand Spence-style signaling, you start to see it everywhere.

In my job, I very regularly get asked to write letters of recommendation — for undergraduates applying to master's and PhD programs, for PhD students applying for grants and jobs, for other faculty trying to get tenure at their schools.

Earlier, I talked about how what people write in recommendation letters could be considered cheap talk. At the same time, however, most people agree to write letters only for employees or students they can say positive things about; I would be hard-pressed to write a letter for a student who was a bottom performer in my class. So simply being able to get someone to write you a recommendation letter is a Spence signal — it is easier for better students than worse students — regardless of what that letter says.

Perhaps the most common form of Spence-style signaling is what economists term *conspicuous consumption*. Conspicuous consumption is an audacious spending of money — think fancy cars, designer watches and jewelry, and expensive experiences — that is done publicly. Sure, the things being bought might have the same price for everyone, but it is much easier (and more feasible) for the wealthy to part with the money needed to buy them. So this consumption serves as a Spence signal of wealth.

Signaling wealth often serves as a way of attracting mates on dating markets. If people are looking for someone who can provide for them financially, observing a potential partner consume conspicuously may make them appear more attractive. And in a culture that often equates wealth with intelligence, a strong work ethic, and other positive characteristics, people who engage in conspicuous consumption may signal that they have those desired traits (even if that's not always the case).

The same can be true for business relationships. As much as we might wish that everyone were judged on merit and ability alone, if you wear high-end clothes and a fancy watch, you might signal wealth or sophistication, which can in turn earn you the trust of other people of means. I remember an employee at a start-up in Los Angeles telling me that he was saving up for a Rolex watch because wearing it would open doors to business deals with wealthier people in his native Mexico. It seems to have worked, because he returned to Mexico City and has had a very successful career in public relations for super-wealthy clients there.

Spence signaling is one reason why companies invest in fancy offices, which can signal to customers or potential business partners that they are doing well; you might worry that a company with dank and dingy corporate offices is struggling to survive. But as many venture capitalists know, spending on a swanky office is not always a clear signal—even companies that are not doing well can use their limited cash to make their offices look swanky (and if you have reason to believe a company is not doing great, an office that is too nice may signal that the leadership is wasting money on frivolous expenses).

I'M NOT DOING IT FOR THE MONEY
An example of signaling good intentions by donating cash

Just as you can use signaling to convince market participants of your enthusiasm and intellect or your wealth and sophistication, you can signal other virtues and that you are doing something for the right reasons.

About two million dogs are adopted from shelters each year. These shelters typically charge adoption fees on the order of fifty to three hundred fifty dollars or more. These fees help cover the costs of caring for the animals while they are in the shelter, but pet adopters who pay these fees are also signaling to the shelter that they want the animal enough and have the means to take care of it.

The same logic—trying to identify suitable adopting families—is why many private pet owners who can no longer take care of a pet but want to skip the shelter and rehome their pet themselves will ask for an adoption fee as well. This practice may serve to reassure those who are giving up the pet, but it poses an issue on the other side of the market. How do the adopting families know they are getting a dog that the owner can no longer care for (what they are looking for) rather than one that was bred to be sold for profit (a seller they might like to avoid)?

Seeing the opportunity for a market design solution, Christine Exley, a dog lover who at the time was a graduate student at Stanford (she is now a tenured professor at the University of Michigan and my regular coauthor), devised a strategy to help potential dog owners differentiate between these two groups—the people who wanted to make sure their dog found a good home and breeders who were just in the market to make a buck.

Together with Stanford alum Elena Battles, Christine started a nonprofit called Wagaroo that allowed people who were giving up their dogs for adoption to commit to donate adoption fees to help find homes for other dogs. This created the perfect Spence signal for the market. The fee would still serve the purpose of weeding out anyone who couldn't afford to care for a dog while also weeding out professional breeders, who would not agree to give the adoption fee to charity, since they were in it for the money.

Wagaroo was so successful that it no longer needs to exist. Christine's idea was adopted by platforms that specialize in dog adoption, and Christine was able to wind it down.

I'LL HAVE MY PEOPLE CALL YOUR PEOPLE

Explaining why even a false signal can be effective
(as long as it's not too easy to copy)

For a signal to be truly effective, it cannot be easily copied. If it were common knowledge that anyone could buy a ten-dollar fake Rolex that was indistinguishable from a ten-thousand-dollar real one, the Rolex would lose its ability to signal wealth, and it would probably stop opening doors to wealthy clientele. Similarly, if anyone could purchase a college degree without having to be accepted to a school, let alone graduate, it would lose its value as a signal.

Thanks to the rise of large language models like ChatGPT, this is essentially what is happening to the value of previously costly signals like personalized cover letters and college-specific application essays. When it can take seconds to produce a piece of writing that looks like it took hours, recipients will start to assume it did indeed take seconds rather than hours. The signal will lose its luster.

Perhaps my favorite example of a signal that has not yet lost its luster but probably soon will, as AI is already beginning to learn how to copy it, is the personal assistant. Having an assistant is a signal of being too busy and important to handle your own administrative tasks and of being successful enough that you can afford to hire someone to do them for you.

Over the past few years, a series of magazine and newspaper pieces have highlighted the professional and personal benefit of having a personal assistant—or, more accurately, of pretending to have a personal assistant. These authors found that having an assistant (albeit a fake one) signaled that they were more important, earned more, and were willing to spend more; as a result, they were taken more seriously, were paid more for their time or expertise, and had more perks and opportunities available to them.

I suspect this trick is on its way out, because soon artificial intelligence agents may be good enough to take over the role of personal assistant. This will allow more people to have one, thereby negating its value as a signal. Until then, however, a fake personal assistant could be your ticket to that coveted corner table at the hottest new restaurant.

WHEN SIGNALING BACKFIRES

Why sending inauthentic signals in a choose-me market may affect how happy you are with the match

So far, we have been talking about how to increase your chances of getting matched in a choose-me market. But another consideration is whether you are happy with that match in the long run, which may depend on what you signaled when you were chosen.

In preparation for academic job interviews, candidates generally research the faculty on the hiring committees and are often tempted to tailor their answers to questions like "What are you planning to research next?" to the tastes of the faculty in the room. But while expressing a desire to research topics outside of your true areas of interest might help you convince a hiring committee to give you a job, it might not be the job that you actually want or one in which you'll be able to succeed in the long run. (While it's one thing to fake your research interests for a thirty-minute interview, it's another to fake them for years.)

By the same token, if you try to attract a potential partner with your conspicuous consumption (fancy clothes, big tips, bottle service at the club, and so on), you might worry that this potential partner is interested in you for your bank account rather than for who you are. And this dynamic may not result in the kind of meaningful relationship you want in the long term.

This is the beauty of the advice "Be yourself." Your goal, whether on the dating scene or in the job market, should not be merely to end up with the match that seems most desirable in the moment. For the match to be truly successful, you want to be sure that whomever you end up with likes you for you.

I cannot say "Be yourself" without picturing the scene from the Disney movie *Aladdin*—an old favorite—where the Genie (voiced by Robin Williams), in the shape of a bee, tells Aladdin to "Bee yourself." The Genie is trying to convince the title character to come clean with Princess Jasmine and tell her that he is the street urchin Aladdin rather than wealthy Prince Ali. This is good advice. Better for Aladdin to find out now whether Jasmine loves him for who he is (spoiler alert: she does) than to pretend to be someone he is not forever.

The job search that started for me in Denver was just the first step on a long academic path. Sure, I wanted a job that was in or close to New York, but that wasn't the only factor. I would be going up for tenure within a decade, and I knew that getting tenure would require the strong support of the members of my department. So I needed to pick a school where I would be encouraged and rewarded for doing the research that I wanted to do, not just a school in the best location.

As the process unfolded, it became more and more clear that Wharton was the school that fit that bill. The campus might have been ninety minutes by Amtrak from New York's Penn Station, but more important, it was the place where I could pursue my true research interests—where I could be myself—and succeed. When they offered me a job, I jumped at the opportunity.

THE BOTTOM LINE

*Takeaways from this chapter to help you
succeed as a market participant*

In choose-me markets, you want to make yourself look as attractive as possible to participants on the other side of the market. This surely involves putting your best foot forward and likely also involves investing in costly signals that show off your positive traits.

In these markets, you can gain an edge by signaling your *idiosyncratic* preference for matching with a particular employer, graduate program, or romantic partner (rather than signaling a *general* preference that is likely to be shared by most other market participants). By investing in a costly signal of your genuine interest, you can convince your potential matches that you are attainable and therefore worth the necessary investments for them to decide whether to choose you.

But your signals should be authentic, or you might end up with a match who is more interested in the image you have presented than in who you are. Being yourself—albeit the best version of yourself—is how to make a productive match for the long term.

COULD THE MARKET DESIGNERS DO BETTER?
Describing possible improvements to choose-me markets

Participating in choose-me markets is not necessarily easy. But research suggests that this lack of ease helps make these markets efficient, since costly signals communicate things about you to participants on the other side of the market and, as long as the signals are honest, help ensure that you end up with the best match. And when choose-me markets generate successful matches—in particular, matches that last for the long term—this is a sign that they are efficient.

One way market designers are making the dating market more efficient is through a growing number of niche apps, like SilverSingles (for people fifty and over), Christian Mingle (for devout Christians), and Veggly (for vegetarians and vegans). There are also apps, like The League and Raya, that heavily screen potential users and have high price tags, long waiting lists to join, or both. By narrowing the pools to a subset of others who share common interests or backgrounds, market designers are giving participants more confidence that investments in learning about potential matches will be well spent: A lot of the signaling has already been done for them, through the screening process to get onto each app.

There are still improvements that designers can make by developing rules that allow market participants to signal their idiosyncratic preferences more accurately. This includes finding replacements for signals that have become obsolete due to technological advancements like large language models as well as optimizing the number and type of signals that participants are allowed to send.*

If you run a dating app, work in college admissions, or do a lot of hiring and are looking for a market designer to help with that endeavor, feel free to reach out to my (admittedly fake) personal assistant, Benjamin.

---

* There is not yet consensus on how many signals are appropriate for certain markets. Different residency specialties use a different number of signals for their markets, ranging from two to thirty signals, and some markets have separate tiers of signals, like (rare) gold and (more common) silver signals. When the European Economic Association, the European equivalent of the AEA, added signals to their market for new professors, they piloted giving everyone ten signals rather than two. They expected their members to also participate in the AEA market and wanted to create a set of signals that would be less costly than the AEA ones (like a silver tier in addition to the AEA gold one).

CHAPTER 7

Speculation and the Aftermarket

I DID A LOT OF THEATER IN HIGH SCHOOL.

The school I attended—Hunter College High School, a publicly funded magnet school in New York City—is known for its strength in the performing arts. Notable alumni include the actress Cynthia Nixon, the rapper Young MC, and the songwriter Robert Lopez—the only person ever to win all four competitive EGOT (Emmy, Grammy, Oscar, and Tony) awards twice.

When I attended, the high school put on three theater productions a year: a play in the fall, a musical in the winter, and a production of five student-written, student-acted, and student-directed one-act plays in the spring.

During my sophomore year, I was cast as the best friend of the main character in one of the one-act plays, *Moon over Manhattan*. The student playing the lead was a gifted actor whom I knew from theater and other student clubs.* But despite our prior interactions, I was intimidated by my popular and talented costar. That dynamic did not help my confidence in pretending to be his best friend onstage.

---

* Including the Simpsons Appreciation Club: basically, a group of kids watching VHS-taped episodes of the popular cartoon during lunch (remember, this was in the late 1990s).

The director had a solution. He said that, to establish onstage chemistry, whenever the lead and I saw each other in the hallways of the school, we should imagine we were best friends who hadn't seen each other in years; we should loudly shout each other's names and rush toward each other for a bear hug. Miraculously, the strategy worked, and in addition to acting like friends onstage, we became friends offstage as well.

While *Moon over Manhattan* improved by opening night, 1998's spring production was more notable for another of its five one-acts. The lead of my play, my new friend Lin, had written a musical called *Seven Minutes in Heaven*, about seventh-graders going to their first unchaperoned party.

It was a hit.

Since then, Lin-Manuel Miranda has written and starred in the Tony Award–winning shows *In the Heights* and *Hamilton* and has had an extraordinary career in television and movies as an actor and—even more prominently—as a songwriter. (If you have a kid near the age of any of mine, you have no doubt heard his songs in the Disney movies *Moana* and *Encanto* and in the live-action *The Little Mermaid* many, many, many times. He's the reason we don't talk about Bruno.)

Hamilton, Lin-Manuel's 2015 smash Broadway hit, was a masterpiece. It holds the record for the most Tony nominations, at sixteen; it won eleven of those along with a Grammy for Best Musical Theater Album and the Pulitzer Prize for Drama. It was such a rousing success that it became a cultural phenomenon and part of the zeitgeist in a way that no other piece of theater in my lifetime has.

Much of the buzz about *Hamilton* had to do with how good it was, but the show became famous for one other thing too: It was impossible to get tickets to it.

According to an article in the *Wall Street Journal*, the difficulty of getting tickets meant that seeing the show was "an essential barometer of professional coolness." Because tickets sold out instantly each time they went up for sale on Ticketmaster, if you managed to snag one, it likely meant that you were famous or powerful enough to know someone who could get you in. (The tickets were so coveted that when Lin-Manuel's father, political strategist Luis Miranda Jr., attended social events at the time, he was "besieged by people begging for tickets. When the demands [became] particularly taxing," the same *Wall Street Journal* article reported, he would seek refuge by hiding in a nearby kitchen or bathroom.)

Lin-Manuel and the producers of *Hamilton* knew they had a hit when the show reached Broadway. Even though they were doing eight shows a week, it was obvious that there would be excess demand for tickets at regular Broadway show prices.

They could have charged much more for their tickets and still sold out every performance. But like in the Eras Tour example we talked about in the introduction, they did not want to make the show unaffordable. If anything, they wanted the opposite. They wanted to keep the face value of the tickets (the price the box office charges) attainable for regular theatergoers. In addition, they developed a program to make twenty thousand tickets available at ten dollars apiece (the ten-dollar bill is graced by Hamilton's image) to juniors in New York City high schools. They targeted schools with a high proportion of low-income families for the program.

Once it became clear that higher prices were not going to resolve the excess demand, it was inevitable that a market would arise to allocate the available seats—a type of market that we have not yet talked about.

If you have ever purchased theater or concert tickets through StubHub or SeatGeek, you have participated in what economists call an *aftermarket* or a *secondary market,* one in which a scarce resource—in this case, a theater ticket that has been purchased at face value—is resold, often at a much higher price.

AFTER THE MARKET IS THE AFTERMARKET

Explaining what happens when something has value outside of its original market

When you buy a *Hamilton* ticket, you are buying the right to sit in a particular seat—to be in the room where it happens—for a particular performance. And until the moment you enter the theater, you can sell your right to sit in that seat to another person. In many places, it is legal for you to charge more than you paid for the ticket, allowing you to make a profit from the sale.

When demand is high enough that it is possible to resell tickets for a profit, the conditions are ripe for what economists call *speculation*.

Unlike people who put their tickets up for resale because they can no longer use them (and who are happy if they get more than they initially paid), speculators never intend to see the show. They buy tickets with the specific intention of reselling them. These speculators are more commonly known as brokers or scalpers, and they can make a significant profit by inserting themselves between the sellers of tickets to a performance and the fans who want to see it.

Speculation arises because something can be traded outside of the market that allocates it. But not all hidden markets offer the possibility of aftermarket transactions. If someone is allocated a deceased donor kidney, gets assigned a seat in an elementary school, or receives a job offer, he cannot reassign it to someone else the way he can a theater ticket or a pair of high-end sneakers or even, nowadays, a restaurant reservation. But if the thing being allocated can be reassigned—given, traded, or sold—to someone else, it almost always ends up with an aftermarket.

The existence of an aftermarket invites additional opportunities to strategize in the primary market—by regular market participants, but also by speculators. If I think I can trade my reservation at another fancy restaurant for one at the French Laundry in an aftermarket, I might go for the reservation that I do not value that much but know other people value with the intention of trading it for the French Laundry reservation that I prefer but that I cannot get in the primary market.

When I lived in Cambridge, Massachusetts, during the many years I spent earning my PhD, my rental building had a parking garage. Each apartment, including mine, had a dedicated parking spot. I went a few years without a car, but I eventually got an old beater that had been passed down (like a family heirloom, only much less valuable) from my grandfather to my father and then to me.

Since the occasional out-of-town visitor would no longer be able to park in my now-occupied parking spot, I applied for and received a visitor parking permit, which allowed the holder (me or any guest upon whom I temporarily bestowed it) to park on certain Cambridge streets that were otherwise restricted.

I kept the permit in my apartment for its very rare use. But in doing so, I was squandering its aftermarket value. If I had been savvier (or more motivated), I could have swapped it for the visitor parking permit of a friend who lived in the neighboring town of Somerville, where I went frequently. Assuming the friend used his permit as infrequently as I did, that swap would have been a win-win, giving each of us free street parking in each other's neighborhoods.

My favorite aftermarket swap strategy was honed during the years before Ilana and I had kids and would periodically travel, just the two of us (those were the days), when I was on a semester break and Ilana could get away from work.

When I booked the plane tickets, I did so well in advance, both because it was cheaper and because it gave me more choice in which seats to select. My go-to move was to pick a row near the back of the plane and select the window (seat A) for Ilana and the aisle (seat C) for me.

• Speculation and the Aftermarket •

I wasn't trying to avoid sitting next to my wife or relishing the chance to converse with a random seatmate at thirty-five thousand feet. Booking the window and aisle at the back of the plane was a strategy to try to get the whole row to ourselves. Since most people prefer to sit near the front of the aircraft so they can deplane faster at the end of the flight, and no rational person would ever pick a middle seat unless it was the only available option, sitting in the back and leaving the middle seat unoccupied increased the chances we'd get the extra room afforded by an empty middle seat.

This strategy, however, was a gamble. If the flight turned out to be completely full, we would be packed in like sardines; worse, we'd be packed in like sardines with a stranger sandwiched between us. I was comfortable with this risk only because of the opportunity for post-market trades. If a stranger did end up in that middle seat, I was confident that he or she would be happy to trade for the window or aisle seat. Who would want to sit in the middle seat, let alone between a young couple who might be talking or handing things back and forth the whole flight, when they could have the window or aisle seat instead? In all my years of using this strategy, I never came across a single person who was not eager to make this trade.

In the case of seats on an airplane, the aftermarket is restricted to swapping seats with those who are already on the plane. Airplane tickets must be purchased from the airline (even if you go through an intermediary like Expedia.com, you are still purchasing them from the airline) and have your name on them. If it turns out you are not going to fly, you cannot sell your seat on the plane to someone else, so a speculator couldn't buy up a bunch of aisle seats and resell them to passengers who would otherwise be stuck in middle seats.

But in less restricted markets, the ability to resell invites an influx of speculators who want to participate in the market only for the chance to get something valuable that they can sell for a profit.

SPECULATION MADE SIMPLE

Explaining the origins and evolution of speculation in ticket markets

Speculation in ticket markets has a storied history that stretches back over a hundred and fifty years. When Charles Dickens sold tickets to a reading of *A Christmas Carol* for two dollars apiece in 1868, tickets sold out in less than a day; there were reports of them swiftly being resold for ten times that in advance of the performance.

Anytime there is enough demand that people are willing to pay twenty dollars for a ticket that originally cost two dollars (or $1,599 for a ticket that originally cost $159, in the case of *Hamilton*), speculators will try to elbow their way into the market. In the era of in-person lines, they quite literally elbowed their way to the front of the box office line to buy desirable tickets or—if they were more dignified—paid people to stand in line for them.

More brazen strategies involved bribing box office clerks (or record store clerks, who were often responsible for selling concert tickets to fans) to sell them the best tickets even before the doors opened for fans who might have been waiting in line overnight.

Once tickets could be purchased over the phone, speculators set up boiler rooms where their army of callers would flood the Chargit and Telecharge lines, trying to get through to operators before other ticket buyers. They would then sweet-talk the operators into selling them as many desirable tickets as possible.

The internet put ticket speculation on steroids for two reasons. First, it made the process of reselling tickets much easier. Online marketplaces like eBay and StubHub simplified the experience for anyone interested in buying secondhand tickets while also giving speculators easy access to many potential buyers, which allowed them to charge higher prices.

Second, sites like Ticketmaster made it substantially easier for speculators to buy up face-value tickets in the first place. In chapter 3, I noted that the internet turned ticket lines into ticket races, replacing the ordeal of waiting in line with a few clicks on a website. But perhaps more important, it also opened the door for speculators to do all that clicking on an exponentially larger scale through automated computer programs called bots, which could buy up tickets from Ticketmaster and other sites in a tiny fraction of the time it took humans to complete the same transaction.

When ticket buying was in person, a box office could, and often did, limit the number of tickets each customer was allowed to buy (say, four tickets each). A speculator who wanted more inventory needed to send many buyers so each could secure a few tickets at a time. But bots can be easily copied and made to appear like different customers, which means that a speculator can create dozens of Ticketmaster accounts, assign each one a bot, and deploy all these bots to buy tickets simultaneously.

And because Ticketmaster preserved the first-come, first-served allocation rule that was used in the pre-internet days, bots have a massive added benefit for ticket speculators: They are incredibly fast.

Competing against an army of bots in a first-come, first-served ticket race is like competing against a fleet of Ferraris in the hundred-meter dash. Your ability to buy tickets when they are released for sale is constrained by the speed of your fingers and your brain's capacity to visually process information shown to you on each page of the Ticketmaster website. Because a well-coded computer program does not have these limitations, even if you click on the Buy link at the precise moment tickets go on sale, bots will claim many—if not most or all—of the seats before you (or any other human) can. This is exactly what happened in the market for *Hamilton* tickets.

Shortly after *Hamilton* premiered, in August 2015, the average price paid for a ticket at the box office was $159. That was the second-highest price on Broadway, but it wasn't much higher than theatergoers were accustomed to paying to see a Broadway show and certainly far from high enough to eliminate the excess demand.

But most people who saw *Hamilton* paid far more than $159 due to bots that were buying up face-value tickets and reselling them for a massive profit on resale sites like StubHub. By 2016, the average price for a *Hamilton* ticket on the resale market was around $1,200.

According to a *Hamilton* producer, early in the show's run, a staggering 78 percent of the tickets were purchased by bots. A lawsuit later filed by Ticketmaster alleged that during the same period, *a single ticket brokerage* managed to buy 30 to 40 percent of all the *Hamilton* tickets that were released.

In short, the bot problem was rampant, and its reach wasn't limited to *Hamilton* tickets or even to other ticketed performances and events.

When I unsuccessfully tried to get a birthday reservation for my wife at the French Laundry, I may have also been competing with bots. Recently, websites have started popping up that allow people to sell their desirable restaurant reservations. And while some diners might welcome the opportunity to earn a bit of money for a reservation they would otherwise have had to cancel at the last minute, this active aftermarket has, unsurprisingly, attracted speculators who book tables for the sole purpose of reselling them to others.

If all reservations were successfully resold, restaurateurs might not hate this innovation. After all, diners who are willing to spend a few hundred dollars just to secure a reservation in the aftermarket may also be willing—and able—to splurge during their meal, perhaps by springing for an expensive wine pairing or ordering a pricey menu item that most regular diners would not.

However, if the speculators cannot or do not resell all the reservations, it can cause major problems for restaurants. Restaurants that expect to be packed but have many last-minute cancellations (from reservations that were not resold) end up with empty tables, lost revenue, and staff with fewer tips, a clearly inefficient outcome, particularly if customers would have happily claimed the tables if reservations had been available for free, as the restaurants intended.

• Speculation and the Aftermarket •

Industry advocates have pushed for bans on unauthorized restaurant reservations; New York State enacted such a law in 2024.

Most theaters don't offer audiences opportunities to spend extravagantly while at the show, which means that a production likely earns roughly the same amount of revenue regardless of whether a theatergoer can afford a $1,200 ticket from StubHub or can only swing the face value of $159.

If speculators were not allowed to enter the market, there would still be a race to buy tickets, but the race would at least be ex-ante equitable and efficient, since tickets would get sold at relatively affordable prices to real fans. But once speculators and their bot army enter the picture and people who want to see the show end up getting their tickets almost exclusively from speculators on secondary markets, ticket prices rise to the point where only the rich can afford them, and speculators earn hundreds or thousands of dollars on each ticket despite contributing nothing to the production.

BEATING BACK THE BOTS

Attempts to regulate ticket bots and eliminate secondary markets

About a year after *Hamilton*'s Broadway premiere, Lin-Manuel wrote an op-ed for the *New York Times* titled "Stop the Bots from Killing Broadway." In it, he cited a report from New York State's attorney general that found that ticket bots were buying a large share of the tickets to many popular shows.

While these bots were already illegal in New York, enforcement of the existing law was lax, and the penalties were small compared to the amount of money that speculators could make from breaking it.

Lin-Manuel's proposed solution was to make the penalties harsher. He supported a bill that would create criminal penalties, including prison time, for ticket brokers caught repeatedly using bots. A few months later, New York passed a bill making the use of bots to buy tickets for resale a misdemeanor rather than a violation, which meant that ticket brokers who used bots could face incarceration; soon after, President Obama (a big fan of the show) signed the cleverly named Better Online Ticket Sales (BOTS) Act into law. It made reselling tickets bought by bots illegal at the federal level, with potentially hefty fines.

But despite the flurry of new legislation, a continued lack of enforcement and the challenge of tracking down bot developers—who are hard to trace and could easily set up shop across state lines or overseas—have allowed bots to proliferate. In the first six years after the BOTS Act was signed, the Federal Trade Commission, which enforces the law, had done so only once, against a trio of New York brokers. And the resale ticket market is now estimated to be a fifteen-billion-dollar-a-year industry, with 20 percent of all tickets purchased from venues being resold.

Around this time, Ticketmaster tried to take matters into its own hands and introduced a new program, Verified Fan, to help solve the bot problem. The idea was to identify real live fans and create a presale period during which only they could buy tickets (or perhaps a randomly selected subset of them, if demand from fans exceeded the available tickets).

One of the program's earliest uses was for Taylor Swift's 2017 Reputation Stadium Tour, the one that preceded the Eras Tour. Swift took the *fan* part of the Verified Fan program seriously and saw an opportunity not just to eliminate bots but also to prioritize customers based on the extent of their fandom.

The Verified Fan program allowed Swift to introduce ways for fans to signal their dedication: by watching Swift's music videos and posting about Swift on social media. Fans who did so got a better spot in the virtual line for tickets, making it more likely that they would get to buy tickets during the presale period.

The strategy was reminiscent of an earlier one: Back when seeing the Grateful Dead in concert required sending in mail-order requests for tickets, some dedicated Deadheads decorated their envelopes with colorful, elaborate, and often super-impressive art, in the hope that doing so would increase the chances their envelopes would be selected and their ticket orders filled. (Decades later, photos of many such envelopes have surfaced on social media and in a coffee-table book dedicated to Deadhead art.)

But this system of rewarding the most dedicated Swifties with a better chance of snagging coveted Reputation Stadium Tour tickets turned out to be controversial, in large part because the algorithm gave the biggest boost to fans who bought Swift's latest album or tour merchandise through her online store or from one of her partner retailers. As a result, critics denounced the Verified Fan system as a cash grab that unfairly favored wealthier fans who could afford to buy the album or thirty-five-dollar T-shirts, perhaps multiple times for bigger boosts. If part of the reason to price tickets low in the first place was to avoid the inequity of tickets going to those able to pay the most, this part of the Verified Fan program backfired.

Yet the Verified Fan program lives on, albeit in a modified form. For the now-infamous presale of her Eras Tour, Ticketmaster used the program to weed out bots. People who registered as fans proved their identity as real people and became eligible to receive a code that would allow them to purchase tickets.

It did not go well.

Ticketmaster reported that 3.5 million people registered as Verified Fans for the Eras Tour. They used a lottery to select 1.5 million Verified Fans who would be lucky enough to receive a code to buy tickets and put the other 2 million on a waiting list.

People who got codes were assigned a purchase time, and upon clicking on a link (within thirty minutes of their designated purchase time), they were ushered into a virtual waiting room, which then created a virtual line for purchases. The problem was that so many people logged in to buy tickets on the day of the presale that it overwhelmed Ticketmaster's servers and slowed their website to a crawl. To reduce the unprecedented amount of traffic on the site, Ticketmaster paused sales at certain venues, forcing customers to wait in the virtual line, staring at their computer screens, for hours. Some customers experienced errors with their Verified Fan passcodes, causing them to lose out on purchasing tickets they had put into their carts even after their excruciating waits.

In the aftermath, Ticketmaster said that they had received 3.5 billion total system requests, four times their previous peak. But as it turned out, it wasn't just the Verified Fans who were creating all this website traffic. Ticketmaster attributed the problem to a "staggering number of bot attacks."

While Ticketmaster claims that the bots were unsuccessful at buying up many Eras Tour tickets, its attempt to limit ticket speculation still failed, albeit in a different way, by making the process painful for market participants. Which leads one to wonder: Would we all be better off if ticket sellers adopted the policies of some other markets and just banned resale altogether?

ON THE OTHER HAND...
The plus side of resale markets

Speculation aside, resale markets can make allocations more efficient by providing people with an easy way to unload tickets after buying them or pick up tickets at the last minute.

People might buy tickets to a live event but get sick before the show, or their babysitter might cancel, or they might get a last-minute work project dropped in their lap. Resale markets may allow them to recoup what they paid so they don't have to eat the cost if they cannot attend.

The ability to resell is not just good for the buyer who unexpectedly cannot attend the performance; it can also benefit producers, particularly when their shows are not major hits. Ticket buyers with unpredictable schedules or unreliable babysitters might be less likely to buy advance tickets for a performance if they know they will have no recourse if they have to miss the show. It is much safer to buy a ticket if you know you can resell it if you need to.

Put differently, by eliminating risk, the option of resale makes the ticket more valuable to you as a buyer even if you are not planning to resell the ticket for a profit. So the existence of a resale market allows venues to charge more for tickets in the first place.

There is another way in which allowing resale makes a market more efficient. If resale was banned and people with last-minute conflicts could not repurpose their tickets, desirable seats would just sit empty during a show. This infamously happened when organizers of the 2012 London Olympics limited the resale of tickets, which resulted in some athletes competing in embarrassingly empty stadiums while fans who would have been ecstatic to fill those seats were unable to get tickets. If there are people without access who want to attend, any empty seat is an opportunity wasted.

The resale market can also benefit buyers in that market, even when they pay high prices. After all, people who spend thousands of dollars on *Hamilton* or *Eras Tour* tickets are choosing to do so. By making the purchase, they are revealing that they prefer the tickets to the money. If the alternative is a hidden market like a first-come, first-served race or a lottery for a Verified Fan code where they have only a slim chance of getting tickets, these buyers may prefer a market where they are more likely to get tickets, even if they have to pay a lot to secure them.

Back when Ilana and I were dating, I wooed her by snagging tickets for myself, her, and her parents to see Prince perform at Madison Square Garden, a feat I was able to execute thanks to an active resale market on StubHub. Sure, we paid about triple face value for seats in the very last row of the arena, where our views were partially obstructed by the skyboxes. But the value I got from those tickets—the enjoyment of the concert, getting to see the elated look on Ilana's face all evening, and knowing I did something nice for my future in-laws—made the higher-than-face-value price well worth it.

ON THE *OTHER* OTHER HAND...

How money resolves scarcity when we do not want it to

But the issue with the secondary market—and the reason it poses a problem in the three-*E* framework—is that it allows money to resolve scarcity in settings where market designers had explicitly tried to avoid letting money do that important job.

As we talked about in the introduction, a key reason we often avoid letting money determine who gets what in certain markets has to do with equity considerations. Namely, it is unfair to let wealthier individuals get access to things most people think should be distributed more evenly.

But as the ubiquity of secondary markets demonstrates, unless we fight hard to prevent it, money will almost always work its way into markets to help allocate scarce resources.

In many public health-care settings around the world, appointments with doctors are offered on a first-come, first-served basis: People in need of medical care arrive, enter into a queue, and wait their turn (although factors like urgency of condition can influence prioritization). In China, however, public hospitals issue tickets indicating one's place in line, and these tickets are often secured by speculators early in the morning and then sold later in the day to real patients. In a viral video from 2016, a girl complained that an appointment that was initially 300 yuan ($45) was being resold for over 4,500 yuan ($600).

Other examples abound. In Berlin, appointments at the Citizens' Registration Office are available on a centralized website with first-come, first-served rules. Sensing an opportunity, three friends built software that quickly scooped up canceled appointments and sold them to Berliners who needed them on short notice and were willing to pay twenty-five or forty-five euros a pop.

Around this time, Iranians hoping for a visa to visit Germany might have had to pay for an appointment at the German embassy in Tehran, thanks to speculators snagging available appointments via the embassy's online portal. When a paying customer came along for a slot, the broker would cancel his appointment and immediately rebook it for the customer on the embassy's website. Evidence suggested similar schemes were playing out elsewhere, including at the Irish Naturalisation and Immigration Service, where foreigners might have had to pay a third party for an appointment to extend their visa for the Emerald Isle.

What these examples have in common is that market designers intended a scarce resource to be allocated equitably, either without prices or at prices low enough that the benefits could be spread widely. But the existence of an aftermarket in which one could resell these scarce resources created the incentive for speculators to enter the market.

This is a lose-lose situation for regular market participants, who are being made to pay dearly, and for the market designers, who are trying to equitably allocate their scarce resources, be it appointment times at the consulate or visits with a medical specialist. The only reliable winners are the (often wealthy) buyers, who would rather pay an exorbitant price to secure an appointment for sure than risk not getting one when it is offered for free or at a low price, and, of course, the speculators, who benefit themselves at the expense of the market.

In these cases, speculators are violating the rules of the market for financial gain. But not all speculation involves money, and even when the rules allow it, speculation can wreak havoc on markets.

WHAT, ME SPECULATE?

Introducing the concept of option value and explaining how we speculate as market participants

My local Jewish Community Center (JCC) is a hub of activity in the neighborhood for Jews and non-Jews alike. It has day-care options, afterschool classes, and gym facilities. All my kids have learned or are learning to swim in its twenty-five-meter swimming pool. And I am a member of its reasonably affordable health club.

The main health-club room at the JCC has the treadmills, bikes, ellipticals, free weights, and weight machines that are common to most gyms. In my younger years, I would have spent my time at the gym lifting weights on those machines and running on those treadmills. Now, in my forties, I find myself gravitating toward the multipurpose room on the side of the gym where the JCC's group fitness classes are held.

Given the demographic of JCC members, I may be the only person under sixty in these classes, which have names like Yoga Flow and Sculpt and Contemporary Mat Pilates. As most of the physical activity I do outside the gym involves child wrangling, the classes suit my lifestyle reasonably well, and when I attend them regularly, they keep me limber and my core strong.

The only problem with the classes is that, because they are free with a JCC health-club membership, they tend to fill up fast. My classmates might move gingerly through the JCC lobby, but they are world-class sprinters when it comes to racing to sign up for class slots.

The JCC allows members to register for classes two weeks before they take place, and some popular classes fill up on the day they open. On any given Monday, most popular classes for the week are already full. This can put potential participants in a bind if—like me—they do not have a clear picture of their week's schedule that far in advance.

Because my availability depends on childcare, Ilana's schedule, and the amount of work I have, I might not be sure if I can attend an evening Pilates class until the day before or sometimes the day of the class. But if I wait to sign up until I am sure I will be able to attend the class, it will already be full.

Since classes are free and there is no penalty for signing up and then not attending, the optimal strategy is to secure my spot in advance so that I have the option to take the class if my evening turns out to be free. This would give me what economists call *option value:* a benefit you get from having access to something down the road. Even if you do not yet know whether you will want to or be able to consume that resource in the future (in this case, a yoga or Pilates class), there is value in preserving the option to consume it if you end up wanting to do so. Unfortunately, many other JCC members also use this strategy, which is one of the reasons that the classes fill up so quickly.

If we all waited to sign up for classes until we knew for sure we could attend, spots in the classes might still be open once people became certain they could go. But while we would collectively benefit if everyone waited until their schedule had crystallized to sign up, each individual person is better off snagging one of the spots while it is still available.

The other problem is that many market participants taking advantage of option value can make the outcome inefficient, in that classes for which there is high demand can wind up with empty spaces—a wasted resource—when people bail at the last minute or forget to cancel. Those who are slow to sign up can end up on a waiting list designed to fill those empty spots. But because attending an evening yoga class requires some advance planning—I need to bring gym clothes to the office and avoid scheduling any late meetings that would prevent me from getting to the JCC on time—even if people are considerate and withdraw from a class as soon as they realize they cannot attend, the news that a spot is available may come too late for someone on the waiting list to actually use it.

The same dynamics arise in education and labor markets. A star student holding acceptances to two colleges and taking time to weigh her options will eventually turn one down. Meanwhile, the students on the waiting lists for those schools may face deadlines to accept slots at other schools. By taking extra time to choose between two offers, the star student is making the market work less well for others, who may end up accepting a less desirable option before the preferred spot opens up (when the star finally decides to turn it down). Similarly, a candidate mulling over a job offer—or perhaps using it to negotiate with other potential employers—may be burning time that the employer could be using to recruit other candidates or onboard their second-choice candidate for the role.

So while taking advantage of option value is the right strategy for any one individual, it can be inefficient and disadvantageous for the market as a whole.

FREE DISPOSAL

Introducing the concept of free disposal to explain why option value is a problem

The dynamics described above are sustained by another economic concept called free disposal.

Free disposal means you can get rid of something you no longer want—whether you paid for it originally or not—at no cost to you. There is no penalty imposed by the JCC if I withdraw from a class or even if I skip it without canceling. So it makes sense for me to sign up early and bail if the class does not suit me.

Many of the things that we acquire from hidden markets have free disposal. If I make an appointment at my local Department of Motor Vehicles and then do not show, I do not pay a fee, and I can still get my driver's license another day. I can also freely turn down a job offer, and my children can decide not to matriculate at a particular elementary school, high school, or college without incurring a penalty.

To deal with the problem of people speculating for option value, many markets have introduced rules to make disposal more costly. For example, half a block up the street from the JCC is Equinox, a higher-end gym with nicer facilities and a wider variety of classes (and a price tag to match). Equinox classes are also free for members and allow you to sign up in advance, which makes them susceptible to the problem of people taking up spots in classes they ultimately don't attend.

To combat this practice, Equinox has added a small cost of disposal. If you fail to show up to a class or if you cancel within three hours of the start time, you get a ding on your account. Accrue three dings in thirty days and you won't be allowed to sign up for classes for a week. Abuse the system too often, and you lose the chance to use it.

Because Equinox offers more classes per day than the JCC, they have other problems related to option value. For example, members who want flexibility in their schedule might try to keep their options open by booking multiple classes on the same day. Say you are not sure if a 5:30 p.m. meeting is going to get added to your schedule today. You might be tempted to book one yoga class at 6:00 p.m. and another at 7:00 p.m. so you will have a class to attend regardless of whether you need to stick around for that late meeting. And if you find out about your schedule by 3:00 p.m., you can cancel one of them with enough notice to avoid being dinged—but possibly too late for someone on the waiting list to take your spot.

To prevent its members from employing this strategy, Equinox limits sign-ups to one class per category per day. So you can still preserve some option value, but you might need to book a Pilates class at 6:00 p.m. and a yoga class at 7:00 p.m.

ClassPass, a membership program that lets you book classes across various gyms without being a member at each one, goes even further in making disposal more costly. ClassPass pays the partner gyms for your spot even if you fail to show up, so they charge members up to sixty-two dollars for canceling late or skipping classes—a financial cost designed to dissuade people from scheduling classes just for their option value.

Discouraging people from speculating for option value is also why airlines typically do not let you return your ticket for a full refund (or charge much more for refundable tickets). If you could return your ticket at the last minute, you might book multiple tickets early to have options about which flight to take on a particular day. A $250 cancellation fee makes that potential strategy much less appealing.

Restaurants, too, must worry about people booking reservations primarily for their option value; they lose out on revenue if they end up with empty tables during a prime dining hour.

People with young kids know how difficult it can be to get out of the house on date night. When there are endless ways your planned exit could get derailed, it can be hard to predict whether you will be able to make it to a 6:30 p.m. dinner reservation or if you should aim for 7:00 p.m. (or 7:30 p.m.), so having two different reservations might put your mind at ease. Or maybe you're not sure what you'll be in the mood to eat on a Saturday night three weeks from now. If you know you can easily dispose of a reservation at no cost, you might be tempted to book one reservation at a sushi place and one at a steak house for the same night so you can decide later.

While both are perfectly understandable strategies, it is equally understandable that a restaurant does not want to hold a table for someone who is not coming, potentially turning away paying customers calling for a reservation later or walking in without one.

If you called a restaurant and asked to make two reservations at different times on the same night, they would politely (or not so politely) decline to let you. But they can't prevent you from making another reservation for that same night at another restaurant. Or can they?

· Speculation and the Aftermarket ·

In a sense, they can, thanks to the rise of online booking services like OpenTable and Resy, which manage reservations for tens of thousands of restaurants across the country (and, increasingly, the world) and which also prevent you from making reservations that overlap. Once you have a 7:00 p.m. table for the sushi place, the app will not let you book an 8:00 p.m. reservation at a steak house for the same evening.

But because these rules are easy to work around—for example, a diner can book reservations under different names or using different apps—restaurants have started to become more aggressive about eliminating free disposal by taking a credit card at the time you book so they can charge you a fee (sometimes the price of a meal) if you cancel within twenty-four hours of your reservation.

These restaurants are following in the footsteps of doctors' offices that penalize you—often with a hefty fee—if you fail to show up when you said you would. While I might not be booking doctor appointments for their option value (*Am I in the mood to see my cardiologist or orthopedist today?*), it is still disruptive and a drain on their revenue if I don't show, and the fees help discourage me from being a flake. This is also why hotels charge you, typically the cost of the first night or the first few nights, for last-minute cancellations. By imposing a fee if you skip out on your reservation or miss your appointment, businesses are encouraging you to cancel while they still have time to fill your slot.

As online bookings become more common, I expect fees for being a flake to proliferate as well. It may be annoying to give a credit card to make a reservation and face the threat of a charge if you do not show up, but those fees are actually helpful to you as a market participant. The more people are discouraged from making reservations they won't use, the more likely it is that you will be able to find a reservation. And the more people who know they will be penalized for canceling a reservation within twenty-four hours, the better your chances of coming off the waiting list with enough notice to attend.

THE BOTTOM LINE

Takeaways from this chapter to help you succeed as a market participant

Speculators like ticket brokers benefit themselves by hijacking the market. They increase the price that customers pay and make the outcome less equitable. But although you are a market participant, it is not your job—nor is it within your power—to improve the market outcomes unilaterally. So if you want something that can be secured only by paying exorbitantly in a secondary market, and if you are willing to pay the high price for it, you should buy it. You may have to hold your nose and close your eyes at the thought of the broker making so much profit on the purchase, but you should not feel guilty about your part.

Along the same lines, when the rules allow it, you should take advantage of *option value* that benefits you. If you do not book your gym class or restaurant reservation early, someone else will. And if you can secure multiple job offers or favorable admission decisions, do not rush or skip out on negotiating just because you know someone else is next in line.

But when you speculate, do it responsibly. Cancel an appointment as soon as you know that you won't need it. Spending ten seconds canceling an online reservation could give other diners a reservation that they have been desperately trying to secure while generating revenue for a restaurant and tips for its staff (helping to ensure the restaurant will stay open for you to go to another night). Once you have leveraged a job offer you are not taking, let the firm know, even if there is no penalty for waiting longer. Saying no to a job offer in a timely way could mean the firm's second-favorite candidate gets the job and does not have to accept a less attractive offer at another company. These actions might come with a small cost to you, but they can have a big impact on other market participants. Even if those other market participants will never know what you have done for them, you will have made their lives better.

At the same time, beware of the costs that come with being a serial flake. Even when you do not pay a fee, you can still develop a bad reputation, which comes with its own consequences, whether it's a reprimand from the receptionist at your doctor's office or getting your Equinox class privileges paused. And you don't always know who is tracking your behavior. OpenTable, for example, has a policy of automatically canceling accounts of people who no-show four times within twelve months. If you do not know that in advance, you might inadvertently end up on the no-dine list.

But you should not feel guilty for speculating in situations where no one is harmed or when potential harms are very small or very unlikely, like booking the aisle and window seats on an airplane or swapping infrequently used visitor parking passes with a friend when it benefits you both and is not specifically forbidden. If your actions do not make the market less efficient—that is, they don't create waste or make someone else worse off—that's a good sign that you can and should proceed with a clear conscience.

COULD THE MARKET DESIGNERS DO BETTER?

Describing possible improvements to markets with speculation and aftermarkets

Ultimately, you as a market participant can't prevent speculation from occurring, whether you participate in it yourself or not. It is the responsibility of market designers to come up with rules that push speculators out of the market.

Solving the problem with ticket brokers is complex but doable. The goal is to keep the dual efficiency benefits of the secondary market—letting consumers buy with confidence and ensuring tickets do not go to waste—without the damaging effects of speculators and their bots.

A necessary step is for venues to issue tickets that cannot be resold to other market participants but that do not lose all their value if the primary buyer cannot use them. This is what happens when you buy a plane ticket: You have the right to return it to the airline for a partial refund or a flight credit but not to resell that seat to someone else.

Venues can take a similar approach. They can put your name on your theater or concert ticket, just like on a boarding pass. Sure, entering a venue with a named ticket would be slightly more annoying, since you might have to show your ID (and no one wants going to the theater to be more like going to the airport). But as people get used to having their IDs out with their tickets, the scans would be quick. I also expect this process to get much easier over time as facial recognition, which is used at airports and arenas for security purposes, starts replacing ID checks. (This is already happening at certain venues; in 2023, Major League Baseball launched a pilot of Go-Ahead Entry, a program that allows ticket holders to skip the line by uploading selfies linked to their tickets and then having their faces scanned as they enter the stadium.)

To preserve some of the efficiency benefits of the secondary market, however, the optimal rules must also give you the option of returning your ticket to the venue so they can resell it, so it does not go to waste, and so you can recoup at least some of what you paid, making it less risky for you to buy it in the first place. The promise of a full refund might be too much, since it could result in people booking tickets for their option value. But if people could return a ticket for a partial refund (at a fixed fee or, perhaps, for an amount that depended on when it was returned or whether the venue was able to resell the ticket), they would feel more comfortable about their initial purchases.

· Speculation and the Aftermarket ·

Despite the benefits of these measures in mitigating speculation, there is pressure against restricting resale in these ways. Due to lobbying by groups like the Fan Freedom Project, the right to resell tickets to live events is already enshrined into law in certain states, including New York, so laws would have to be changed to introduce resale restrictions. (Perhaps unsurprisingly, these lobbying efforts have been funded by eBay and StubHub, which make substantial profits off resale.)

But banning resale is only one piece of the puzzle. If artists and venues want to fully eliminate the role of middlemen while keeping prices low, the only sustainable solution is to get away from first-come, first-served races for allocating tickets. As long as the best tickets are given out to whoever can click fastest, speculators and their bots will find new and nefarious ways to creep into the market.

Even in a world without resale, under first-come, first-served allocation rules, speculators could sell a service that used the same bot technology to help customers secure tickets faster than everyone else. For some Taylor Swift tour in the future, instead of sitting in front of my computer and trying to click faster than other fans, I could hand my account over to a company that promises to get me primo seats for a hefty fee. This imagined outcome would look quite like the current system: a low face-value sum going to the artist or venue, a high price being paid by the fan, and a big chunk being taken by whoever programmed the fastest bots.

Instead, the key to putting bots out of business is a trick that we have seen before: lotteries, like the ones used to allocate a subset of tickets for *Rent* and, later, *Hamilton*.

For every performance of *Hamilton*, the production reserved forty-six tickets to be sold in the Ham4Ham lottery (the first *Ham* in the name is slang for a ten-dollar bill and the other *Ham* refers to the show). Fans entered the lottery to win the opportunity to buy a pair of tickets for ten bucks apiece. Lottery winners had to pay for their tickets at the theater slightly before showtime, mitigating chances for resale.

While Ham4Ham was designed to provide access to the hit show to people who might not otherwise be able to afford tickets, an online ticket lottery could replace first-come, first-served ticketing more broadly and become the backbone of new and improved market rules for live event ticketing of popular shows and tours.

Fans could enter the lottery for whichever dates and whichever sections of the theater appealed to them, and the market rules could be designed to give die-hard fans a better chance of getting tickets—potentially improving the efficiency of the allocation—by rewarding flexibility.

When it comes to seeing your favorite artist perform, flexibility is a rather good signal of dedication that does not require an ordeal like waiting in line all day. Someone willing to sit in any seat in the theater and cancel any plans he might have on whatever night he gets a ticket probably values the experience more than someone who is interested in coming only if he can get a particular seat for a particular performance.

If lotteries were run section by section, flexible superfans would have more chances to win, because if they were willing to sit in any section, they could effectively enter themselves in more lotteries. To make the market even more efficient, the theater could even allow ticket seekers to rank preferences (for example, they might rank the Saturday-evening performance as more desirable than the Wednesday matinee and the more affordable mezzanine seats higher than the pricey orchestra ones), so if any fans won multiple lotteries, the preference list could determine which tickets they get. And to boost ex-post equity, the lottery could also be designed to remember outcomes from previous lotteries, giving prior losers a better chance of winning a seat this time.

Dispensing with first-come, first-served rules would improve not only efficiency and equity but also ease; since the specific time that you entered the lottery would not affect your chances of winning, there would be no waiting on a hold screen for hours, no race to log on at a certain time, and no massive spike in internet traffic that could force a website slowdown like the one that frustrated fans trying to buy tickets for the Eras Tour.

To prevent speculators, however, the market rules would still need to restrict resale by issuing nontransferable tickets. But an added benefit of that plan is that once they shut down resale, the productions could let winners know far in advance of the date that they have been selected.

The lottery could also have an automated, randomized waiting list for seats that become available due to cancellations. And perhaps the fee for canceling could get larger as the day of the performance approaches, which would encourage initial winners who cannot use their tickets to cancel faster. This kind of policy might give those on the waiting list enough advance notice to cancel existing plans, hire a babysitter, or even travel to a different city to use tickets that come their way.

I am optimistic about these types of improvements coming. Or, as Lin-Manuel sang in his eponymous role in *Hamilton: Just you wait, just you wait*...

CHAPTER 8

You Are a Market Designer

THROUGHOUT THIS BOOK, WE HAVE CONSIDERED HOW TO PLAY IN A variety of markets under various rules from the perspective of a market participant.

But there are many situations where you are a market designer allocating scarce resources that you control rather than a market participant, even if you don't always realize it.

You might find yourself in this role at work, for example, if you are tasked with determining how shared resources (like IT support or marketing dollars) should get allocated to different teams or departments or if you are responsible for coordinating schedules or shifts to decide which staff members get which days off.

You might also be a market designer as a member of a volunteer organization like a parent-teacher association, responsible for deciding who works when and where during the spring carnival or how to run your gala's charity raffle.

If you are a member of a multi-person household, you are part of the market design team that determines how to allocate household chores and tasks. (If you are involved in doing the tasks, you are also a market participant playing under whatever market rules you establish.)

If you are a parent, you are responsible for designing the market rules to allocate things that your kids want, everything from desserts to time on the family iPad to back-to-school shopping budgets to rides to the mall.

More fundamentally, you are the market designer when it comes to allocating the scarce resources that only you control: your time and attention. You decide which colleagues or clients to meet with and which organizations, if any, will get your volunteering hours. You decide which friends will get to enjoy your company, which social media platforms will get your clicks and eyeballs, and which calls, texts, and emails will receive responses before you sign off for the day.

When you are in the role of market designer in these various facets of your life, you will want to keep the three-E framework in mind to make sure your allocations are equitable, efficient, and easy on your market participants. But when you are a market designer, you also have another consideration: what is best for you! You should care about not only what allocations are best for the market participants but also whether you are happy with the outcome. As the market designer, you get to choose market rules that leave you as well off as possible.

This introduces a fourth E into our framework. In addition to market rules that are equitable, efficient, and easy for market participants, they should also *elevate* your needs as a market designer.

USE IT OR LOSE IT

Explaining the importance of getting incentives right when allocating budgets

Sometimes you get to decide how much of scarce financial resources to make available to others, and you must determine rules for accessing those funds. You may have the responsibility of budgeting at work, at a charity where you volunteer, or at home. In these cases, you are a market designer. And when designing rules for using budgets, you want to be cognizant of the incentives you create for market participants.

I want my kids to develop a love of reading, so when they ask me to spend a rainy day at a neighborhood bookstore with them, I happily oblige. And since I want to encourage them to read not just on rainy Saturdays but throughout the week, I usually give them each a budget (say, ten or fifteen dollars a kid) that they can use to buy whatever books they want during that visit.

This is an example of a restricted use-it-or-lose-it budget, meaning that Natalie (who is in her Disney princess phase and will sometimes insist that you call her "Queen Elsa-Ariel") isn't allowed to spend whatever she has left over on a set of plastic figurines from an animated movie or on a cheap plastic tiara from Claire's, the low-priced-jewelry store we pass on the walk home. And while I like to encourage saving money, my priority as a market designer is to get the kids reading on a consistent basis, so I do not want them stockpiling bookstore bucks over many months to save up for a big-ticket item (as much as I might share Cass's desire to have *The Complete Calvin and Hobbes* in our home).

So I set a rule that the money they are allocated can be spent on books only and only on that day; it can't be spent on toys or jewelry or banked for the future.

The problem with use-it-or-lose-it budgeting is that it encourages inefficient spending. Because money that isn't spent is lost (from the perspective of the kids, who are too young to fully internalize the bigger household-budget picture), there is an incentive for them to spend money on books that they might not want much or at all. With use-it-or-lose-it, a kid who can't find a good book this week or who has found one but still has money left in the budget might decide to get a book he or she probably won't read, figuring that a so-so book is better than nothing.

This temptation to use it rather than lose it isn't unique to my kids. In fact, we see it play out on a much larger scale in settings ranging from corporate finance departments to the halls of government.

In the United States, federal budgets run on a fiscal year. Since it is hard for agencies to get additional funds midyear, it makes sense for them to engage in a bit of precautionary saving in the early quarters in case a big expense comes up later. If a big expense doesn't arise, however, the agencies may be left with a bunch of funds that they need to use by the end of the fiscal year or else return to the US Treasury.

When economists Jeffrey B. Liebman and Neale Mahoney analyzed over two and a half trillion dollars of federal procurement spending by US government agencies from 2004 to 2009, they found that agencies spent, on average, five times more during the last week of the fiscal year, when funds were about to expire, than they did during a typical week earlier in the year. And while this pattern arises across the board, spending on information technology is particularly susceptible to this dynamic—it is about six and a half times higher during that last week.

One possible explanation for these findings is that agencies are simply waiting to make sure they have enough money in their budget to fund important programs. But Jeff and Neale's research tells a different story. Based on evaluations from chief information officers and data on project cost and duration, they found that end-of-fiscal-year IT projects were nearly six times more likely to be low quality (rated four or lower on a scale of one to ten) than projects initiated at other times of the year.

They concluded that market rules preventing agencies from rolling over unused funds into the following year encouraged them to waste money on low-quality projects, a highly inefficient allocation of tax dollars.

While none of us has the power to rewrite the market rules for federal spending, we can design rules that mitigate the bad incentives of use-it-or-lose-it budgeting elsewhere. For example, I could discourage wasteful spending while also encouraging sharing and cooperation by telling my kids they can pool anything left over in their personal budgets or that they can give their extra funds to one of their siblings. In this scenario, the kids might still be tempted to use rather than lose the money, but it increases the likelihood that the pooled money will be spent on a book (perhaps one that no one could afford on his or her own) that at least one of them wants rather than on three books that none of them really want.

Or, to get a bit more creative, I might allow Natalie to spend half her leftover bookstore money at Claire's. Such a rule would still prioritize reading over cheap costume jewelry (because a dollar at the bookstore is only fifty cents at Claire's), but it would also disincentivize wasteful spending on a book that does not really interest her since she knows she'll be able to get something she wants more on the walk home.

I could also do what Wharton does with research funds that remain unused at the end of the academic year. Faculty members are allowed to roll the funds over to the next academic year, but not indefinitely. This limited saving eliminates the incentive to spend funds frivolously while ensuring that we can't stockpile research budgets over a decade.

The solutions above—allowing excess budgets to be combined to make more desirable purchases, allowing funds to be repurposed for other things of value, and allowing unused funds to roll over for the future—are designed to elevate your priorities as a market designer (in my case, to raise literate children) without creating incentives that lead to inefficient spending.

These solutions also emphasize a more general point: In the settings where you are a market designer, you need to put yourself in your market participants' shoes and think carefully about the incentives you create for them. Failure to do so can be costly.

THE HIGH COST OF GIVING THINGS AWAY FOR FREE

An example of why you do not want to set a price at zero

In the Wharton managerial economics course that I taught to MBA students for many years and that I currently teach to executives, I reference a type of airline ticket that a few of the major airlines sold back in the 1980s and early 1990s.

The airlines were not doing well at that time, and they needed to raise funds quickly. So in 1981, American Airlines introduced the AAirpass. For $250,000 (and another $150,000 for a companion), a traveler could take an unlimited number of first-class flights to anywhere American Airlines flew for as long as the pass holder lived. Other airlines introduced similar programs. Unfortunately for the airlines, things did not exactly go according to plan.

While this program did generate much needed cash at the time, the airlines severely underestimated how much the lifetime-pass holders would fly. While the initial price tag was hefty, once travelers paid it, all flights were essentially free for them. And with the cost of a first-class ticket at zero, some of the buyers of these passes were happy to fly *constantly*.

For example, one frequent flier profiled by the *Washington Post* paid United Airlines $290,000 for a lifetime pass in 1990 and has flown twenty-four million miles—the equivalent of about fifty round trips to the moon—so far, all the while racking up points that he can redeem for gift cards or other perks. Because each ticket issued to a lifetime-pass holder was a ticket the airline could not sell to an actual paying customer, the airlines ended up losing millions and millions and millions of dollars on these über-frequent fliers.

The mistake that the airlines made was creating an incentive structure similar to that of use-it-or-lose-it budgeting. Because lifetime-pass holders were essentially paying for an unlimited number of flights up front, they preferred to use those flights rather than lose them, even if it meant going on trips that they didn't care about that much.

If you offer services as a lawyer, publicist, consultant, or expert in some other field, you need to be wary of providing membership-style programs with rules that make inefficient use of scarce resources or leave you vulnerable to out-of-control costs. Rather than charging a membership fee that grants unlimited access, you could elevate your needs as a market designer by putting a cap on the number of hours you will spend per customer or specifying a fixed set of services the member can get in exchange for a flat fee.

Another option is to adopt a structure like my favorite membership program (Costco, of course!). They don't charge you a high up-front fee and then let you take whatever you want from the store for free; if they did, customers would quickly strip the warehouse clean. A membership fee gets you into the store, but once you're in, you still have to pay for every item (albeit at low prices).

The other way to protect yourself is to build in cost controls. For example, the JCC and Equinox let members take classes for free, but the size of those classes is capped, and the schedule is set in advance, so the cost of providing the classes is capped as well. Even all-you-can-eat buffets and free refills on sodas have a natural limit on how costly they can be to provide. After all, try as you might to get your money's worth, there is only so much free shrimp one person can safely eat.

Whatever pricing structure you choose, the important thing to remember is that to avoid wasted resources (and bankruptcy), you need to be smart about the incentives you create for your customers or clients.

· You Are a Market Designer ·

THE CREAM OF THE CROP

Using motivation as a criterion to determine who gets what

At the start of each spring semester, I get to design the market for registration in my behavioral economics class.

I teach one section of the course for Wharton MBA students and a separate section for Wharton undergrads. Those groups of students get priority for seats in their designated sections. But Wharton is only one school of the University of Pennsylvania, and the university has many students enrolled in other schools who are interested in learning about behavioral economics, so I end up getting enrollment requests from all around the university.

If there were just a handful of requests, this would be no problem. But each spring, I end up with about ten seats to give away and about two dozen students from outside of Wharton requesting permission to enroll.

Faced with excess demand, I end up designing a hidden market to allocate these seats.

At various points throughout the book, I have extolled the benefits of randomization to allocate scarce resources. That might be ex-ante equitable and easy on the subjects, but when it comes to elevating my interests, I think I can do better.

In choosing which students to admit, I have dual goals. The first is to enroll students who will get the most value *from* the class — those whose academic careers will be most improved by having access to the course and will thereby put my scarce resources to their most efficient use.

The second is to enroll students who will add the most value *to* the class by engaging with the material and speaking up in our discussions, ideally with a unique perspective. This goal might also enhance efficiency, since engaged students will improve the class experience for everyone. It also satisfies the fourth *E*, elevating what I care about. I much prefer teaching the class when it is full of active students who are engaged and speak up—that is more fun and dynamic than lecturing at a bunch of blank stares.

Given these goals and what I know about the students interested in registering, I develop market rules designed to select students who satisfy these two criteria.

First, I aim to prioritize the Penn Law students who are working toward a certificate with my department, the Business Economics and Public Policy Department. Through their enrollment in that joint program, they have already indicated an interest in the topics that my class covers, so I am confident they value and will benefit from the course. I've also noticed that future lawyers usually do not hesitate to speak up, so I can rest assured they'll be active contributors to class discussions.

Similarly, I try to admit students enrolled in Penn's master's program in behavioral and decision sciences. I know they'll learn about quirks of human decision-making in their other classes and be able to bring those insights to mine, and I think of my class as a nice complement to their other coursework.

Second, beyond just what program they are enrolled in, I consider the information that I get about specific individuals and their eagerness to participate in the class. When students email me weeks or months before registration opens to inquire about seats in the class, it suggests they have a sincere interest in the course and have long been thinking about how it fits into their academic goals (in contrast to the students who scramble to fill out the registration form the day of the deadline, thereby sending the signal *I just realized I need another class this semester, and this one looks good enough*). Using when they email me to determine whether to enroll them is reminiscent of a first-come, first-served rule, but I do not apply the rule automatically; this is more of a choose-me situation, where people who email early are signaling more sincere interest in the course.

Another good source of data is the students' reasons for registering, which they are asked to describe on their forms. Some students provide nonanswer answers, like *To enroll*. Others provide summaries of their academic backgrounds, what they anticipate getting from the course, and how the course will set them on a path toward their future career. The more detailed the responses, the more interest the students are signaling in the course.

The timing of their requests and the answers on the registration forms tell me not just how much the students will get out of the class but also how much value they will add to the class. I assume that students thinking months ahead about enrolling in this course and who have a clear vision of why the course will be good for them will be thoughtful and productive members of the class, and I am usually right.

The rules that I have set up have worked for me in the past but might not work forever. Future students, especially ones who read this book, might learn that if they want to get a seat in my class, they need to email me earlier and provide a more detailed response about what they hope to get out of the course. This knowledge might allow students to appear more engaged and more interested in my class than they actually are.

That said, my mechanism simply needs to differentiate the more motivated from the less motivated. Anyone who reads this far into my book to learn this trick for getting into my class and then bothers to do it has clearly signaled they are motivated.

While you may not have to allocate seats in a course, similar principles apply to how you allocate your time and attention. There are only so many hours in a day and only so much energy you can devote to your work, your friends, your family, your partner, and your kids.

In some cases, you may want to allocate more of these scarce resources to those who are most motivated in seeking them, like I aim to do for seats in my class. That said, in other cases, you might want to do the opposite.

I'M JUST BUMPING THIS EMAIL...

How to create market rules that disincentivize others from wasting your time

Those of us with children have easy access to advice—some solicited and some less so—about how to deal with our kids when they are fussy, whiny, or throwing tantrums. But the good advice almost always boils down to this: Do not give in when your kids are acting out.

If you give them what they want when they are throwing a fit, you can stop the screaming in the moment, but the silence comes at a steep cost. You will be teaching your kids that if they really want something, the way to get it is with a tantrum.

The logic for holding firm with a four-year-old is the same reasoning behind countries' policies not to negotiate with terrorists or pay ransom to kidnappers or hackers: When you reward bad behavior, you end up encouraging more of it.

This advice is also worth heeding when it comes to how you dole out the scarce resource of your time and attention—particularly when it comes to your correspondence.

My email inbox is a sacred place, and I consistently try to keep it close to empty. While perhaps not the best practice, I used to treat messages in my inbox as a sort of running to-do list for my personal and professional life, so I would begin to feel overwhelmed when my inbox started to get too full, compelling me to spend a morning sending replies and completing tasks to get emails out of my inbox as quickly as possible.

When deciding which emails to prioritize, I had two criteria: ease and frequency. This meant that the emails that got answered first were generally the ones that took the least amount of time or effort to deal with and the ones that senders had nudged me about or followed up on the most times. But while these rules made me feel like I was being efficient in the short term—helping me get emails and the related follow-ups out of my inbox—they did not serve my interests in the long run. Like giving in to a screaming toddler, they created the wrong incentives for the people who were trying to get my time and attention by email.

The problem with the first criterion is that responding quickly to small requests encourages people to send you more small requests. If an undergraduate student has a question about tomorrow's lecture and shoots me an email about it, she will learn that such emails get answered quickly. I'll respond fast because I know it'll take me only a minute, and I want to knock the email out of my inbox. But in almost every case, the student could have saved us both the trouble by looking up the information on the syllabus. If I were slower to respond, maybe students would decide that it was faster to try to find the information on their own.

Prioritizing tasks for which I have received more frequent follow-up emails also creates perverse incentives by rewarding people who clog my inbox with follow-ups. If students know that sending a second email will get my attention more quickly than the first one did and make me more likely to reply, they will do so. Over time, the result is more emails, creating the kind of stress that I am trying to avoid.

As the market designer allocating your time and attention, you get to set the rules for what is worthy of your time. What should you deal with sooner and what should you do later? What should you totally ignore? I had built a suboptimal system that not only failed to elevate me as the market designer but also failed on the other three *E*s. It was inequitable because it benefited the students who knew they needed to send more emails and left the others with delayed responses. It was not easy, since it put the burden on students to remember to send follow-ups. And it was inefficient, since in responding to simple questions that students could have figured out on their own with a quick Google search, I was unlikely to be using my scarce time and attention optimally—to deal with my students' most pressing and important requests.

Thinking carefully about the principles in this book, however, has helped me optimize the hidden market for my time and attention and improve my email maintenance.

To improve the efficiency of my correspondence, I have stopped tackling emails based on how fast I can deal with them. Instead, I triage them based on level of importance. Less important stuff gets ignored for now, usually by way of a feature that sends an email out of my inbox and returns it at a later date, when I expect to have time to deal with it (admittedly, some emails get ignored forever).

Once I have identified the important stuff I want to do today, how do I decide which important email to respond to first? I respond to emails that came in later before those that came in earlier. This means an email that came in a few hours ago will be ignored until I have addressed the ones I received more recently.

This system—what economists call *last in, first out*—isn't the most equitable; the people who emailed me earlier end up having to wait longer for a reply than the people who emailed more recently, and some important emails get very fast responses while other important emails languish. But it is more efficient, because many of the emails I get are from people working with me on joint projects in real time. If I can reply to their important emails quickly—while they are still working on the task they are asking me about—my response may arrive when it is maximally useful and make them more productive. (Of course, some emails I want to reply to today tell me explicitly that they are not *that* time-sensitive. Those I'll skip—in the name of efficiency—until I've handled everything important that might benefit from a snappy reply.)

That said, last in, first out is not always the most efficient way to handle your work. Sometimes a delay in completing a task gets more and more costly as time passes, which is what economists call *convex costs* of delay. Let's say your team is putting together a report that is due to your boss ASAP, and each of you is responsible for producing one component. If you are waiting on a few team members to submit their portions, the cost of your taking another hour or even another day to finish yours is small, since you are not holding up the group. But if you are the last one to submit your portion, every additional minute you take is holding up the whole project. You usually need to prioritize this work before anything else.

FIRST IN TIME, FIRST IN RIGHT

Why recurring meetings are a bad way to allocate time

The Colorado River stretches approximately fourteen hundred fifty miles, from the Colorado Rockies to the Gulf of California in Mexico. For thousands of years, it has helped sustain the American Indian tribes that lived in its basin. And at the very start of the twentieth century, California began diverting water from it to turn a desert into fertile farmland.

Since then, the Colorado River has continued to fuel population growth and agriculture in the region. In 1936, the Hoover Dam was completed along the river and formed Lake Mead, the nation's largest reservoir by volume. Today, the Colorado River provides drinking water for nearly forty million people in seven states and irrigates over five million acres of farmland.

But over the past twenty years, a megadrought, exacerbated by climate change, has caused the water level in the Colorado River and Lake Mead to drop, making this once abundant resource increasingly scarce. Between 2000 and the time of this writing, the river lost ten trillion gallons of water—about 20 percent of its volume—prompting serious fears that Lake Mead would reach dead pool, the point at which levels are too low for water to flow downstream, by the middle of this decade. If Lake Mead gets that low, millions of people living south of the Hoover Dam, including residents of Los Angeles, Phoenix, and parts of Mexico, will be left without access to water from the reservoir.

In the short term, the only way to keep Lake Mead full and the Colorado River flowing downstream of the dam is to divert less water from the river. But how much water should we take and who should get to use it?

The market rules allocating Colorado River water in times of drought were set by the 1922 Colorado River Compact and were based on the principle of *first in time, first in right*. These rules stated that when the water level of the river dropped, the states that had been diverting the water the longest—such as California, which was the first state to tap the river—got priority over states with more recent claims.

But first in time, first in right is unlikely to be the most efficient or equitable way to allocate a scarce resource. For one thing, in this case, it means that certain states, such as Arizona, must cut back on their water use while similar sacrifices do not have to be made in California. Moreover, much of the water being taken from the river by California is used to grow water-intensive crops, like alfalfa, that primarily go to feed livestock. In a time of a megadrought, when millions of people are at risk of losing drinking water, this is probably not the best use of a scarce life-sustaining resource.[*]

Despite being inefficient and inequitable, the market rules we often use to allocate our time and attention look a lot like first in time, first in right.

Even more than my email inbox, my work calendar determines how I spend my day. The time I have available to respond to emails, not to mention do the research, writing, and course preparation that I really should be prioritizing, must be squeezed in between the meetings and events on my daily calendar.

---

[*] While "first in time, first in right" might sound like "first come, first served," it lacks many of the allocative efficiency and equity benefits of the first-come, first-served rules discussed earlier. It essentially allows a single race—one that was run over 120 years ago—to determine how we do allocations today, even though the entire region has changed dramatically (and everyone involved in the original tapping of the Colorado River is long gone).

Some of the calendar events are sacrosanct, like the hours I am teaching. But other things that appear on my calendar are not nearly as essential.

Early in my career as a professor, I started a bunch of projects with external organizations like health insurers, government agencies, and researchers at various "nudge units" that were trying to use behavioral economics to improve their practices. Many of these projects were organized around recurring weekly or biweekly meetings. The meetings were put on the calendar at the start of the project to ensure regular check-ins, but as projects progressed, we often showed up at meetings only to find that there was not much new to report on or discuss since the previous meeting.

Scheduling all these recurring meetings seemed sensible when they were originally set up. But recently, when I looked at how my time was being spent in any given week, it was clear I was not using my time efficiently.

Recurring meetings allocated time on my calendar according to a first-in-time, first-in-right rule. Just as the first states to divert water from the Colorado River got dibs on future water, those who were first to put recurring meetings on my calendar got dibs on that time slot for all the weeks that followed.

Recurring meetings are attractive because they are easy; once established, they simply pop up without anyone having to schedule them. But as you might have guessed, they are neither equitable nor efficient. First, anyone who wanted to schedule a meeting with me would have to work around the meetings that were already scheduled, which gave the external researchers unfair priority over other people who were requesting my time, including my students and fellow Wharton faculty. Moreover, these weekly meetings were rarely the best use of my time and took me away from the more pressing, higher-value work that I could have done during that hour.

In the same way that Colorado River water rights should be untethered from whoever first diverted water at the start of the last century, you should consider freeing your schedule from the constraints of previously scheduled meetings. While some of your recurring meetings will end up being nonnegotiable—like my teaching schedule is—you will likely find that others can be made shorter or less frequent, or dropped altogether.

Eliminating first-in-time, first-in-right rules will do more than just improve how you allocate your working hours; by working more efficiently, you'll also get more time for yourself, your family, and all the things outside of work that you enjoy doing.

MAKE MORE WITH LESS

How priority policies not only optimize but also increase the resources you have available

At the end of chapter 3, I told you about a rule in the market for organ donations that would grant priority to people who had registered as organ donors themselves. The logic of that policy, a version of which has been adopted in Singapore, Israel, Chile, and China, is that it incentivizes people to take actions that expand the supply of an available resource (in this case, organs) by rewarding them with greater access to it.

This same logic explains why, at the height of the COVID-19 pandemic, when hospital beds and ventilators were in short supply, hospitals prioritized those resources for their own staff. While an opponent of the policy might have argued it was a form of nepotism, both medical ethicists and surveys of the American public agreed that it was fair to prioritize care for people who had been exposed to COVID while trying to save others. Moreover, the promise that the doctors and nurses who were on the front lines would get prioritized might have increased the supply of doctors and nurses on the front lines to treat patients, not only because treatment kept them alive and thus able to return to work if they did get COVID, but possibly also because the knowledge that they would get the best possible treatment if they got sick made doctors and nurses feel safer continuing to work (and putting themselves in harm's way) day after day. Such priority policies likely made COVID care more available.

This is also why, once the vaccine became widely available, if you had asked me which of two equally sick patients should receive the last ventilator or last hospital bed, I would have advocated prioritizing care for the individual who had chosen to get vaccinated over the one who had been medically eligible to receive the vaccine but chose not to get it. I realize this may sound punitive toward people who opted not to get vaccinated. But the purpose of such a rule is not to punish but to provide an extra incentive for vaccination. It seems fairer to me to give first access to care to those who took actions to slow the spread of the disease so that less care was needed overall.

A similar logic extends to how you allocate your time and attention.

You cannot lengthen a day. But although you can't increase the amount of time you have available to spend at work, with your family, and with your friends, you can improve the *quality* of time you spend with them as well as the amount of attention that you devote to those people and activities. Are you focused while working, or is your mind (and internet browser) wandering? Are you engaged and patient with your kids, or are you scrolling your phone and easily annoyed by their antics?

To optimize how you allocate your time and attention, think carefully about whether you are succeeding in prioritizing supportive, upbeat friends, family members, and colleagues who give you energy at the expense of the grouchy or resentful people who drain you of it.

And while you are searching for a person who will boost your energy if granted your time and attention, you might want to look in the mirror—often, that person is you! Prioritizing taking care of yourself is, almost by definition, elevating to you as the market designer. But it is also efficient and equitable for other market participants. By prioritizing self-care, you can bring a better mood and attitude to your other interactions, ensuring you can give quality time and attention to those who request it from you.

WHO DOES WHAT AND WHY

Where I introduce the concept of envy-freeness in allocating household chores

On March 5, 2020, just a week before New York City (and most of the world) all but shut down due to COVID, Ilana and I attended an event at the JCC with the author Eve Rodsky, who had been invited to talk about her bestselling book *Fair Play* as part of the JCC's Conversations on Parenting and Beyond series. The central premise of Eve's book was that even in this day and age, heterosexual couples still split the burden of household tasks unevenly. She had ideas about how they could do it better.

Eve's research showed that in the average American household, women did more of the work—including taking care of children, doing laundry, buying groceries, packing school lunches, and replacing toilet paper—than their male partners and that this inequity persisted even in cases when both partners had full-time jobs outside the home. Economists term that type of work *household production*. A perhaps more apt description that is often used is *invisible labor*, since it is work that typically goes unnoticed and is excluded from measures of productivity like gross domestic product that are designed to capture economic activity.

I was aware of these imbalances. My Wharton colleague, office neighbor, and coauthor Corinne Low studied these topics in her research, and she periodically burst into my office upon uncovering new empirical facts about the extent of the inequity.

As a progressive husband and father, I did my best to avoid

contributing to those statistics. I folded laundry, prepared snacks for the kids to take to school, cleaned up, and made beds. I knew that research from behavioral economics consistently found that people, be they basketball players, business partners, or married couples, regularly overestimated their own contributions to group production. Researchers suggested that this occurred because one's own contribution was easier to observe and remember than one's partner's contribution. It is *invisible* labor, after all.

Even though I was aware of this potential bias, if you had asked me how much work I did in our household, I would have said between 40 percent and 50 percent. I knew Ilana did a lot, but I was confident I did close to half.

Ilana did not agree. In fact, if you had asked her, she would have said she was doing 70 percent to 75 percent of the household labor. That meant either she was overestimating or I was. And if she was right, that meant that the system we had implemented to allocate household chores was not as equitable as we wanted.

Halfway through Eve Rodsky's book talk, I had a realization (had it been a cartoon, a light bulb would have appeared above my head). Before the talk, I had thought that our primary goal was establishing a fair system in which we each spent the same number of hours on parenting duties and other household chores. But it suddenly became clear to me that this was only half the battle.

It turned out that what we really needed, and what our current task-allocation system had failed to achieve, was efficiency.

In her talk, Eve described her CPE framework for how a household chore gets done. For each task, you must conceive, plan, and execute. When signing kids up for summer camp, for example, you conceive by recognizing that it is time to book summer camp (even when it feels early, since there are often first-come, first-served races for summer-camp slots). You plan by researching the camp that might be right for your kids, figuring out if the dates work for their schedules, and making a list of whatever gear they need. You execute by booking the camp, buying the gear, and getting the kids there and back during the summer.

If we wanted to split this work up equitably, we might calculate all the hours that were needed to execute the task and then divvy up the work to make sure the hours were split fifty-fifty. But it turned out that even if we could figure out exactly how long it took to do the registration paperwork, order the necessary gear on Amazon, and walk the kids to the camp bus stop on summer mornings, and even if we could split it all up evenly (a massive logistical challenge), we would almost certainly still end up doing an uneven amount of work.

That's because such a calculation would fail to account for all the additional time and mental energy Ilana would spend on conception and planning: talking to other parents about camp, thinking about the logistics of our summer schedule, researching what should be on the gear-purchase list, and worrying that we would not decide on a camp in time to register before it filled up. In Eve's framework, many of these tasks imposed a *mental load,* a type of work that is truly invisible because it happens inside one's head.

In our household, Ilana was carrying a heavy mental load, doing much of the conception and planning for things that we jointly executed. I might fold laundry or make a lunch for a kid to take to school, but Ilana was still the one to recognize that Isla was out of clean socks and remember that Cass needed to bring lunch from home because there was a field trip (and make sure that we had peanut butter, jelly, and bread in the house so one of us could make him a sandwich). She might also spend time worrying about whether it had gotten done and texting me to confirm it had so she could check it off the giant household-chore list in her head.

I thought about this mental load, and it became clear that Ilana was doing a bunch of extra household work that I had been ignoring. As I sat in the auditorium listening to Eve talk, it was not lost on me that it was Ilana who had found out about the talk, decided we might get something out of it, and coordinated with a babysitter so we could attend.

But my light-bulb moment was realizing that our allocation of household chores was not just inequitable but also highly inefficient. Better understanding the mental load Ilana was carrying made me see that I was carrying a mental load too. While she was doing a mental inventory of what was in the kids' backpacks before they left for school, I might have been thinking about whether those backpacks had full water bottles, anticipating complaints about the afterschool snacks I was about to drop in them, and trying to remember whether or not Cass wanted me to cut his field-trip PB and J. Because the mental load was in our heads, it was all but impossible for either of us to see when we were duplicating effort in an inefficient way.

The system that Eve proposed solved this problem by assigning each task entirely to one partner, who would be totally responsible for conception, planning, and execution. It also required that couples agree on a minimum quality level at which the task would get done, which would theoretically let the other partner stop worrying about whether a task would be executed properly.

Because mental load does not get lighter when someone else is carrying it too, one person handling conception, planning, and execution was necessary to achieve efficiency (and equity) in our allocation of household tasks. The concept is referred to as *total responsibility transfer* by Thomas Phelan in his book *The Manager Mom Epidemic*, and that's what my grad-school classmate, Brown University professor, and bestselling author Emily Oster calls it in her 2021 book *The Family Firm*.

After realizing where we had gone wrong, Ilana and I replaced our old system (splitting the hours of time spent on observable work) with a system that assigned each of us complete tasks. But instead of assigning these tasks randomly or handing them back and forth on a regular basis, we recognized that we would reap additional efficiency gains if we assigned each task according to which of us could do it more easily or effectively. We knew that for most tasks, one of us was better suited to handle it based on our skill sets and personalities.

Of course, we could not use ease of handling a household chore as the only determinant of who got assigned what. It would be inequitable if one person had to do everything just because he or she was better at everything—a phenomenon called *the curse of the capable* or *the curse of the competent.* Such an allocation rule would also create an incentive to feign ignorance to get out of doing undesirable tasks, a phenomenon sometimes called *strategic incompetence* or *weaponized incompetence* (which I am told is a strategy regularly employed by the male partners of some of my female colleagues).

So to distribute tasks in a way that would leverage efficiency gains while also fairly distributing the burden on each of us, we decided to rely on a concept from market design called *envy-freeness.*

A market is free of envy if participants prefer what they get to what other people get; in this case, if we each prefer the chores assigned to us to the chores assigned to the other person. For example, my years collecting and organizing baseball cards make me particularly adept at mind-numbing paperwork. While I wouldn't put paperwork on the list of things I enjoy doing, I also don't hate it nearly as much as Ilana does. Meanwhile, Ilana does enjoy cooking and somehow manages to find serenity shopping at a greenmarket, whereas I do not.

It was clear to both of us that, even though it might reinforce some gender norms that we would have happily shattered, I should be paying our bills, dealing with our medical reimbursements, and signing the kids up for afterschool programs and camp. Meanwhile, Ilana, an incredibly impressive issue spotter and fixer—she's always two steps ahead—should be managing our day-to-day family operations, keeping us stocked in everything (groceries, consumer packaged goods, clothes, and the like), overseeing our family's medical and dental care, and doing the meal prep and cooking to make sure the family was fed.

Once every task had been assigned, all we had left to do was ask ourselves whether either of us would want to swap any of the tasks we had been assigned for what was supposed to be done by the other person. Only when both of us said no would we know we'd achieved envy-freeness.

This system quickly got put to the test when the pandemic started and we were trapped together in our small apartment (which the three kids would more or less destroy each day). Because I've always been a night owl, I would stay up late each night to straighten the house, do the dishes, and fold laundry. On top of her new duties planning for all the uncertainty of the pandemic and procuring newly needed and newly hard-to-get things like hand sanitizer and N95 masks, Ilana, who is more of a morning person, would be on duty for the mornings—waking up the kids each day, getting Cass set up with Zoom kindergarten, trying to find something educational for the girls to do on the weekdays, and making a "special breakfast" (think pancakes and waffles instead of cereal and oatmeal) on the weekends—while I got to sleep in.

Even as the months marched on, I preferred doing my tasks to doing Ilana's. I did not want to swap, and neither did she. Because we appreciated what the other was doing, and because we recognized that the other's chores would be difficult to take on, we avoided feeling resentment about our tasks.

During those dark days, envy-freeness preserved our sanity.

THE BOTTOM LINE

Takeaways from this chapter to help you succeed as a market designer

There are many situations where you are the market designer, responsible for determining how scarce resources get allocated. You might decide who gets what at work or who does what at home. At the very least, you decide who gets how much of your scarce time and attention. In these settings, you should think about the three Es—how to make the markets you control equitable, efficient, and easy for market participants—but you should also think about a fourth E: how to elevate yourself as the market designer.

You will likely want to avoid use-it-or-lose-it budgeting or other policies that give market participants a perverse incentive to consume scarce resources (like your time, attention, expertise, or money) when those resources could be put to better use. Similarly, you do not want to unintentionally reward market participants for placing more demands on you, which can happen if you respond too quickly or liberally to their requests. And you may be able to increase the supply of your scarce resources by spending some on yourself.

When deciding whether to handle tasks according to first-come, first-served rules or the opposite, last-in, first-out rules, consider whether there are convex costs of delay (which suggests first come, first served) or whether close-to-real-time responses are particularly valuable to the recipients (which suggests last in, first out).

You may also want to avoid first-in-time, first-in-right rules for allocating your time; one way to do this is by untethering yourself from old recurring meetings that should no longer get priority.

Finally, when assigning household chores, keep in mind that even when allocations appear equitable, one partner may be carrying a heavier mental load than the other, or you might be duplicating efforts, particularly on the conceiving and planning parts of tasks, where labor is more likely to be invisible. To avoid this, consider allocating each person complete tasks, making one individual responsible for the conception, planning, *and* execution rather than splitting tasks down the middle. And to make sure that household chores are assigned efficiently, you might want to assign them to those who see them as less of a burden—just as long as this is done equitably—to avoid the resentment that comes from carrying more than one's fair share.

You can also apply the other principles you've learned throughout this book to the markets you control and find creative ways to make sure you and your market participants end up as well off as possible.

I would say good luck, but I'm confident you'll be lucky by design.

Coda

THROUGHOUT THE BOOK, WE SAW HOW DIFFERENT TYPES OF HIDDEN markets operate.

We saw how understanding the market rules can help you decide what strategy to play to get the most of what you want.

Now you can go out into the world, see the hidden markets around you, and play your optimal strategy.

Like Natalie after I finally explained rock-paper-scissors strategy, you are now equipped with the tools you need to have the best chance of success under any set of market rules.

Rock, paper, scissors—shoot!

Acknowledgments

THERE ARE A HANDFUL OF PEOPLE WITHOUT WHOM THIS BOOK WOULD not exist and a handful more who dramatically improved the finished product.

A story about my mother and father, Randy Osofsky and Stephen Kessler, kicks off chapter 4 (and a passing reference to them letting me go to an early-morning movie on a school day—thanks again!—is in chapter 3). But while they appear only briefly in the text, their imprint is all over this book.

Who I am and how I think about the world are due to their influence on me over my four-decades-and-change. My mother likes to claim credit for the academic success of her children: Her theory is that my brother and I developed analytical minds because she would regularly tell stories with a million tangents, and we needed to be smart to figure out what in the world she was talking about.

Of course, any success we have had—academic or otherwise—is actually a direct result of the loving and supportive environment our parents created for us. Their devotion and encouragement allowed us to develop our interests fully. (It may have also helped that they raised us in an apartment above a Barnes & Noble.)

I am incredibly indebted to Ryder Kessler, the best younger brother anyone could ask for. Ryder is a phenomenal editor of my writing and a trusted sounding board for anything life might throw at me. People who know us both will, to my slight chagrin, regularly refer to him as "the smart one." I would like to believe that they make this comparison because, while we look very similar, he wears glasses; but when pressed, I have to admit that the ranking is fair.

· Acknowledgments ·

There is no one who has had (or ever will have) as profound an impact on my professional life as Alvin Roth. Al allowed me to take his PhD class even though I was still an undergraduate. Then, in an interaction I will never forget—our first real conversation—he agreed to advise me on my undergraduate thesis. Al signing on as my adviser (on that Friday in mid-October 2003) put me on a path that led to a love of academic research, to a PhD (also under Al's tutelage), to Wharton, and to this book. I hope the preceding chapters make it clear how big an impact Al has had on the field of market design and on me personally.

My debt to Al is one I can never repay, although—in his usual generous way—he has encouraged me to pay it *forward* to my own students. This is fitting, since any good advice I give them no doubt originates from Al.

Thanks in no small part to Al, market design is a field brimming with talented academics, many of whom I cite throughout the book. I am grateful to these researchers for their work and especially to those kind enough to review my references for accuracy and comprehensiveness.

I am additionally grateful to two stars of the field of market design—my academic coauthors and friends Eric Budish and Colin Sullivan—who both read an early version of this book. They have each taught me a great deal through their own academic work, through our writing research papers together, and now also through the insightful, helpful comments they gave me during this process.

When I first thought about writing a book, I reached out to another of my academic coauthors, Wharton colleague and friend Katy Milkman. Katy's guidance was instrumental, and she continues to provide help and support as I navigate this chapter of my professional life.

While I have only ever had one book agent, I am very confident that Margo Beth Fleming is the best in the business. After leading me through every step of the process, from turning a vague idea for

· Acknowledgments ·

a book into a finished product, she continues to provide excellent advice and counsel for which I am exceedingly grateful.

I am similarly indebted to my amazing editor, Talia Krohn, at Little, Brown Spark. I did my best to provide her with a decent hunk of marble to work with, but it was her skill and dedication to her craft that sculpted it into this finished product (of which I am very proud).

I am also indebted to Heather Kreidler for thorough fact-checking, Tracy Roe for her careful and clarifying copyedits, and Stephanie Dodd for her diligent review of the galley.

Three friends (all of whom I was lucky enough to meet at Hunter College High School) were kind enough to read a far-from-polished version of this book. I am grateful to Laura Weidman Powers, Vanessa Adriana Nadal, and Marion Billings (i.e., "Doctor Marion") for their decades of friendship and for the many hours they each devoted to this particular endeavor.

I dedicated this book to my amazing and incredibly talented wife, Ilana Turko, and our three quick-witted and bighearted kids. Ilana's support as I worked on the manuscript was unending. She patiently let me read aloud early chapter drafts and provided constant positive reinforcement about whatever I had gotten down onto the page (even when it may not have deserved it). She encouraged me to go on writing retreats and carried the burden of holding down the home front in my absence. I could never have finished this book without her.

Ilana is a phenomenal partner — not just in bringing this book into existence but in all things, most importantly in creating and raising Cass, Isla, and Natalie, our three greatest accomplishments. I am grateful to them for providing me with such excellent fodder for this book, and I promise to grab more Hold the Cones the next time I pass a Trader Joe's.

Notes

Chapter 1: The Three *E*s in Ice Cream

28 **the Wong-Baker FACES Pain Rating Scale:** "Wong-Baker FACES History," Wong-Baker FACES Foundation, February 2025, wongbakerfaces.org/us/wong-baker-faces-history.

32 **market participants rarely have a currency besides money:** Some organizations create virtual currency to solve their allocation problems. Feeding America, a nonprofit network of US food banks, uses a virtual currency that allows individual food banks to buy food donated to the national network (on the order of three hundred million pounds of food a year in 2017) in regularly held auctions. This method helps each bank ensure it has a diversity of food options for the families it serves. The currency is artificial in that it has no value outside of the food-bank network, but the fact that the network uses it and plans to continue using it allows it to have and retain value. Perhaps unsurprisingly, Feeding America partnered with a team that included an academic economist, Canice Prendergast, to develop this system. See Canice Prendergast, "How Food Banks Use Markets to Feed the Poor," *Journal of Economic Perspectives* 31, no. 4 (2017): 145–62.

Chapter 2: The Need for Speed

51 **estimate that five billion dollars a year:** Matteo Aquilina, Eric Budish, and Peter O'Neill, "Quantifying the High-Frequency Trading 'Arms Race,'" *Quarterly Journal of Economics* 137, no. 1 (2022): 493–564.

52 **data transmission approaches the speed of light:** Eric and his coauthors have suggested a market innovation to reduce the value of speed: replacing the first-come, first-served market rules with auctions that are run every second or even every tenth of a second (that is, every one hundred milliseconds), which would give all traders' automated algorithms ample time to send messages to the exchanges about the prices at which they want to trade. These updated bids and asks would generate a trading price using an auction mechanism. This type of market innovation—what the researchers call *frequent-batch auctions*—would eliminate the costly investments in getting information to flow infinitesimally faster. See Eric Budish, Peter Cramton, and John Shim, "The High-Frequency Trading Arms Race: Frequent Batch Auctions as a Market Design Response," *Quarterly Journal of Economics* 130, no. 4 (2015): 1547–1621.

| 62 | **people are more focused on themselves:** Clayton R. Featherstone, Eric Mayefsky, and Colin D. Sullivan, "Learning to Manipulate: Out-of-Equilibrium Truth-Telling in Matching Markets," working paper (2021).

Chapter 3: The Waiting Game

| 81 | **these improvements could increase patient welfare:** Nikhil Agarwal et al., "Equilibrium Allocations Under Alternative Waitlist Designs: Evidence from Deceased Donor Kidneys," *Econometrica* 89, no. 1 (2021): 37–76.
| 98 | **published in a top economics journal:** Judd B. Kessler and Alvin E. Roth, "Organ Allocation Policy and the Decision to Donate," *American Economic Review* 102, no. 5 (2012): 2018–47.
| 99 | **campaign alerting Israelis to the policy:** Avraham Stoler et al., "Incentivizing Organ Donor Registrations with Organ Allocation Priority," *Health Economics* 26, no. 4 (2017): 500–10.
| 99 | **In addition, next of kin:** Avraham Stoler et al., "Incentivizing Authorization for Deceased Organ Donation with Organ Allocation Priority: The First Five Years," *American Journal of Transplantation* 16, no. 9 (2016): 2639–45.

Chapter 4: That's So Random!

| 103 | **"all Army troops killed in action":** National Advisory Commission on Selective Service, *In Pursuit of Equity: Who Serves When Not All Serve?* (Washington, DC: US Government Printing Office, 1967).
| 127 | **academic research—including mine:** Alexander Gelber, Adam Isen, and Judd B. Kessler, "The Effects of Youth Employment: Evidence from New York City Lotteries," *Quarterly Journal of Economics* 131, no. 1 (2016): 423–60; Judd B. Kessler et al., "The Effects of Youth Employment on Crime: Evidence from New York City Lotteries," *Journal of Policy Analysis and Management* 41, no. 3 (2022): 710–30.
| 127 | **Bloomberg News uncovered a rampant case of cheating:** Eric Fan et al., "How Thousands of Middlemen Are Gaming the H-1B Program," Bloomberg.com, July 31, 2024, https://www.bloomberg.com/graphics/2024-staffing-firms-game-h1b-visa-lottery-system/.

Chapter 5: Ranks a Bunch

| 142 | **solving the school-choice problem:** Atila Abdulkadiroğlu and Tayfun Sönmez, "School Choice: A Mechanism Design Approach," *American Economic Review* 93, no. 3 (2003): 729–47; Michel Balinski and Tayfun Sönmez, "A Tale of Two Mechanisms: Student Placement," *Journal of Economic Theory* 84, no. 1 (1999): 73–94.
| 142 | **the DOE to adopt deferred acceptance:** Atila Abdulkadiroğlu, Parag A. Pathak, and Alvin E. Roth, "Strategy-Proofness Versus Efficiency in Matching with Indifferences: Redesigning the NYC High School Match," *American Economic Review* 99, no. 5 (2009): 1954–78; Atila Abdulkadiroğlu, Parag A. Pathak, and Alvin E. Roth, "The New York City High School Match," *American Economic Review* 95, no. 2 (2005): 364–67.

143 **That was unfair:** Atila Abdulkadiroğlu et al., "The Boston Public School Match," *American Economic Review* 95, no. 2 (2005): 368–71; Atila Abdulkadiroğlu et al., "Changing the Boston School Choice Mechanism: Strategy-Proofness as Equal Access," working paper (2006); Parag A. Pathak and Tayfun Sönmez, "Leveling the Playing Field: Sincere and Sophisticated Players in the Boston Mechanism," *American Economic Review* 98, no. 4 (2008): 1636–52.

143 **undergraduates at the Ohio State University:** Shengwu Li, "Obviously Strategy-Proof Mechanisms," *American Economic Review* 107, no. 11 (2017): 3257–87.

145 **improve on most people getting their first:** Alvin E. Roth, *Who Gets What—and Why: The New Economics of Matchmaking and Market Design* (Boston: Houghton Mifflin Harcourt, 2015).

147 **This was very inefficient:** Ibid.

148 **parents systematically overestimate the quality:** Claudia Allende et al., "Biased Beliefs and Search in Education Markets," presentation, Market Design Working Group Meeting, Cambridge, MA, October 2023, patrickagte.github.io/patrickagte/search_slides.pdf.

148 **academics also found that when parents:** Patrick Agte et al., "Search and Biased Beliefs in Education Markets," working paper (2024).

149 **assigns medical school graduates to residencies:** Alvin E. Roth, "The National Residency Matching Program as a Labor Market," *Journal of the American Medical Association* 275, no. 13 (1996): 1054–56.

149 **even well-informed, highly motivated applicants:** Alex Rees-Jones, "Suboptimal Behavior in Strategy-Proof Mechanisms: Evidence from the Residency Match," *Games and Economic Behavior* 108 (2018): 317–30.

150 **who misreported earned over 20 percent:** Alex Rees-Jones and Samuel Skowronek, "An Experimental Investigation of Preference Misrepresentation in the Residency Match," *Proceedings of the National Academy of Sciences* 115, no. 45 (2018): 11471–76.

150 **some students ended up being admitted:** Avinatan Hassidim, Assaf Romm, and Ran I. Shorrer, "The Limits of Incentives in Economic Matching Procedures," *Management Science* 67, no. 2 (2021): 951–63.

150 **college applicants fail to appropriately rank:** Ran I. Shorrer and Sándor Sóvágó, "Dominated Choices in a Strategically Simple College Admissions Environment," *Journal of Political Economy Microeconomics* 1, no. 4 (2023): 781–807.

151 **Researchers are still trying to understand:** Avinatan Hassidim et al., "The Mechanism Is Truthful, Why Aren't You?," *American Economic Review* 107, no. 5 (2017): 220–24.

152 **many parents incorrectly believed that listing:** Betheny Gross, Michael DeArmond, and Patrick Denice, "Common Enrollment, Parents, and School Choice: Early Evidence from Denver and New Orleans," Center on Reinventing Public Education (2015).

154 **posted an interactive feature:** Roque Ruiz, Juanje Gómez, and Alexa Corse,

"What Is Ranked Choice Voting? NYC's Ballot Explained, with Bagels," *Wall Street Journal*, June 22, 2021, wsj.com/articles/confused-by-nycs-ranked-choice-mayoral-primary-practice-with-bagels-11622631601.

161 **But starting in 2001:** Yan Chen and Onur Kesten, "Chinese College Admissions and School Choice Reforms: A Theoretical Analysis," *Journal of Political Economy* 125, no. 1 (2017): 99–139; Yan Chen, Ming Jiang, and Onur Kesten, "An Empirical Evaluation of Chinese College Admissions Reforms Through a Natural Experiment," *Proceedings of the National Academy of Sciences* 117, no. 50 (2020): 31696–705; Yan Chen and Onur Kesten, "Chinese College Admissions and School Choice Reforms: An Experimental Study," *Games and Economic Behavior* 115 (2019): 83–100.

162 **people have trouble recognizing this fact:** Alex Rees-Jones, Ran Shorrer, and Chloe J. Tergiman, "Correlation Neglect in Student-to-School Matching," *American Economic Journal: Microeconomics* 16, no. 3 (2024): 1–42.

162 **fail to get into the better schools on their lists:** S. Nageeb Ali and Ran I. Shorrer, "Hedging When Applying: Simultaneous Search with Correlation," *American Economic Review* 115, no. 2 (2025): 571–98.

162 **the large majority of provinces made:** Binzhen Wu and Xiaohan Zhong, "Matching Mechanisms and Matching Quality: Evidence from a Top University in China," *Games and Economic Behavior* 84 (2014): 196–215.

166 **had developed in his dissertation:** Eric Budish, "The Combinatorial Assignment Problem: Approximate Competitive Equilibrium from Equal Incomes," *Journal of Political Economy* 119, no. 6 (2011): 1061–103.

168 **improvements seemed more equally spread:** Eric Budish et al., "Course Match: A Large-Scale Implementation of Approximate Competitive Equilibrium from Equal Incomes for Combinatorial Allocation," *Operations Research* 65, no. 2 (2017): 314–36; Eric Budish and Judd B. Kessler, "Can Market Participants Report Their Preferences Accurately (Enough)?," *Management Science* 68, no. 2 (2022): 1107–30.

168 **allow couples to submit preferences:** Seth S. Leopold, "A Conversation with…Alvin E. Roth, PhD, Economist, Game Theorist, and Nobel Laureate Who Improved the Modern Residency Match," *Clinical Orthopaedics and Related Research* 479, no. 5 (2021): 863–66; Fuhito Kojima, Parag A. Pathak, and Alvin E. Roth, "Matching with Couples: Stability and Incentives in Large Markets," *Quarterly Journal of Economics* 128, no. 4 (2013): 1585–632.

Chapter 6: Choose-Me Markets

177 **employers generally prefer candidates:** Along with my Wharton colleague Corinne Low and University of Pittsburgh professor Colin Sullivan, I have done work exploring the preferences of employers recruiting recent college graduates at the University of Pennsylvania. In our study, when we randomly gave a résumé a higher GPA or more prestigious work experiences, we saw that, on average, employers rated the candidate as more desirable. See Judd B. Kessler, Corinne Low, and Colin D. Sullivan,

- Notes -

"Incentivized Resume Rating: Eliciting Employer Preferences Without Deception," *American Economic Review* 109, no. 11 (2019): 3713–44.

181 **partnered with a South Korean dating website:** Soohyung Lee and Muriel Niederle, "Propose with a Rose? Signaling in Internet Dating Markets," *Experimental Economics* 18, no. 4 (2015): 731–55.

189 **called love letters:** Estela B. Diaz, "Parents and the Priceless Child in Elite Early Childhood Admissions," PhD diss., Columbia University (2023).

193 **a certain type of signal:** Michael Spence, "Job Market Signaling," *Quarterly Journal of Economics* 87, no. 3 (1973): 355–74.

197 **authors found that having an assistant:** Ella Quittner, "Life Is Easier with a Fake Assistant," *New York*, March 6, 2023, thecut.com/article/fake-assistant-tiktok.html; Fortesa Latifi, "I Have a Fake Personal Assistant," *Business Insider*, May 22, 2023, businessinsider.com/i-have-a-fake-personal-assistant-2023-5; Kate Sloan, "I Hired a Fake Male Assistant and My Income Doubled," *M Dash*, June 7, 2019, mdash.mmlafleur.com/fake-male-assistant-experiment.

Chapter 7: Speculation and the Aftermarket

204 **"When the demands [became] particularly taxing":** Erica Orden, "What's Worse Than Getting Shot by Aaron Burr? Not Having Seen *Hamilton*," *Wall Street Journal*, March 6, 2016, wsj.com/articles/whats-worse-than-getting-shot-by-aaron-burr-not-having-seen-hamilton-1457298388.

208 **Charles Dickens sold tickets:** Eric Budish and Aditya Bhave, "Primary-Market Auctions for Event Tickets: Eliminating the Rents of 'Bob the Broker'?," *American Economic Journal: Microeconomics* 15, no. 1 (2023): 142–70.

211 **Lin-Manuel wrote an op-ed:** Lin-Manuel Miranda, "Stop the Bots from Killing Broadway," *New York Times*, June 7, 2016, nytimes.com/2016/06/07/opinion/stop-the-bots-from-killing-broadway.

216 **Other examples abound:** Rustamdjan Hakimov et al., "How to Avoid Black Markets for Appointments with Online Booking Systems," *American Economic Review* 111, no. 7 (2021): 2127–51.

229 **seats that become available due to cancellations:** Ibid. Research suggests a randomized waiting list rather than a first-come, first-served race for waiting-list spots might also be necessary to mitigate speculation. As we saw with German embassy visits, markets that do not allow resale but have first-come, first-served races for waiting-list slots allow brokers to speculate for appointments and then sell them by returning them to the platform at a low-traffic time and immediately claiming them back for a paying customer.

Chapter 8: You Are a Market Designer

233 **analyzed over two and a half trillion dollars:** Jeffrey B. Liebman and Neale Mahoney, "Do Expiring Budgets Lead to Wasteful Year-End Spending? Evidence from Federal Procurement," *American Economic Review* 107, no. 11 (2017): 3510–49.

248   **Eve Rodsky, who had been invited:** Eve Rodsky, *Fair Play: A Game-Changing Solution for When You Have Too Much to Do (and More Life to Live)* (New York: Putnam, 2019).

249   **regularly overestimated their own contributions:** Michael Ross and Fiore Sicoly, "Egocentric Biases in Availability and Attribution," *Journal of Personality and Social Psychology* 37, no. 3 (1979): 322–36.

251   ***total responsibility transfer:*** Thomas Phelan, *The Manager Mom Epidemic: How Moms Got Stuck Doing Everything for Their Families and What They Can Do About It* (Naperville, IL: Sourcebooks, 2019); Emily Oster, *The Family Firm: A Data-Driven Guide to Better Decision Making in the Early School Years* (New York: Penguin, 2021).

Index

AAirpass, 235
acting, and onstage chemistry, 202–3
Adams, Eric, 154–56
Ad Hoc, Yountville, California, 60
aftermarkets
    market design and, 225–29
    restrictions on, 207
    scarcity and, 204
    speculators and, 205–6, 210, 217
    swap strategies and, 206–7
aftermarket transactions, 205
aftermarket value, 205, 206
AI, 197–98
airlines
    aftermarket swap strategy for tickets, 206–7
    boarding groups and, 91
    partial refund for cancellation of tickets, 226
    seat prices of, 15–16, 17
airports
    CLEAR Plus, 93, 94
    Global Entry status and, 93, 94
    TSA PreCheck and, 93, 94
Aladdin (film), 199
Alaska, hunting tag lotteries in, 113
allocation mechanisms. *See also* equitable allocation mechanisms
    easy mechanisms, 21–22, 23, 24, 33–36, 39, 105, 231
    efficient mechanisms, 21–22, 24, 25–32, 36
    high-stakes randomized allocation, 101–5
    trade-off realities and, 23–25, 33
    waiting lists and lines and, 71, 74
allocative efficiency
    auction types and, 31–32
    cheating and, 34, 127–28
    first-come, first-served and, 33–36, 57, 87, 88, 93, 96, 211, 244n
    loopholes and, 90
    lotteries and, 39–40, 105, 109–10, 126–28, 228–29
    market design and, 125–26
    market rules and, 33, 78, 81–82, 88, 96
    opportunity costs and, 82–83
    quantification and comparison of value and, 27–31
    scarcity and, 26–29, 244
    value and, 27–32, 33
AMC theaters, Sightline program of, 15
American Airlines, 91, 235
American Economic Association (AEA), 170, 171–72, 174, 184–85, 201n
American Museum of Natural History, 110–11
amusement parks, 93
apartments, waiting lists for, 79–80
Apple stores, 35, 85–86
Aquilina, Matteo, 51
Armstrong, Neil, 102
Ashkenazi, Tamar, 98

Index

assortative matching, 177–78
attention
   allocation of, 231, 239, 240–43, 247, 254
   market for, 18
auctions
   allocation of scarce resources and, 30–31
   allocative efficiency and, 31–32
   excess demand and, 113
   format of, 30, 31–32
   frequent-batch auctions, 261n
   Wharton's Course Match for university courses, 165–68
Austen, Jane, 138

Battles, Elena, 196
Beatles, 13
Belvedere Castle, 87, 87n
Berlin, Germany, 216–17
Better Online Ticket Sales (BOTS) Act, 212
bison, overhunting of, 111–12
Bloomberg News, 127–28
Boston Marathon, 118
bot technology, 227. *See also* ticket bots
budget allocation
   incentives and, 231–34, 236
   market design and, 231–36
   market rules and, 232, 233–34
   pricing structure and, 235–36
   rollover of unused funds, 233–34
   use-it-or-lose-it budget, 232–34, 235, 254
Budish, Eric, 51, 69, 166–67, 261n

Cachon, Gérard, 167
Chalamet, Timothée, 46
chance
   allocations determined by, 117
   strategy decisions and, 55–56, 58
Charles III, king of England, 48
charter schools, lotteries for enrollment in, 105, 126–27, 173
ChatGPT, 185, 187, 197

cheating, 34, 127–28
Cherokee Nation, 33
Cherokee Outlet Opening, 33–35, 36
Chicago Housing Authority, 80
Chicago Mercantile Exchange, 51
Chile, 99, 246
China
   Beijing license plate lottery, 38–40
   Gaokao scores and, 160–61, 162, 173
   hybrid immediate/deferred acceptance in, 161–62
   medical care in, 216
   organ transplants and, 99, 246
   ranked-performance list and, 161
   university students' priority status in, 161
choose-me markets
   assortative matching and, 177–78
   general versus idiosyncratic preferences and, 177–79, 264n
   labor market as, 172, 173–76
   market design and, 200–201, 238, 239
   market rules and, 18, 173
   overqualified candidates and, 175–76
   signaling and, 171–72, 174, 179–82, 198, 199–200, 201, 238, 239
   subjectivity of, 173
   top-coding and, 175–76
   universities and, 170–72, 173, 174–75, 186–89, 201
Civil War, 102
ClassPass, 221–22
climate change, 243
Colorado, hunting tag lotteries in, 116
Colorado River, 243–46, 244n
Colorado River Compact, 244
combinatorial assignment problem, 164–65
competition
   excess demand and, 60–63
   of ticket bots, 209–10, 211, 212, 214
computerized ticketing systems, 96
conspicuous consumption, 194–95
contests, as allocation mechanism, 22–23
Coppola, Sofia, 139

Index

Costco
  membership fee for, 236
  parking lot spots for, 57–59, 62
COVID-19 pandemic
  excess demand for ebooks and, 77
  excess demand for treatments and, 12
  household chore allocation and, 253
  priority policies and, 246–47
  recovery from, 155
  school enrollment and, 133
COVID-19 vaccine, 12, 66–67, 247
Creedence Clearwater Revival, 102–3
currency
  reputation as, 190
  types of, 32, 165–66
  virtual currency, 261n
curse of the capable/curse of the competent, 252

dating markets
  as choose-me markets, 174
  conspicuous consumption and, 194–95, 198
  dating apps and, 179–82, 200
  efficiency of, 180, 200–201
  general preferences and, 177, 178
  idiosyncratic preferences and, 177, 178, 182–84
  love letters and, 190
  public gestures of courtship and, 191
  signaling and, 180–83, 185–86, 190–91, 194–95, 198, 201
  top-coding and, 176, 183
  value and, 13–14
DaVita dialysis centers, 73
day-care centers, waiting lists for, 79, 80
de Blasio, Bill, 155, 158
demand. *See also* excess demand
  for doctor appointments, 45, 72
  future demand, 9
  law of, 7–8
  for university courses, 5–6, 11–12, 24, 48, 69, 164–68
  for university housing options, 48–50, 52

Dempsey, Patrick, 13
dialysis treatment, for end-stage renal disease, 73–75
dibs, 35–36
Dickens, Charles, 208
Diversity Visa Lottery, 107, 108
doctors
  appointment waiting lists and, 63–64, 64n, 72
  demand for appointments with, 45, 72
  fees for dropped appointments, 223
  hidden markets and, 17
double-dipping strategy, for lotteries, 106–8, 113, 116, 117, 120, 124

eBay, 208, 227
ebooks, 77–78
economics
  market design as subfield of, 6
  signaling strategy and, 182
  traditional models of profit maximization, 9–10
education. *See* charter schools; private preschools and elementary schools; public-school systems; universities
efficient mechanisms
  allocative efficiency, 27, 39–40
  Hold the Cone example and, 22, 27–29, 31, 32, 41
  introduction to, 25–32
  market design and, 231
  Pareto efficiency, 25–27, 39–40, 41, 105
  resale markets and, 215
  three Es and, 21–22, 24, 25–32, 105
effort, allocative efficiency and, 33–35, 36
80-20 rule, 26n
Encanto (film), 203
end-stage renal disease, 73–75
equality, equity distinguished from, 89
equitable allocation mechanisms. *See also* ex-ante equity; ex-post equity
  all or nothing allocation and, 36–38
  lotteries and, 104–5, 106, 110, 113–15
  market design and, 231

equitable allocation mechanisms *(cont.)*
  market rules and, 68, 217
  randomization and, 38–40
  secondary markets and, 216
  sharing and, 21–24
  strategy-proof systems and, 143
  taking turns and, 40–42, 41n
  three *E*s and, 10–12, 23–24
  waiting lists and lines and, 77–78, 83–85, 89, 96, 98
e-readers, 77
European Economic Association, 201n
ex-ante equity
  first-come, first-served races and, 211
  lotteries and, 38–39, 104, 105, 110, 125
  random choice and, 38–40
excess demand
  estimating of, 87
  first-come, first-served races and, 43–44, 45, 60–63, 66, 86–87
  future demand and, 9
  hunting tags and, 112–15, 113n
  marathons and, 117
  prices and, 7–8, 9, 16, 209
  races and, 46, 60–63, 66
  scarcity and, 7–8, 70–71, 85–87
Exley, Christine, 196
ex-post equity
  indivisible goods and, 38
  lotteries and, 110, 113–14, 125, 228–29
  taking turns and, 40
  university class schedules and, 165–66
ex-post inequity, 104

facial recognition, 226
failure, pain of, and strategy decisions, 56, 58, 59, 60, 68, 164
Fan Freedom Project, 227
fantasy-football drafts, 41n
Federal Trade Commission, 212
Feeding America, 261n
financial crisis of 2008, 51
first-come, first-served races
  allocative efficiency of, 33–36, 57, 87, 88, 93, 96, 211, 244n
  ex-ante equity and, 211
  excess demand and, 43–44, 45, 60–63, 66, 86–87
  hunting tag lotteries and, 114
  loopholes and, 64–67, 68
  market design and, 35, 68–69, 90, 91, 96–99
  market rules and, 33–36, 43–44, 45, 71, 88, 106, 173, 261n
  New York City Summer Youth Employment Program and, 105
  recognition of, 45–47, 67, 72
  speculation and, 227
  speed and, 48–52
  theater tickets as, 96, 208–9, 227, 228
  waiting lists and lines and, 63–64, 64n, 68, 72, 72n, 82–83, 85, 87, 95, 96, 265n
first in time, first in right principle, 244, 244n, 246, 254
fishing, 112
fitness classes
  free disposal and, 220–23, 236
  option value and, 218–20, 221
"Fortunate Son" (Creedence Clearwater Revival), 103
free disposal, 220–23
French Laundry, Yountville, California
  aftermarket trading and, 205–6
  first-come, first-served reservations and, 43–44, 45, 54, 55, 60, 65, 69, 71, 210
frequent-batch auctions, 261n

gain, and strategy decisions, 56–57, 58
Garcia, Kathryn, 155–56
Giamatti, Paul, 177, 183
Go-Ahead Entry, 226
goals
  market rules and, 18
  for registering students in class, 237–39
  social goals, 108
  wildlife population goals, 112

Index

Grateful Dead, 212–13
grocery stores, waiting lines in, 83–84, 84n

Ham4Ham lottery, 227–28
Hamilton, Alexander, 204
Hamilton (musical), tickets for, 203–4, 205, 208, 209–10, 215, 227–28
happiness/unhappiness, comparison of, 28–29
hidden markets
  aftermarket transactions and, 205
  free disposal and, 220–21
  identification of, 17, 42
  introduction to, 5–6
  lotteries and, 102, 116–17
  market design and, 6, 17
  market rules and, 16–17, 18, 19, 42, 242, 257
  parking spots and, 57–58
  resource allocation and, 6, 17, 24, 42, 237
  school choice and, 134, 160
  stakes of, 18–19
  Vietnam war draft as, 102
highways, 93, 94
Hill, John R., 34
Hold the Cone example
  easy mechanisms and, 22, 35
  efficient mechanisms and, 22, 27–29, 31, 32, 41
  equitable mechanisms and, 22, 38, 40–42
  snake draft and, 41n
  three *E*s and, 21–22
  trade-offs and, 24, 25
Homestead Act of 1862, 33–34
homophily, 129
household chores
  allocation of, 16, 248–53, 254
  conceive, plan, execute (CPE) framework for, 249–50, 251, 254
  hidden markets and, 17
household production, 248

hunting
  environmental conservation and, 111–13, 112n
  excess demand for hunting tags, 112–15, 113n
  tag lotteries and, 105, 113–15, 116

immediate-acceptance system, 138
incentives, and budget allocation, 231–34, 236
income inequality
  allocative efficiency and, 31
  inequitable allocation and, 10–12, 13, 31
indivisible objects, distribution of, 24, 38
interconnected preferences, 168–69
internet
  speed of, 48–52
  ticket speculation and, 208–9, 229
In the Heights (musical), 203
invisible labor, 248–49, 254
Iran, 217
Ireland, 217
Israel, 97, 98–99, 246

Jobs, Steve, 75

Keats, Ezra Jack, 76
Keller, Thomas, 43, 60
kidney transplants, 73–74

labor market
  cheap talk and, 184–86, 194
  as choose-me market, 172, 173–76
  college graduation as signal, 193–94
  cover letters as signals of interest, 185
  efficiency of, 14, 180
  general versus idiosyncratic preferences, 177–79, 183–84, 264n
  in-person meetings and, 185
  signaling and, 183–86, 199
  top-coding and, 175–76
Lake Mead, 243–44
large language models, 185, 187, 197, 201

Index

last in, first out system, 242, 254
latency arbitrage, 51
Lavee, Jacob, 98
Lee, Soohyung (Soo), 181–83
Leonardo da Vinci, 30
Li, Shengwu, 143
Liautaud, Jimmy John, 113n
Liebman, Jeffrey B., 233
Lincoln, Abraham, 33
Little Mermaid, The (live-action film), 203
London Marathon, 116–19
London Olympics (2012), 215
loopholes
  first-come, first-served races and, 64–67, 68
  for lotteries, 102–3, 117–19, 124, 163
  for Vietnam war draft, 102–3
  waiting lists and lines and, 89–91
Lopez, Robert, 202
lotteries
  as allocation mechanism, 22, 69, 104
  allocative efficiency of, 39–40, 105, 109–10, 126–28, 228–29
  banking your wins and, 116–17, 125
  bending rules for, 108–10, 124–25, 127
  bonus-point systems and, 114
  for charter school enrollment, 105, 126–27, 173
  controlling who else enters and, 121–24, 125
  double-dipping strategy for, 106–8, 113, 116, 117, 120, 124
  early-and-often strategy for, 110–15, 116, 125
  hidden markets and, 102, 116–17
  as high-stakes randomized allocation, 101–5
  hunting and, 105, 113–15, 116
  loopholes for, 102–3, 117–19, 124, 163
  for marathons, 105, 116–19
  market design and, 125–28, 229, 265n
  market rules and, 113–15, 116, 118, 124–25
  multiple entries rules and, 108–10, 124
  New York City Summer Youth Employment Program and, 104–5
  options in strategy choices and, 119–21
  priority-based systems for, 114–15, 117
  probability rules and, 100–101
  random choice and, 38–40, 101–5, 125–26, 130
  school choice and, 134, 136
  university housing lotteries, 129
  for visa applications, 105, 107–8, 110, 127–28
Low, Corinne, 248, 264n
loyalty, 9–10
luck, 5, 19, 39–40, 74, 121–24, 125, 166

Ma, Huge, 66
Machiavelli, Niccolò, 14
Mahoney, Neale, 233
marathons
  lotteries for, 105, 116–19
  qualifying times for, 118
marijuana markets, lottery for license applications, 108
market-clearing prices, 8, 9, 10, 15
market design
  budget allocation and, 231–36
  choose-me markets and, 200–201, 238, 239
  disadvantaged groups and, 89
  first-come, first-served rules and, 35, 68–69, 90, 91, 96–99
  hidden markets and, 6, 17
  incentives and, 231–34, 236
  inequities addressed by, 68–69, 88–89, 124, 217
  interconnected preferences and, 168
  motivation as criterion and, 237–39
  pricing structure and, 235–36
  priority policies and, 246–48
  randomization and, 125–28, 237
  ranked-preference lists and, 164–69

research on market rules and, 96–98
resource allocation and, 6, 217, 230–31, 253–55
school choice and, 137, 142, 144, 146, 163
signaling and, 196
speculation and, 225–29, 265n
three *E*s and, 231, 254
university housing allocation and, 132, 146, 163
waiting lists and lines and, 96–97, 229
market participation, ease of, 33
market rules
allocative efficiency and, 33, 78, 81–82, 88, 96
budget allocation and, 232, 233–34
creation of, 18
email management and, 240–43
enforcement of, 18
equitable allocation mechanisms and, 68, 217
first-come, first-served and, 33–36, 43–44, 45, 71, 88, 106, 173, 261n
formalization of, 17
hidden markets and, 16–17, 18, 19, 42, 242, 257
historical accident and, 17
for live event ticketing, 228
lotteries and, 113–15, 116, 118, 124–25
operational expediency and, 17
organ transplants and, 96–98, 99
psychological harm to market participants and, 32
ranked-choice voting and, 154
recurring meetings and, 243–46, 254
resource allocation and, 17–18, 21–22, 24, 25, 173, 230–31, 238
speculation and, 18, 217, 229
three *E*s and, 18, 21–23, 24, 25
for university housing allocation, 130
unstated rules, 17
waiting lists and lines and, 18, 71, 72, 78, 79–82, 89–91

markets. *See also* aftermarkets; choose-me markets; dating markets; hidden markets; secondary markets; stock markets
prices and, 6, 8
market shamans, 144
medical care, first-come, first-served basis of, 216
medical students, residency programs for, 149–52, 168, 184
Medicare, 73
mental load, 250–51, 254
Michelangelo, 70
Michigan, hunting tag lotteries in, 114, 116
Miranda, Lin-Manuel, 203–4, 211, 229
Miranda, Luis, Jr., 204
misreporting
risks of, 148–53, 156, 157
short-listing and, 151, 152–56, 163–64
swapping and, 151, 152, 163
Moana (film), 203
Mohammed bin Salman, Saudi prince, 31
money
inequity associated with, 31–32, 216
as measure of resource value, 29–31
as resolution to scarcity, 216–17
Moon over Manhattan (play), 202–3
movie tickets, as first-come, first-served races, 86–87, 96
Muir, John, 111
multi-listing, 72–78

Nasdaq, 50–52
National Advisory Commission on Selective Service, 103
National Guard, 102
national parks, and lotteries, 119–21, 162
National Resident Matching Program (NRMP), 149–50, 168
National Wildlife Refuge System, 112
Newsom, Gavin, 43–44n
Newton, Isaac, 48

· Index ·

New York City Department of Education (DOE), 133–37, 142, 145, 146, 148, 157, 160, 163
New York City Summer Youth Employment Program, 104–5, 127
New York Passport Agency office, 84n
New York Public Library, 76–78, 79
New York State lottery, 100–101
New York Stock Exchange, 50–52
Niederle, Muriel, 181–83
Nixon, Cynthia, 202
nursing homes, waiting lists for, 79

Obama, Barack, 212
Oklahoma, Cherokee Outlet Opening and, 33–35, 36
O'Neill, Peter, 51
online dating. *See* dating markets
OpenTable, 223, 225
opportunity costs
  allocative efficiency and, 82–83
  of time, 94
  waiting lists and lines and, 82–83, 85–89, 95, 96
option value, 218–20, 221, 222, 224, 226
organ donors, 97–98, 246
organ transplants
  biological complexity of, 74
  excess demand for, 12, 73
  hidden markets and, 17, 24
  inequities in, 75
  market rules and, 96–98, 99
  multi-listing and, 72–75
  priority policies for organ donors and, 97–98, 246
  regional transplant centers and, 74–75
  surgeon's role in decisions and, 80–81
  viability of organ and, 81
  waiting list strategies and, 72–75, 79, 80, 81–82
Orwell, George, 79
Oster, Emily, 251
outside option, and strategy decisions, 59–60, 67, 68

pain, comparison of, 28–29
Pareto, Vilfredo, 26, 26n
Pareto efficiency, 25–27, 39–40, 41, 105
Pareto principle, 26n
parking spots, allocation of, 57–60, 62
Peele, Jordan, 46
personal assistants, 197–98
Phelan, Thomas, 251
power, hidden markets and, 17
preferences. *See also* ranked-preference lists
  general versus idiosyncratic preferences, 177–79, 182–84, 200–201, 264n
  interconnected preferences, 168–69
  market rules for, 18
  school choice and, 135, 137, 139–41, 144, 145, 146
  waiting-list rules and, 72
Prendergast, Canice, 261n
prices
  difficulty with, 15–16, 18, 21
  excess demand and, 7–8, 9, 16, 209
  face-value prices, 9
  hidden costs of, 16
  inefficiency of, 12–14, 16, 18, 21
  inequity of, 10–12, 13, 15, 16, 18, 21
  market-clearing prices, 8, 9, 10, 15
  market design and, 235–36
  markets and, 6, 8
  as measure of resource value, 29–31
  problems with, 8–10
  resource allocation and, 7–8, 11, 12–14
Prince, 215–16
private preschools and elementary schools
  admissions consultants and, 190
  admissions love letters as signaling, 189–90, 191
  as choose-me markets, 173, 174
  high yield admissions rates and, 189
  market design and, 144
  public signals and, 191

274

probability theory, rules of, 100–101
profits, maximization of, 9–10
public housing, waiting lists for, 79, 80
public libraries
   ebooks and e-readers and, 77–78
   first-come, first-served waiting lists for, 76–77
   multi-listing for materials from, 75–78
public-school systems. *See also* school choice
   afterschool programs, 46–47, 60–62, 68–69
   equitable mechanisms and, 36–39
   gifted-and-talented programs and, 37–38
   hidden markets and, 17
   parent-teacher conference slots and, 53, 64
   resource allocation and, 11, 12, 24

races. *See also* first-come, first-served races; strategy decisions
   advance decisions and, 52–53, 67–68
   excess demand and, 46, 60–63, 66
   loopholes and, 64–67, 68
   multiple options and, 53–56, 67
   outside options and, 59–60, 67, 68
   recognition of, 45–47, 49, 53, 67
   speed and, 48–52, 261n
   waiting lists and, 63–64, 64n
raffles, 121–22
randomization
   ex-ante equity and, 38–40
   lotteries and, 38–40, 101–5, 125–26, 130
   market design and, 125–28, 237
   market rules and, 18
   waiting lists and lines, 229, 265n
ranked-choice voting, 153–56
ranked-preference lists
   market design and, 164–69
   market rules and, 18, 132, 147
   misreporting risks and, 148–53, 156
   online ticket lotteries and, 228
   school choice and, 132–34, 141, 143, 145, 146–48, 156, 163–64

university courses and, 166–67
university housing allocation and, 130–32
voting and, 153–56
Rank the Vote NYC, 153–56
Rees-Jones, Alex, 149–50
relationships
   hidden markets and, 17
   inefficient prices and, 13–14
Rent (musical), 106, 227
repeated games, 190
resale markets, 210, 214–16, 226–27, 228, 229
resource allocation. *See also* allocation mechanisms
   algorithmic expression of, 172
   hidden markets and, 6, 17, 24, 42, 237
   market design and, 6, 217, 230–31, 253–55
   market rules and, 17–18, 21–22, 24, 25, 173, 230–31, 238
   prices and, 7–8, 11, 12–14
   scarcity and, 4–5, 7, 11, 13, 16, 17–18, 24, 25, 45, 98, 160, 231, 237, 254
restaurant reservations
   first come, first-served rules and, 43–44, 45, 53, 71
   free disposal and, 223
   option value and, 222
   paid line standers and, 93
   speculation and, 210–11
   waiting lists and, 63–64
Resy, 223
rock-paper-scissors game
   possible outcomes of, 3, 4, 17, 156
   settling disagreements with, 3–4, 16
   strategy for, 257
Rodsky, Eve, 248–51
romantic partners. *See* dating markets
Roosevelt, Theodore, 110–13, 119
Roth, Alvin, 5–6, 96–98, 98n, 142, 144, 146, 168
Rudd, Paul, 177–78, 182, 183
rules. *See also* market rules
   hidden and complex rules, 5

Index

runoff elections, 153, 154
Rybolovlev, Dmitry, 30

San Francisco, California, rental conversions lotteries and, 115
scarcity
  aftermarkets and, 204
  allocative efficiency and, 26–29, 244
  excess demand and, 7–8, 70–71, 85–87
  money as resolution to, 216–17
  resource allocation and, 4–5, 7, 11, 13, 16, 17–18, 24, 25, 45, 98, 160, 231, 237, 254
  secondary markets and, 204, 216
school choice
  algorithms for, 136–41
  deferred-acceptance system and, 138–40, 142, 145, 147, 160
  gameable mechanisms and, 160–62, 164
  hidden markets and, 134, 160
  immediate-acceptance system and, 138, 139, 140–41, 142
  lottery numbers and, 134, 136, 137, 139, 142, 146, 147, 148, 160, 163, 173
  market design and, 137, 142, 144, 146, 163
  options available for, 145
  performance-based priority in, 159–60
  preferences and, 135, 137, 139–41, 144, 145, 146
  priority level and, 134–36, 137, 139, 140, 146, 147, 148, 157–59, 173
  ranked-preference lists and, 132–34, 141, 143, 145, 146–48, 156, 163–64
  strategy-proof mechanisms for, 140, 142–45, 160, 164
SeatGeek, 204
secondary markets
  dual efficiency benefits of, 225–26
  elimination of, 211–14
  market rules introducing, 18
  resale markets, 210, 214–17, 224
  scarcity and, 204, 216

serial dictatorship, for university housing allocation, 130–32
Seuss, Dr. (Theodore Seuss Geisel), 76
Shakespeare in the Park, New York City, 87–89
sharing
  easy mechanisms and, 23
  efficient mechanisms and, 24
  equitable mechanisms and, 21–24
  three-E properties of, 23–24
short-listing, misreporting and, 151, 152–56, 163–64
signaling
  admission to private preschools and elementary schools, 189–90, 191
  authentic signals, 200
  cheap talk and, 184–86, 190, 194
  choose-me markets and, 171–72, 174, 179–82, 198, 199–200, 201, 238, 239
  college graduation as signal, 193–94, 197
  conspicuous consumption and, 194–95, 197, 198
  costly signals, 185–86, 192–95, 200
  dating markets and, 180–83, 185–86, 190–91, 194–95, 198, 201
  early application to university and, 186–89
  false signals, 197–98
  good intentions and, 195–96
  idiosyncratic preferences and, 200–201
  inauthentic signals and, 198–99
  labor market and, 183–86, 199
  number and types of signals, 201, 201n
  personal assistants and, 197–98, 201
  private preschools and elementary schools and, 189–90, 191
  signals of disinterest, 191–92
  strong signals, 187–89
  tiers of signals, 201n
Simpsons, The (television show), 72n
Singapore, 97, 246

Sistine Chapel, Vatican Museum, 70, 82, 93
Skip The Line, 92
Skowronek, Samuel, 149–50
Smith, Adam, 97
snake draft, 41n
South Dakota, hunting tag lotteries in, 114
speculation
　conditions for, 205–6, 207
　first-come, first-served races and, 227
　market design and, 225–29, 265n
　market rules and, 18, 217, 229
　medical care and, 216
　option value and, 218–20, 221, 222
　responsible use of, 224–25
　ticket markets and, 208–11, 214, 224, 225–26
　visa applications and, 217
speed
　first-come, first-served races and, 48–52
　internet speed, 48–52
　marathons and, 118
　market rules and, 18
Spence, Michael, 193–95
Spread Networks, 51
stadiums, seat prices of, 15, 24
Star Wars: Episode I (film), 86–87
stock markets
　first-come, first-served market rules for trades, 50–52, 261n
　internet speed and, 50–52
　latency arbitrage and, 51
Stoler, Avraham, 98
Storage Wars (television show), 30
strategic incompetence, 252
strategy decisions
　chance and, 55–56, 58
　excess demand and, 60–63
　factors determining, 58, 144–45
　gameable mechanisms and, 160–62
　go-for-gold strategy, 55, 56–59, 60, 62, 63, 67, 141, 151
　outside option and, 59–60, 67, 68

　pain of failure and, 56, 58, 59, 60, 68, 164
　settle-for-silver strategy, 55–58, 59, 63, 67, 68, 121–24, 141, 151
strategy-proof mechanisms
　misreporting risks and, 148–53, 156, 157
　priorities and, 157–59
　ranked-choice voting and, 153–56
　for school choice, 140, 142–45, 160, 164
　technological advances and, 164
StubHub, 204, 208, 210, 211, 215, 227
Sullivan, Colin, 264n
supply
　limited supply, 7
　prices and, 8
swapping, 151, 152, 163, 225
Swift, Taylor, 8–11, 13, 24, 204, 212–13, 215, 227

taking turns, 40–42, 41n
theater prices, 15
theater tickets
　as first-come, first-served races, 96, 208–9, 227, 228
　lotteries for, 106–7, 108, 109, 110, 227–28
　sharing and, 24
　speculation and, 205, 208–11
　waiting lines for, 88, 93
three *E*s
　distribution of indivisible objects and, 24
　easy mechanisms, 21–22, 23, 24, 33–36, 39, 105, 231
　efficient mechanisms, 21–22, 24, 25–32, 105
　equitable mechanisms, 10–12, 23–24
　lotteries and, 105, 109
　market design and, 231, 254
　market rules and, 18, 21–23, 24, 25
　school choice and, 160
　secondary markets and, 216–17
　sharing and, 23–24

three *Es (cont.)*
  strategy-proof system and, 142–45
  trade-off realities and, 23–25, 33
  university course auctions and, 165
ticket bots
  competition of, 209–10, 211, 212, 214
  regulation of, 211–14, 226, 227
ticket markets. *See also* movie tickets; theater tickets
  nontransferable tickets and, 229
  online ticket lotteries and, 227–29
  resale market and, 212, 229
  speculation and, 208–11, 214, 224, 225–26
Ticketmaster, 204, 208–10, 212–14
time
  allocation of, 231, 239, 240–46, 254
  allocative efficiency and, 33–35
  equitable allocation and, 40–42
  market for, 18
  opportunity costs of, 94
  priority policies and, 247–48
  waiting lists and lines and, 93–95
top-coding, 175–76
total responsibility transfer, 251
trade-off realities
  allocation mechanisms and, 23–25, 33
  sharing and, 23–24
Trader Joe's, 21–22
TurboVax Twitter account, 66
two Xs, ex-ante and ex-post equity, 38–49

unfair advantages, 35
US federal budgets, 233–34
US Fish and Wildlife Service, 112
US passports, renewal of, 94
US Supreme Court, paid line standers, 92–93
universities
  application essays for, 190, 197
  choose-me markets and, 170–72, 173, 174–75, 186–89, 201
  college graduation as signal, 193–94
  combinatorial assignment problem and, 164–65
  demand for courses and, 5–6, 11–12, 24, 48, 69, 164–68
  early action and, 187–89
  early decision and, 187, 188
  hidden markets and, 17
  high yield admissions rates and, 173, 186–87, 188, 189
  student-matching system for, 161
  value of education and, 14
university housing allocation
  automation of, 132
  centralized clearinghouse for, 132
  demand for housing options, 48–50, 52
  interconnected preferences for, 168–69
  lottery numbers and, 147–48, 162, 168–69
  market design of, 132, 146, 163
  process of, 129–30
  serial dictatorship for, 130–32
  strategy-proof systems and, 143

vaccine access, 17
Valentine's Day, and equitable mechanisms, 36–37
value
  aftermarket value, 205, 206
  allocation of scarce resources and, 13, 29–31
  allocative efficiency and, 27–32, 33
  dating markets and, 13–14
  easy mechanisms and, 33–36
  immediate acceptance system and, 139
  inequity associated with money and, 31–32, 216
  lotteries and, 109, 126
  option value, 218–20, 221, 222, 224, 226
  priority level and, 11
  quantification and comparison of, 27–28
Vatican Museum, Vatican City, 70
Verified Fan system, 212–14, 215

Vietnam war draft
   anti-war movement and, 104n
   exemptions and deferments to individuals and, 102–3, 104
   as hidden market, 102
   inequities in, 102–4
   random selection and, 101–4
visa applications
   lotteries for, 105, 107–8, 110, 127–28
   speculation and, 217

Wagaroo, 196
waiting lists and lines
   excess demand and, 70–71
   first-come, first-served races and, 63–64, 64n, 68, 72, 72n, 82–83, 85, 87, 95, 96, 265n
   line cutting and, 89–91, 93–95
   line maintenance and, 90–91
   lists distinguished from lines, 71, 72
   loopholes and, 89–91
   market design and, 96–97, 229
   market rules and, 18, 71, 72, 78, 79–82, 89–91
   multi-line strategy and, 84–85
   multi-listing for library books, 75–78
   multi-list opportunities and, 72–78, 95, 106
   one-line-for-all system, 84, 84n
   opportunity costs and, 82–83, 85–89, 95, 96
   organ transplant strategies and, 72–75, 79, 80, 81–82
   paid line standers and, 92–93, 95
   randomized waiting lists, 229, 265n
   rule enforcement and, 89–91
   separate-line policies and, 88–89
   special line for complicated cases and, 84n
   strategies for waiting lines, 85–89, 95–96
   strategies for waiting lists, 71–72, 79–82, 95–96
   targeted lists, 81–82
Wanamaker, John, 146
Washington Express, 92
weaponized incompetence, 252
Wharton, Edith, 138
Wiley, Maya, 155
Williams, Robin, 199
Winkler, Henry, 46
Wong-Baker FACES Pain Rating Scale, 28
World Marathon Majors, 117, 118

Yang, Andrew, 155
Yosemite National Park, 111, 119–20, 162
Young MC, 202

About the Author

JUDD KESSLER IS THE INAUGURAL HOWARD MARKS PROFESSOR IN the Business Economics and Public Policy Department at the University of Pennsylvania's Wharton School. In 2021, he was awarded the prestigious Vernon L. Smith Ascending Scholar Prize for his groundbreaking scholarship. For his work on organ allocation, Kessler was named one of the "30 Under 30" in Law and Policy by *Forbes*. He is an award-winning teacher whose courses are popular among undergraduates, MBAs, PhD students, and executives, and he is a sought-after speaker. His research and writing have been featured in leading media such as the *New York Times*, the *Wall Street Journal*, the *Washington Post*, the *Los Angeles Times*, *Scientific American*, the *Harvard Business Review*, *Politico*, NPR, *Hidden Brain*, and *Freakonomics*, among others. He received an AB, an MA, and a PhD from Harvard University and an MPhil from the University of Cambridge. At Harvard, he trained with Nobel laureate Alvin E. Roth, one of the founders of market design, an area in which Kessler has been conducting research for the past fifteen years.